Your Right to Know

Your Right to Know

A Citizen's Guide to the Freedom of Information Act

Second Edition

Heather Brooke

PLUTO PRESS
www.plutobooks.com

First published 2005
Second edition 2007 by Pluto Press
345 Archway Road, London N6 5AA and
175 Fifth Avenue, New York, NY 10010

www.plutobooks.com

Distributed in the United States of America exclusively by
Palgrave Macmillan, a division of St. Martin's Press LLC,
175 Fifth Avenue, New York, NY 10010

British Library Cataloguing in Publication Data
A catalogue record for this book is available from the British Library

ISBN-13   978 0 7453 2583 5 hardback
ISBN-10   0 7453 2583 1 hardback
ISBN-13   978 0 7453 2582 8 paperback
ISBN-10   0 7453 2582 3 paperback

Library of Congress Cataloging in Publication Data applied for

This book is printed on paper suitable for recycling and made from
fully managed and sustained forest sources. Logging, pulping and
manufacturing processes are expected to conform to the environmental
standards of the country of origin. The paper may contain up to
70 per cent post-consumer waste.

10 9 8 7 6 5 4 3 2

Designed and produced for Pluto Press by
Chase Publishing Services Ltd, Fortescue, Sidmouth, EX10 9QG, England
Typeset from disk by Stanford DTP Services, Northampton, England
Printed and bound in the European Union by
Antony Rowe Ltd, Chippenham and Eastbourne, England

Contents

Foreword

Last year Heather Brooke was shortlisted for the Paul Foot Award, a prize set up in honour of the late campaigner and investigative journalist, and the first edition of this book was highly recommended by the judging panel. Paul Foot would certainly have approved of this choice as one of his favourite quotations came from a poem by Hilaire Belloc, a copy of which he pinned above my desk. The poem is called 'A Ballad of General Misapprehension' and the refrain at the end of each verse goes:

> But these are things that people do not know:
> They do not know because they are not told.

This for Paul Foot was the essence of journalism, to give people information that is being denied them, and he would have been delighted to see the principle extended further to embrace not just the professional reporter but the ordinary citizen too. There is a great deal we do not know about the workings of our own government and our public services and the reason we don't know is that no-one tells us. In fact they go out of their way not to tell us and despite the introduction of the Freedom of Information Act they are still finding reasons not to tell us. Heather Brooke makes it clear that the important thing is to keep asking the questions and her handbook is a terrific guide to how to put these questions to the right people. And how to keep going with them until you get some sort of answer.

The good news is that answers are being given, to all sorts of enquiries that might previously have been considered as too important, too sensitive, or just too impertinent. The bad news is that the opponents of Freedom of Information are claiming that the whole process is too expensive and that people are asking silly questions and merely wasting officials' time.

Heather Brooke's accounts of the successes of Freedom of Information and her analysis of why transparency could actually prevent mismanagement and even disaster are a convincing riposte to such allegations and affirm the genuine value of the public's right to know. This book was sufficiently successful first time out to now be called YRTK but if we are talking acronyms it should actually be called DIYFOI. Brooke does not merely want to conduct investigations herself. She wants you, the general public, to go out and find out about issues that concern you – whether it is policing terrorism, awarding private companies public contracts, EU farm subsidies, local councils selling playing fields or anything else that comes to mind. If this is not exactly a call to arms, it is certainly a call to write a letter. Belloc's poem contains the memorable line:

So grin and bear it, Stupid, do not bleat.

In this country we have perhaps been too good at the grinning and bearing it and not very good at the bleating bit. And maybe it has taken an American like Heather Brooke (I got this piece of information without recourse to FOI legislation) to alert us to what we should and can do to correct our 'general misapprehension' and exercise our right to know.

Ian Hislop
2006

Acknowledgements

This is a book for citizens so firstly I would like to thank all the people who wrote in with suggestions, queries, experiences and even praise for the first edition of the book and the www.yrtk.org website. It's always heartening as an author to know that the work one does in solitary confinement is read and used by others. There would not be a second edition without the team at Pluto Press, so thanks to all the editors and staff, particularly David Castle.

I am very grateful to Ian Hislop for graciously agreeing to write the new foreword. Tom Young was a blessing for helping with research, interviews and fact checking. Thanks also to various FOI officers, too many to name, for sharing their experiences with me. Steve Wood at Liverpool John Moores University deserves praise for assiduously maintaining a fantastic FOI blog that continues to set the standard for the FOI community. As ever, continued appreciation to Maurice Frankel and Katherine Gundersen at the Campaign for Freedom of Information for their work and to David Banisar who keeps me informed about what's happening in the wider world of FOI. There are lots of other people to thank including all those mentioned in the first edition.

Finally, the biggest thank you, as always, goes to my husband, Vaci, who continues to inspire and support in equal measure. Behind every great woman, there is sometimes an even better man.

Introduction

*'There is not a crime, there is not a dodge, there is not a trick, there is
not a swindle which does not live by secrecy. Get these things out in the
open, describe them, attack them, ridicule them in the press, and sooner
or later public opinion will sweep them away.'*

Joseph Pulitzer

The new second edition of *Your Right to Know* comes almost two years
after the first. Writing the original, I often felt like a fortune-teller,
trying to predict how people would use the Freedom of Information
Act and the subsequent reaction by politicians to being held directly
accountable to citizens.

Now, after two years, it is much easier to see the good and bad
points of the law in practice. This new update takes into account
all the many and varied requests made in the first two years by
campaigners, journalists, politicians, lawyers, trade unionists,
historians, consumer groups, researchers and citizens. It's satisfying
to see that many of the issues I campaigned for in the first edition
have come to pass. For the first time, the British public can now see
restaurant inspections, MPs' expenses, contracts for public services
provided by private companies and police incident reports. But these
are just the basics of accountable government, a chink of light in a
very dark cavern! Fortunately, there are many people asking their own
questions and setting new precedents for greater openness. That's the
purpose of this book. The government and practitioners have plenty
of books and experts advising them on the law, but *Your Right to Know*
remains the only publication by, and for, the citizen.

The Freedom of Information Act and its sister the Environmental
Information Regulations came into force on 1 January 2005. The laws
cover more than 100,000 public authorities and mean a wealth of
previously secret information is now accessible for the first time – but
only if you know where to look and how to ask the right questions.

Already, we are seeing power shift back into the hands of people as
they use the laws to ask searching questions about our public services.
While not quite the sword of truth some had hoped, the new laws are
an effective chisel against government secrecy and corruption. Some
of the major disclosures in the first year and half include:

- Lists of all those receiving farm subsidies from the EU. The big surprise was that Nestlé, Unilever, Tate & Lyle, the Royals and the Duke of Westminster pocketed the most.
- Mortality rates for all Scottish surgeons and some English surgeons
- A full listing of all Post Office closures in the coming years
- Taxi receipts for Scottish MSPs leading to the resignation of Tory MSP leader David McLetchie over questions about taxi misuse. (Other MSPs were forced to reimburse the taxpayer for abusing the system.)
- The cost of policing Abu Hamza's street pulpit for almost a year = £900,000. Hamza was later found guilty of inciting murder and racial hatred.
- The amount councils have earned from selling off playing fields
- Documents that showed De Montfort University had lowered pass grades so pharmacy students could continue to study even though they had failed their exams
- The release of a Suffolk policeman's notebook to a motorist who complained about his behaviour.

WHAT'S NEW?

This edition includes a new chapter 'FOI in Practice' that discusses the implementation and enforcement of the new laws. It pinpoints the major problems that have developed and how best to overcome them. You'll find new references to case law from the Scottish and UK Information Commissioners and Information Tribunal along with precedent-setting disclosures that you can use in your own quest for answers.

This book does not need to be read cover-to-cover. You'll find an explanation of your rights and how to use them in the Laws of Access chapter, but if legal discussion daunts you, skip directly to the chapter that deals with the type of information you seek. Each chapter includes a selection of interesting FOI disclosures and a discussion on that sector's response to the law, tips for digging out information, where the trouble spots are and how to overcome them. All contact details have been thoroughly updated and will continue to be monitored via the Your Right to Know website, www.yrtk. org. I've included internet sites where you can obtain answers and wherever possible, named FOI contacts for relevant agencies. There are a few exceptions where public bodies are so mired in secrecy they refuse to even disclose the name of their openness officer (e.g. The Highways Agency)!

A few public bodies are new to this edition, namely the Charity Commission, the BBC, Channel 4 and the Royal Mail (Post Office). These public bodies have become popular targets for requests and while not strictly part of central government you will find their contacts in Chapter 4. Scotland gets its own section as it has taken the lead on issues of freedom of information due to its competent and decisive Commissioner and the progressive view taken by Parliament on the issue of MSPs' expenses. Important precedents are being set in Scotland that will influence what happens in the UK.

The chapter on private companies includes more information on getting contracts, tenders and performance evaluations. As public authorities contract out more of their services, freedom of information is one of the only ways to monitor how taxpayers' money is spent. In America, businesses are major users of FOI, and it is likely they will be in the UK, too. British commerce is a very cosy coterie with the same big businesses getting all the big government contracts. Small and new businesses often have little chance of landing a contract, even when their services are superior and better value for money. FOI can expose the informal lobbying and uncompetitive practices that stifle the free market.

There are new template letters at the back of the book for most types of requests. Feel free to use them or adapt them as you see fit. And please do let me know about your successes, failures or frustrations via www.yrtk.org

TIME FOR CHANGE

Getting information out of government is not always easy. For every disclosure there are hundreds of refusals. Parliament is still far from open with our own MPs refusing to release their detailed expense claims, in contrast to the new transparency of Scottish MSPs. A catalogue of intelligence failures that culminated with the London bombings and subsequent shooting of an innocent man on the London Underground have not led to the needed reforms in the security and police services. The courts, too, need a major overhaul as they remain secretive, unaccountable and unjust with little regard for the law-abiding public's right to see justice being done.

Already some of the battle lines between citizen and state are becoming entrenched. You ask a question: lawyers for the public authority (funded by the public) devise reasons to refuse, you argue that the information is in the public interest, they demand an extension to consider this. You wait. They refuse. You appeal to the Information Commissioner and wait some more. If you're very lucky he makes a decision.

But this is a battle worth fighting. As the saying goes – the cost of freedom is eternal vigilance. Politicians have taken advantage of our indifference by imposing ever more draconian and restrictive laws that increase their power while diminishing ours. Asking questions of our public bodies is the best way to ensure they are working for our interests and not those of politicians. Through FOI we can go behind political rhetoric to see the true state of affairs. For example, in Doncaster residents discovered that Mayor Martin Winter wasn't exactly truthful when he told them he hadn't interfered in planning matters. Documents released under the FOIA showed him personally intervening in a planning application from a developer who helped fund his election campaigns.[1]

A notable result of the law is that any refusals must be accompanied by legal reasoning. The burden is now on secretive officials to justify their behaviour rather than on citizens having to justify their right to know. Of course it's a shame that one must adopt an almost warrior-like mentality to get information out of government, but history has shown that those with power are eager to hold on to it, and the main way of maintaining power is to restrict access to information. The harsh reality is that governments have an interest in keeping secret the information that proves their policies are wrong, and many of the organisations who give evidence on policy decisions are self-interested parties who may present biased or slanted data.

In the first few years, what has become clear is that the determination and hard work of an individual *can* produce remarkable results. It was Paul Hutcheon's relentless pursuit of detailed taxi receipts from Scottish politicians that exposed the numerous abuses in the system. His determination is largely responsible for the amazing new transparency in the Scottish Parliament.

The success of any freedom of information regime depends on two main factors: A tightly drawn law with a clear statement of intent that makes clear a presumption of openness, and a bold regulator who is

1. *Yorkshire Post*, 31 March 2006, 'Mayor said one thing but did another'.

tough and not afraid to exert his authority and challenge government interests. Many of the problems I predicted in the first edition have come to pass; specifically, the abuse by secrecy-loving bureaucrats of the many and vague exemptions and the time extensions. The law is only as good as its enforcement and there has been precious little of that. There are no fines or penalties for non-compliance and what little powers the UK Commissioner has, he has not used them. A dangerous message is being sent to negligent officials that they can ignore the law.

Instead of focusing on these major problems, the government has instead dredged up the wholly ridiculous notion that FOI is too expensive and used by people making vexatious requests. The cost of making government more responsive to the people who fund it and in whose name it exists should not be attributed solely to FOI, but even if it is, surely that is a cost worth bearing? Making government transparent and accountable to the public directly increases the efficiency of the public sector more than any number of government regulators or watchdogs. Already we have seen that FOI has led to efficiency savings from investment in better-trained staff, records management systems and customer service. FOI also highlights problems early, before they become catastrophic mistakes. A strong FOI regime means fewer regulators and public inquiries that eat up public money. The BSE inquiry cost £27 million while the Bloody Sunday inquiry was in its sixth year in 2006 and the last official estimate put its cost at £155 million, though £200 million is probably more accurate.

We all live in a community and therefore all of us have some interest in the way things are run. Even those who are not interested in politics cannot escape the ubiquitous presence of government. What if you suddenly find yourself in bad health? You might want to know:

- The trust with the shortest waiting times for your operation
- The hospital with the least incidents of MRSA
- The best surgeon for your particular malady
- The trust's budget for certain drugs such as Herceptin

Or perhaps you're looking for the best school for your child. You might like to know:

- How many teachers face disciplinary action
- How many teachers or children at the school are on the sexual offenders register?

- How many children are excluded from school and why?
- What is the school's record on dealing with bullies?

You shouldn't be shy about requesting even seemingly trivial information. If something bothers you, chances are that it bothers someone else too. You may even uncover a more serious problem. For example, you may find that your council is ineffective at dealing with noise complaints and this may be a problem in other councils. Whatever your concern, whether it be intensely personal and local, national or even global (such as arms trade figures or sea pollution data), you'll find this book gives you the means to investigate your complaints, concerns and curiosities.

A word of caution – the Freedom of Information Act isn't the cure-all for secrecy many had hoped for, and it's certainly a much weaker version than that proposed by the government in its initial White Paper, but combined with a number of other initiatives, the FOIA does mark a significant shift in the relationship between the government and the governed. For the first time the government's 'Right to Secrecy' is replaced in law with the public's 'Right to Know'. This change took place several decades ago in most other developed countries, but it is to be hoped that Britain will quickly catch up. How quickly things change depends on how the government, the media and the public react to the new rights.

The British state is a complex and unwieldy beast. Bureaucratic agencies, one grafted upon the other, meander this way and that; their vast number and medieval secrecy making them an unaccountable mystery to the people they govern. The government has evolved into thousands of quangos, departments, committees and oddly divided local authorities, some hidden inside others like a set of Russian dolls. The rise of the quangos (quasi-autonomous non-governmental organisations) and public-private partnerships (PPPs) has further dissolved public service accountability. So the first purpose of this book is to help you work out where to direct your query – this can prove the most frustrating part of any request.

The public has had to put up with a sorry state of affairs in which policies are formulated in secret, using facts and figures hidden from public view. Our only input in most cases is to hand over our money to pay for it all. The greatest myth perpetuated by successive British governments is that secrecy somehow benefits society – that it is essential for 'free and candid debate'. Nothing could be further from the truth. Time and again, we've seen that secrecy leads to bad decisions and bad government.

Huge sums of public money have been wasted due to corruption, inefficiency or bad decisions on projects such as the Millennium Dome, the constant restructuring of the railways, the part-privatisation of the Tube, the Trident submarine weapons system, the Jubilee Line extension, and numerous delayed and over-budget IT systems. It is also important to consider the real human cost of Britain's policy of official secrecy. We pay for our public services and yet until now we have had almost no rights to know how safe and efficient they are. Public agencies and the private companies that work with them may be wasting our money and putting our lives at risk. It is essential that we have a right to see every safety inspection, fire and accident report made about a public service. A short list of the tragedies that might not have happened if an FOIA had been in place earlier include the Potters Bar and Hatfield train crashes, the numerous Tube derailments, the Matrix Churchill scandal where the government secretly lifted a ban on selling weapons to Saddam Hussein, the *Marchioness* ferry disaster, and, for secrecy in the NHS, the Harold Shipman case, the Bristol deaths and the Alder Hey hospital scandal in which organs were taken from dead children without their parents' consent. Inquiries into all these events showed there was enough information available beforehand to signal what was to come, but by keeping it secret, the problem was allowed to fester.

The BSE crisis provides a good example of the short-term allure of secrecy and how damaging it proves in the long term – not just to public confidence in government but also to the public's health and livelihood. The inquiry showed the government had suppressed the truth and failed to inform the public about the extent of the epidemic, so vets and farmers didn't know the symptoms or the seriousness of the disease until it was too late. Officials were afraid that being honest and open would lead to a panic and a collapse of the beef trade. The reality is that people are more likely to act rationally and believe a government's advice if all the information has been put forward.

What is finally being realised is the hidden costs of secrecy – it allows bad practices to continue unchecked. One reason government officials hate openness is that it highlights their mistakes, and that's embarrassing. However, avoiding embarrassment should not be the guiding principle of any government; running an efficient and well-run system should be. We only improve by making mistakes, and as it is with people, so it is with government. So if an agency is never held accountable, it is never faced with its mistakes, it can never really learn anything and thus will never improve. Exposure then comes in the form of a crisis or scandal. The problem then is the public's loss of trust.

The priority of all those engaged in public service needs to be first and foremost to serve the public. What a simple thought, and yet if you've ever had dealings with those in the public sector, you'll know that that's not always the case. Ringing the council can lead to total frustration as you find that (a) no one knows who it is you need to talk to; (b) you're transferred to various people then cut off; (c) you get the name of the right person, but they're either off sick, on flexi-time, on holiday, on strike, or generally never around; or (d) you manage to speak to the person who holds the information you want, but they won't give it to you!

Novel concept: the public pay for and elect the government and it is only by the public's will that those in public office hold power. Public servants' primary responsibility is to serve the public.

The litmus test of any FOI law is getting information about more sensitive subjects such as health and safety, law enforcement, commercial dealings, national security and defence – it is on these topics that the law will be judged. How these exemptions will be interpreted is still being decided. That is why it is important for people to test the new law and see what's available. This book is not just a primer on how things work; I hope it inspires action and that you'll file actual requests.

So have a go, and push the boundaries of public accountability. Make a few requests and if you don't get what you want, appeal and keep appealing. Even if your efforts are not rewarded with the information you requested, your case could be used as evidence as to why the law should be amended.

Getting information is only the beginning. Transparency in government must be accompanied by the public's right to be heard and to influence government policy. The first objective is to get the facts, for without facts we are powerless to oppose government decisions or bring about change. The next step is to open up the decision-making process so we finally have a government accountable to those it serves. This should be our right and not a privilege.

I
FOI in Practice

Freedom of Information is a fantastic tool for improving democracy and equality, but there are also tremendous benefits for improving the professionalism, integrity, honesty and value for money of all public services. The continual state of crisis management that haunts many public services is often the result of problems that were allowed to fester and grow in the traditional climate of secrecy.

Contrary to expectation, FOI was not used solely by journalists in the early years, though they were first off the mark on 1 January 2005 putting in requests. Very quickly, citizens took over to become the main users of the Act. In the first year, FOI requests broke down like this:

- 70,000 requests to English councils[1]
- 40,000 to central government and associated public bodies[2]
- 21,000 to police forces nationwide[3]
- 2,083 requests to higher education[4]
- 400 to the General Medical Council
- 18,000 voluntary groups used the Act at least once in the first year and 50,000 bodies plan to use it in the future[5]

That's a lot of people exercising their right to know, especially considering there was almost no promotion of the Act from Whitehall. Information Commissioner Richard Thomas told me his office spent just £218,000 promoting the Act over a three-year period up to March 2006. Perhaps as a result, only 11 per cent of people knew about the FOIA without prompting, according to a survey done by his office. Awareness does rise to 79 per cent when prompted, however, usually by mentioning stories in the media where the law is cited for a major disclosure. Awareness was higher in Scotland, due to the Scottish Commissioner's more proactive role promoting the Act.

1. Survey by the Improvement and Development Agency.
2. Statistical bulletins compiled by the Department for Constitutional Affairs.
3. DCC Ian Readhead, FOI Unit, Association of Chief Police Officers.
4. Survey conducted by Joint Information Systems Committee, www. jiscinfonet.ac.uk/foi-survey/foi-survey-results-2005
5. Survey by the National Council for Volunteer Organisations.

The new openness laws have not overloaded public services or led to the collapse of government. The Commissioner's survey found that 81 per cent of FOI practitioners cited the Act as a positive piece of legislation and only 3 per cent thought it particularly troublesome. Even more noteworthy, 79 per cent of public authorities said releasing information under FOI had increased trust in their service and improved records. As a result of the greater accountability they said public relationships had improved.

The *Yes, Minister* aphorism that you can either be open or have government but not open government is simply not true. History shows that those countries with a strong free press and freedom of information laws are the best run and most economically successful, while the ones adhering to the '*Yes, Minister*' view are badly run dictatorships.

Ironically, in 2006 the UK government was involved in a secret review of the FOI Act and there was concern that politicians were laying the groundwork for weakening the law further. The Lord Chancellor Charlie Falconer claimed public bodies were being overwhelmed with vexatious FOI requests and that fees would need to be introduced to cope. Yet, the Chancellor only knew of six such requests – out of more than 150,000 across the public sector.

The real problems with the law do not come from the public, but from those in power who are neither adhering to nor enforcing the law in a timely way.

Heather's tips for getting results

- Some public authorities will claim they never received your request. If you think this might be the case, send your letter by registered mail or put a receive receipt on your email.
- If the information you seek is lost or destroyed ask for the organisation's records disposal policy. If the policy states that all meeting minutes are kept for five years and you find the minutes from a controversial meeting three months ago were destroyed, you have a legitimate complaint. If a private company stores the records, ask for its name and any correspondence related to the destruction of records.
- If the public body says they need more time to consider the public interest, make them tell you the criteria they are using for this test. You may find that they don't have any criteria as they're simply using the extension as an excuse to delay your request. Or they may be using factors such as 'embarrassment to politicians' that are not applicable.
- Internal reviews should normally take no more than 20 working days. If yours is taking longer, ask to see the public body's complaints handling policy. In the worst instance, you can complain to the Commissioner about the delay and he may begin investigating your complaint directly.   ▶

- When appealing to the Commissioner, make sure your application contains your original request and all subsequent correspondence with the public authority. The Information Commissioner's Office (ICO) now has a model complaint form and checklist available online that you should consult.
- Check the websites of the Scottish and UK commissioners and the Tribunal to see if there are any existing decisions that support your case and cite these in your appeal. Currently the UK Commissioner's website does not offer a search facility, though one is promised by 2007, so look at www.ucl.ac.uk/constitution-unit/foidp/resources/ICO-Cases/foi-index.html
- If your case is held up at the Commissioner's Office, ask for 28-day status reports as specified in the ICO's memorandum of understanding. If you face extreme delay, perhaps of a year or longer, you might try approaching the Information Tribunal to see if it will intervene, or write to your MP.

PROBLEMS IN THE EARLY YEARS AND HOW TO OVERCOME THEM

Delay

Information is a highly perishable commodity so undue delay diminishes its usefulness. Delay has been the number one problem with the law. Unfortunately, the regulator meant to tackle this problem is only adding to it with more delay and a backlog of cases. Nevertheless, the minister in charge of FOI told the Parliamentary committee investigating the first year of FOI: 'There's nothing I see that is a systemic problem in relation to delay' (Baroness Ashton of Upholland speaking to the Constitutional Affairs Committee, 18 April 2006).

Delay is endemic in all stages, and is likely to get worse before it gets better. Firstly, some public authorities are failing to respond within the 20-working day limit. The Home Office is a persistent offender. The department waited until 19 September 2005 to respond to a request sent on 3 January 2005, and then the answer was to refuse the request because answering would exceed the cost limit. The complainant then refined the request to bring it into the cost limit, only for the Home Office to say the information was exempt! The Information Commissioner's ruling on 2 November 2005 stated only: 'the Home Office has breached the time limit for compliance under the Act and has advised the ICO that it expects to provide a substantive response to the complainant by 14/12/04' (Case Ref: FS50073711).

Then there is the whole appeals process that can take up to a year or longer. Before you take a case to the Commissioner, you first have to seek an internal review from the same public body that originally refused your request. You won't be surprised to learn that in 78 per cent of cases[6] the public body agrees with its original refusal. The law does not specify a deadline for internal reviews, but all public authorities should have a complaints policy that states their performance targets.

Another delaying tactic adopted by bureaucrats is a loophole in the law that allows public bodies a time extension if they need to consider the public interest. The Metropolitan Police cited this extension three times while delaying my request for documentation about the shoot-to-kill policy. In total, I waited four months for their answer, which was only a partial disclosure.

Unless this loophole is closed, I predict that it will become widely abused as a means of discouraging the public from asking questions. Ultimately it is up to the Commissioner or Parliament to step in and set strict time limits. The current failure to impose *any* deadline sets a bad example that will only encourage these delaying tactics.

Ironically, it is within the Commissioner's Office itself that one encounters the greatest delay. Out of seven cases I put through to the Commissioner, just one had been processed after more than a year. By March 2006 there were 1,372 cases still open. Friends of the Earth discovered that of all the cases pending as of 15 January 2006, 586 cases were older than six months and 106 had not even been allocated to a caseworker.

This delay is frightening because only a fraction of refusals go to the Commissioner (0.72 per cent to be exact).[7] Only the most tenacious citizens are taking their cases to the Commissioner, so if there is already such delay, it can only discourage others from seeking review. Finally, in March 2006, the Commissioner announced that he was implementing a performance target of closing 50 per cent of cases within 60 working days.

The Commissioner's Office should communicate with applicants every 28 days,[8] yet this is not happening. Stephen Gradwick, a consultant in Merseyside who has made almost 40 FOIA requests, told me the only way he has been able to keep track of his cases is by telephoning the Commissioner's Office. 'They are just not being helpful or user-friendly, and I'm given no information about the status

---

6. DCA quarterly statistics (Q4) 2005.
7. Survey conducted by Joint Information Systems Committee, www. jiscinfonet.ac.uk/foi-survey/foi-survey-results-2005
8. Section 19, Memorandum of Understanding between the ICO and Department for Constitutional Affairs.

of my cases unless I ring. At one point, the Deputy Commissioner then sent me an email telling me to stop enquiring about my cases.' It's not clear what rights, if any, applicants have in the face of such poor performance. All I can suggest is that you badger the Commissioner's Office every 28 days and demand to know the status of your case.

The Commissioner told me that he is committed to reforming his Office before his term expires on 30 November 2007. A newly designed website would finally include a searchable list of cases under investigation and decisions issued. This is good to hear, because the only way to judge the effectiveness of the regulator is to have regular access to caseload statistics.

A severe lack of enforcement

If you or I were to ignore, say, the parking rules in our town, we would most likely find a ticket for £50 slapped on the windscreen of our car – if it hadn't been clamped or towed. But when the state breaks its own law on freedom of information it faces no penalty whatsoever. This is partly due to the laxity of the law, but also the laxity of the regulator charged with enforcing it.

'The point of the law is not to punish public authorities,' the Commissioner told me. 'The court can penalise them, but I cannot.' While technically true, the Commissioner does have the power to name and shame those who disobey the law. Yet he has refused to use even this limited power.

The UK Commissioner received 2,385 complaints during 2005. The public authorities subject to complaints were:

- Local government – 39 per cent
- Central government – 29 per cent
- Health – 7.5 per cent
- Police – 7 per cent
- Quangos – 7 per cent
- Education – 4.5 per cent
- Publicly-owned companies – 2 per cent
- Others – 4 per cent

As of March 2006, the Commissioner had made 155 decisions, but of these only 23 per cent (36) dealt with exemptions while 77 per cent (119) involved procedural issues such as a public authority failing to reject the request properly (i.e. not issuing a proper 'refusal notice'). This is troublesome because what we all want to know is what sort of information should be disclosed. The public wants to know this, but so, too, do public bodies. For example, it took the Commissioner almost a year to decide that restaurant inspections should be made public even though he was aware this would be a test case. In the meantime, hundreds of councils across the country spent tens of thousands of pounds consulting their lawyers on this issue.

It's worth noting that in Scotland, which has its own Commissioner, 120 decisions were made in the same time period of which 54 per cent (65) dealt with exemptions and 46 per cent (55) were about technical issues.

One of the few powers the Commissioner has, besides making rulings, is to issue practice recommendations that set out how public bodies should respond to certain types of requests. Yet by March 2006, the UK Commissioner had not issued any. He can also issue enforcement notices, demanding compliance on a certain issue, but none of these were issued either.

There is also a danger that in an effort to offload as many cases as possible, the Commissioner is using informal resolution or rejecting cases that he classifies as academic. An 'academic' case might be one where there are no steps he can take to remedy a breach of the Act, for example because the information requested has already been released, albeit late. The problem is that no formal record exists of how the cases were resolved so members of the public who may be in an identical situation don't benefit. Of course, if similar cases come to the Commissioner, one would expect they would be dealt with jointly, but this has not always happened.

Matthew Davis, news director of John Connor Press Associates Limited, was one of the first people to take his appeal to the Information Tribunal after the UK Commissioner upheld the National Maritime Museum's refusal to disclose to Davis the cost of a public sculpture. His impression of the Commissioner's Office, shared by many with cases under review, was of an office in disarray with poor management. 'One of the first cases I sent to the Commissioner's Office was lost,' he told me. 'I only discovered it when I received an acknowledgement letter for another complaint. When I called up they said it had been lost and that I'd need to re-send the file, so I did – this time by registered post.' Many of the Tribunal's early rulings were highly critical of the Commissioner's investigations and processes. Letters were often lost in the system and investigators failed to talk to either party in the case.

A further indictment came in June 2006 when the Information Commissioner was forced to issue the first decision notice against his own office for failing to comply with the Freedom of Information Act. Friends of the Earth brought the complaint after the Commissioner failed to follow both the legislation and code of practice in response to their request for information.[9]

It's illegal for us to release that to the public

The most striking evidence of the culture of secrecy operating in the UK is the existence of more than 200 laws making it an offence to release information to the public. These prohibitions on disclosure cover all manner of things and there is no regard for the public interest. The Official Secrets Act is probably the most notorious prohibition on disclosure but there are many more such as section 21 of the Fire Precautions Act 1971, which makes it a criminal offence to publish fire safety inspection reports! Part 9 of the Enterprise Act 2002 could be seen as making it illegal for councils to give out any information they hold on businesses even when those businesses are dangerous to the public (see Chapter 13 for more about the Enterprise Act). Normally, new legislation, such as the FOIA, amends the old automatically, but government officials were so worried about freedom of information they created an exception whereby the old laws had precedence over the new. They are a major obstacle in advancing openness. They are also superfluous in light of the many and broad exemptions in the FOIA.

The first Parliamentary Order to amend these prohibitions was made in November 2004, affecting just eight pieces of legislation, and came into force on 1 January 2005. But a second Order to address the remaining 200+ laws remains outstanding. It should have been published on 1 January 2005, but was deferred to March 2005 and then delayed indefinitely. Even finding all the laws has been a task that has kept the Department for Constitutional Affairs busy for more than five years.

One way to avoid this obstacle is to frame your request as an environmental question. That way, it is covered by the Environmental Information Regulations 2004. This law is the domestic version of an EU Directive and EU law supersedes all domestic legislation. So EIRs override these prohibitions on disclosure.

We don't hold that information

If a public authority comes back to you saying they don't hold the information you want, you should ask them why. Is it because

9. Case Ref: FS50116262, 31 May 2006.

someone else has it? Is it because it's been destroyed? Or perhaps it's simply lost in a basement of boxes! FOI has highlighted what is often an appalling state of records management operating in many public bodies. If the information you want can't be found, or was destroyed, then you should probe the public authority for more information. They should be able to provide an audit trail for the destruction, and if they can't, then you are right to be suspicious.

The Code of Practice issued under section 46 of the Act (I mention it by name, only because it's a useful reference) states that:

> An authority should have in place an overall policy statement... on how it manages its records, including electronic records. This policy statement should provide a mandate for the performance of all records and information management functions... and provide a framework for supporting standards, procedures and guidelines; and indicate the way in which compliance with the policy and its supporting standards, procedures and guidelines will be monitored. [6.1–6.2]

Quote this paragraph to any public authority who claims they can't find what you need, and ask them why they don't have their records in order.

Spin Central

People face additional delay and difficulty getting information from central government due to the creation of a centralised clearinghouse run jointly by the Department for Constitutional Affairs and the Cabinet Office. Requests from the press, round-robins, and pretty much anything remotely controversial will likely be referred to the clearinghouse. The official line is that the clearinghouse 'acts as a source of expert advice for all central government departments, ensuring the Act is applied correctly and consistently'. A spokeswoman said advice is provided within a few days of referral. The reality is that it introduces another level of delay and executive control of information.

All departments and a number of quangos are instructed to approve any disclosure with the clearinghouse. No reporting data on the cases referred to the clearinghouse and how they are dealt with is published. From an answer to a Parliamentary question we know that it received 3,006 referrals between 1 January and 31 October 2005. If the assumption is made that the majority of the referrals were made by central government departments this could mean that as many as 20 per cent of requests are overseen by the clearinghouse. A spokeswoman from the DCA told me the DCA planned to publish monitoring data for the clearinghouse for 2005 in the first annual report on FOI implementation in central government.

You can have it, but you can't use it

If you're lucky enough to get the information you sought, there are still difficulties if you want to use or reuse it. It is not unusual to receive your answer to an FOI request accompanied by an intimidating copyright statement. Such statements serve to stifle the wider dissemination of official information. Along with seeking to restrict the reuse of information, public authorities often like to charge for its use. This is covered in more detail in the 'Copyrighting public information' section of Chapter 4. The good news is that in March 2006, the *Guardian* newspaper launched an excellent campaign to 'Free Our Data' (www.freeourdata.org.uk) to abolish restrictive copyright and fees for public information. Combined with an Office of Fair Trading investigation into public sector information, momentum seemed to be building for the abolition of restrictive copyright.

SOME IMPORTANT DECISIONS

The Information Tribunal

The Information Tribunal had made seven FOI rulings and just one under the Environmental Information Regulations as of May 2006. They may be few, but the rulings involved substantial issues and set important precedents that advanced the cause of greater openness.

One strange fact to come to light is that the Information Commissioner is listed as respondent in all cases. This means that if you are appealing a council's refusal to release, say, a list of planning inspectors' qualifications, your case at Tribunal is actually against the Information Commissioner (for his decision upholding the council's refusal) rather than the council itself. This is odd. It means one party in the case is always effectively excluded. In this example, it would be the council, but it could equally be you if the Commissioner had ruled in your favour and the council had appealed his ruling. It would be better if both parties were directly involved in the Tribunal case and the Commissioner remained an impartial observer. The current system puts at risk his objectivity and independence.

John Connor Press Associates Limited* v. *Information Commissioner (25 January 2006). This Tribunal ruling overturned the Commissioner's decision that the National Maritime Museum could withhold the cost of a publicly funded artwork under section 43 of the Act (information prejudicial to commercial interests). Journalist Matthew Davis had asked for documents and correspondence relating to any payments made to an artist Conrad Shawcross for his exhibition 'Continuum'. While supplying much of the information, the museum refused to release the costs paid to the artist stating that to do so would prejudice future procurement. The Tribunal found the museum had not demonstrated sufficient risk of prejudice to their commercial interests to justify the exemption and the figures were released. This is a case worth citing for all requests regarding procurement details.

Barber v. *Information Commissioner* (11 November 2005). The Tribunal ruled that requests using critical language did not invalidate the information sought. In this case, a taxpayer had asked the Inland Revenue for details on what action it had taken to deal with what he described as 'maladministration' and 'failed standards' in relation to the refunding of overpaid Self Assessment tax. Inland Revenue did not accept that it had failed and so it said it held no information that met Mr Barber's request. The Commissioner ruled in favour of Inland Revenue, but the Tribunal disagreed, noting that the Revenue had apologised in 2000 for shortcomings and failings. It stated: 'If Public Authorities are permitted under the FOIA to pick and choose which requests they respond to on the basis of whether or not they approve of the language used by requesters, this would make a mockery of the legislation.' The Tribunal also criticised the laxity of the Commissioner's investigation stating it found no evidence that anyone from his office had contacted either party. It also instructed the Commissioner to ensure that public authorities were providing advice and assistance to those seeking requests.

Harper v. *Information Commissioner* (15 November 2005). This important judgment overturned guidance issued by the Information Commissioner and the Department for Constitutional Affairs that stated deleted information was not considered to be held. The Tribunal stated that information on a back-up system is 'held' for the purposes of the FOIA. Mr Harper asked the Royal Mail whether there had been any requests to access his personnel file. The Royal Mail said they no longer held the file as it had been deleted. The Tribunal accepted that the information was deleted and was not retrievable within the cost limit. However, it then went on to state that: 'Simple restoration from a trash can or recycle bin folder, or from a back-up tape, should normally be attempted, as the Tribunal considers that such information continues to be held.'

***Alistair Mitchell* v. *Information Commissioner* (10 October 2005).** This decision answered the question of whether court transcripts are exempt under FOIA. Bridgnorth District Council spent taxpayers' money to buy a transcript of a court case in which one of its councillors and two officials had been prosecuted for perjury. The proceedings were recorded by Cater Walsh, court reporters, and the council reputedly spent £7,000 on the written transcript of the 2001 trial. Mr Mitchell wanted the transcripts but the council refused, claiming the documents were exempt under section 32 as they were court records. The Commissioner ruled in the council's favour but the Tribunal overturned this ruling. It specified that a 'court record' for the purpose of the Act applied to:

(i)   'documents created by a court' which meant created by the judge himself;
(ii) documents created by the administrative staff of a court.

Since the recording had not been produced by a member of the court staff or by the judge but by an outside agency, it did not fall within either of these two categories, and was not exempt under this provision. This sets a good precedent. Unfortunately, Mr Mitchell did not benefit from the ruling as the council had already shredded the documents prior to his request! The Tribunal made clear that in similar cases it would order disclosure.

***Mr David Markinson* v. *Information Commissioner* (28 March 2006).** This case has major implications for the amounts charged by public bodies to those seeking access to environmental information. In this case, David Markinson sought to make copies of planning documents at King's Lynn and West Norfolk Borough Council. The council charged £6 for the first A4 black and white sheet and 50p thereafter. Mr Markinson said this was unreasonable and complained to the Information Commissioner. After a botched investigation in which the Commissioner mislaid several letters, the Commissioner made his ruling using the incorrect law – the FOIA instead of the EIRs. The Tribunal then made its own decision notice under the EIRs and directed the council to adopt as a guide price the sum of 10p per A4 sheet, as identified in the good practice guidance on access to and charging for planning information published by the then Office of the Deputy Prime Minister and as recommended by the Department for

Constitutional Affairs. You will find a new letter challenging excessive fees for environmental information in the back of this book.

Scottish decisions of note:

Decision 033/2005, Paul Hutcheon of *The Sunday Herald* **and The Scottish Parliamentary Corporate Body,** Case No: 200501974, Decision Date: 6 October 2005. The Commissioner ordered the disclosure of taxi journey destinations for MSP David McLetchie's travelling claims. He resigned after the disclosure.

Decision 066/2005, Mr Peter MacMahon of *The Scotsman* **and the Common Services Agency for the Scottish Health Service,** Case No: 200501123, Decision Date: 8 December 2005, **and Decision 065/2005, Mr Camillo Fracassini of** *The Sunday Times* **and the Common Services Agency for the Scottish Health Service,** Case No: 200500906, Decision Date: 8 December 2005. These important judgments will have repercussions for health services in the UK. The Scottish Commissioner ordered the release of information about the mortality rates of all surgeons since 2000, including the name of each surgeon, his/her speciality, the hospital in which he/she is based, and the number of patients the surgeon has operated on, by year. The Commissioner accepted that while the information was personal data, its release would not breach any of the data protection principles. The Commissioner also decided that release of the information would not prejudice substantially the effective conduct of public affairs as the public authority had claimed.

Decision 052/2005, Balfour & Manson Solicitors and the Scottish Executive, Case No: 200502019, Decision Date: 9 December 2005. The Commissioner ruled that the Scottish Executive must release details of all fees paid to lawyers. Balfour & Manson Solicitors made the request and the Scottish Executive refused on grounds that the material was exempt personal data as its disclosure would breach the data protection principles. The Commissioner ruled that it would not breach the principles and ruled that the Executive should release the total figure for each Counsel.

UK Commissioner decisions of note:

Department for Education and Skills (Notice FS50074589, 4 January 2006). IC ordered disclosure of minutes of senior management meetings and the identities of civil servants noted at the meeting.

Derry City Council (Notice FS50066753, 21 February 2006). IC ordered disclosure of details about Derry City Airport's agreement with Ryanair for the use of its airport, as well as how much Ryanair paid to Derry City Council for the use of its airport facilities. The Commissioner considered that the information did not fall within the stated exemptions – section 29(1)(a) (the economy), section 41 (information in confidence) and section 43(2) (commercial interests).

House of Commons (Notice FS50071194, 22 February 2006). IC ordered disclosure of a breakdown of the travel expenses claimed by individual MPs over the past three years in the following three categories: car travel, rail travel and air travel. The Commons has appealed to the Tribunal. Several other cases seeking detailed expense claims were still under investigation by the Commissioner at the time of going to press.

Ministry of Defence (Notice FS50073980, 19 April 2006). IC ordered disclosure of the staff directory of arms sales officials in the Ministry of Defence's Defence Exports Services Organisation. The ruling is likely to have a significant effect in opening up secretive government departments who have used a variety of loopholes to stop the public knowing the identities of staff. The decision means departments may soon be required to publish their internal phone books, as happens in America.

2
Scotland

Scotland is taking the lead in freedom of information case law and setting precedents for the rest of the UK, so it's worth being familiar with the law even if you don't live in Scotland.

The UK Act is applicable in England, Wales, Northern Ireland and for UK government departments in Scotland. All other Scottish public authorities are covered by the Freedom of Information (Scotland) Act 2002, which was passed on 28 May 2002 and came into force on 1 January 2005.

The Scottish Act is similar to the UK law, but there are a few important differences (see box), and wherever the laws differ, the Scottish Act is usually superior in terms of the public's right to know. Combined with a strong and efficient Information Commissioner and more progressive Parliament, Scotland's freedom of information regime is significantly more open than the UK system.

The decisions coming out of Scotland mean that it is sometimes worth directing your requests to that country rather than to the UK government. Your chances of success may be greater and you can use the Scottish case as a precedent for forcing open public bodies south of the border. For example, the Scottish Parliament now puts all MSPs' detailed expense claims online after a slew of FOI requests. Now that such details are available in Scotland, it makes the House of Commons' continued refusal to do the same look very poor indeed.

Scottish public authorities are releasing and distributing full minutes of board meetings, which is still not common practice among UK public authorities. It's worth taking a little time to see if the information you want from a UK organisation is already available at its Scottish equivalent and using this as a lever to force greater openness.

There are 10,000 Scottish public authorities covered by the Act, including Scottish Ministers and the Scottish Parliament, Her Majesty's Chief Inspector of Fire and Rescue Authorities, the Commissioner for Public Appointments in Scotland and regional transport partnerships.

Scotland vs UK Freedom of Information laws	
Scotland	**UK**
A harm test of *substantial* prejudice	A lesser harm test of prejudice
No time extension for considering the public interest	Unlimited time extension
Legal right for internal review within 20 working days	No time limit for internal reviews
No section 23 equivalent (material supplied by security bodies)	s.23
Commissioner appointed by Queen on nomination of *Parliament*	Commissioner appointed by Queen on nomination of *Government*
Commissioner more powerful. No Tribunal. Can only appeal on point of law to Court of Session. Doesn't deal with Data Protection Act.	Commissioner oversees FOI and DPA. Can be overruled by Tribunal.
Scottish Commissioner must by law reach a decision generally within four months from receiving the appeal	UK Commissioner under no such statutory performance target
Fees: £600 cap, first £100 free, 10 per cent thereafter	Fees: Caps £600 central/ £450 other. Only pay cost of supplying info, usually free.
Info intended for publication – s.27 specifies future date 'not later than twelve weeks' from request	Applies even when no specific date decided (s.22)
No equivalent	Section 34 exempts information whose disclosure would infringe Parliamentary privilege

(A full description of the differences between the laws is available at the Scottish Commissioner's Office: www.itspublicknowledge.info/legislation/comparativetable.htm)

There is a much greater level of scrutiny going on in Scotland partly because of the number of journalists covering the Scottish Parliament compared to Whitehall. There are all the usual national papers with journalists focusing on Holyrood but in addition there are ten Scottish daily newspapers. And Scottish journalists have used the Act with exuberance.

The Scottish Information Commissioner is Kevin Dunion, a former director of Friends of the Earth Scotland. As you might expect from someone with a campaigning background, Mr Dunion has actively promoted the public's right to know and has held free workshops for journalists, activists and citizens on the Act. His office spent almost £369,000 on promotion in the three years up to April 2006. It's not a great deal of money but still more than the UK Commissioner's £218,000 for the same time period. The Scottish Commissioner rules

---

First 'head to roll' from FOI

Paul Hutcheon, political editor of the *Sunday Herald* (Scotland) was named Journalist of the Year at the 2006 Scottish Press Awards for his FOI investigation that led to the resignation of David McLetchie in what became known as 'Taxigate'. Hutcheon sought to verify rumours that the Scottish Conservative leader was taking publicly funded taxis for personal and legal business by making FOI requests for his detailed travel expense claims. His battle took almost a year and led to the landmark decision from the Scottish Commissioner and the introduction of one of the most transparent political expense systems in the world. Hutcheon has himself made more than 400 FOI requests.

Since his investigation, Brian Monteith, a former Tory MSP, was forced to pay back £250 in wrongly claimed taxi bills. *The Scotsman* revealed how Alex Salmond claimed £8,500 to commute by taxi from his home in Linlithgow to the Scottish Parliament, and Keith Raffan, the former Liberal Democrat MSP, claimed mileage expenses for driving round his constituency when he was out of the country.

The Scots can be proud of the proactive approach taken by their government. Politicians could have easily reacted defensively to the revelations of expense abuse. Instead, George Reid, the Presiding Officer, announced he would reform the expenses system to make it more transparent and accountable. The online system uses a series of easy links from the name of the MSP, to their general expenses claims, then to specific areas such as taxi bills and finally to individual receipts.

---

on FOI and EIR cases. Data protection cases are handled by the UK Commissioner. There is no Information Tribunal in Scotland and the Commissioner's decisions can only be appealed to the Court of Sessions on a point of law.

The situation in Scotland shows what a difference a strong and competent Commissioner can make in changing the culture of secrecy. The Scottish Commissioner has not been afraid to adjudicate on controversial issues. His website is clear and easy to use with an online listing of all the cases under consideration. 'I thought it would be useful to put up our database of cases under investigation because it helps people to see what kind of information others are asking for and hopefully that encourages the public to use the Act,' the Scottish Commissioner told me.

The Scottish office operates on the presumption of openness with complainants named unless they ask not to be, whereas the UK Commissioner assumes that secrecy is better for everyone and complainants have no choice but to remain anonymous in his decision notices. This speaks volumes about the differing philosophies of the two regulators toward the benefits of openness.

The Scottish Information Commissioner had only two years to prepare for the 1 January 2005 start date of the law, yet his management of cases has been more efficient than his UK counterpart (see Chapter 1). He has also shown a willingness to use his powers. In May 2006, he conducted a review of those public authorities showing a systematic failure to abide by the Act. Among those he named and shamed for failing to uphold the law on at least one occasion were the Scottish Executive, the Strathclyde, Tayside and Grampian police forces, the Scottish Public Services Ombudsman, the Crown Office, Audit Scotland, Scottish Water, the Scottish Prison Service and 14 councils, including Edinburgh and Glasgow.

Scotland has its own Codes of Practice (section 60 and 61) that mirror those of the UK. The codes are available online at www. scotland.gov.uk/Topics/Government/FOI or from the Scottish Executive's FOI Unit. The code on the discharge of functions makes clear that any confidentiality clauses in public authority contracts should only be accepted on exceptional grounds and they must be justifiable to the Scottish Commissioner.

FEES

The Scottish fees schedule is different from the one operating in the UK. The upper cost limit for all requests is £600; above this amount and requests can be refused. The costs are made up of search time and supplying the information. The first £100 is free and the remaining amount can be charged at 10 per cent of the value. Then the full cost after £600. So a request costing the public authority £690 would cost the applicant £140 (first 100 free, 10 per cent of £500 + £90); a request costing £290 would cost £19 (£290 − £100 = 190 at 10 per cent).

At the time of going to press, the Scottish Executive was in the process of reviewing the Act, a similar exercise to that being carried out by the Department for Constitutional Affairs in the UK. One of the main questions being considered was changing the fee structure. The Scottish Commissioner has spoken out strongly against any changes that would hinder people's ability to make requests. Check the Commissioner's site for the latest details on fees.

WHERE TO GET INFORMATION IN SCOTLAND

The Scottish Executive
www.scotland.gov.uk/topics/government/foi
St Andrew's House, Edinburgh EH1 3DG
Tel: 0845 774 1741
Head of FOI Unit: Tim Ellis

FOI Unit, Scottish Executive, G-A North, Victoria Quay, Edinburgh EH6 6QQ
Tel: 0131 244 4615
Fax: 0131 244 2582
Email requests to: ceu@scotland.gov.uk or foi@scotland.gsi.gov.uk
Publication scheme: www.scotland.gov.uk/Topics/Government/FOI/19260/18084
Disclosure log: www.scotland.gov.uk/Topics/Government/FOI/Disclosures

Scottish Executive – Environment Group
www.scotland.gov.uk/Topics/Environment
Sustainable Development Directorate, Environment Group,
Scottish Executive, Victoria Quay, Edinburgh EH6 6QQ
Tel: 0131 244 7034
Fax: 0131 244 0195
Email: environmental.information@scotland.gsi.gov.uk

Scottish Executive – Health Department
www.show.scot.nhs.uk/sehd/
FOI: www.show.scot.nhs.uk/sehd/cso/foi/foiintro.htm

The Scottish NHS is overseen by the Scottish Executive's Health Department with 15 unified NHS Boards in Scotland that look after all NHS services in the area, along with local health councils that provide a forum for local input.

Office of the Commissioner for Public Appointments in Scotland
www.scotland.gov.uk/Topics/Government/public-bodies/commissioner
9–10 St Andrew's Square, Edinburgh, Scotland, EH2 2AF

The Public Appointments Unit
The Scottish Executive, 3-G (Dockside), Victoria Quay, Edinburgh EH6 6QQ
Tel: 0131 244 4297
Fax: 0131 244 3875
Email: public.appointments@scotland.gsi.gov.uk

The Scottish Parliament
www.scottish.parliament.uk
Information Access Manager, The Scottish Parliament, Edinburgh EH99 1SP
Tel: 0131 348 6913
Fax: 0131 348 5378
Email: foi.officer@scottish.parliament.uk
Directorate of Access and Information, Carol Devon
Publication scheme: www.scottish.parliament.uk/cnPages/foi/spcb-pub-00.htm
Disclosure log: www.scottish.parliament.uk/cnPages/foi/log_index.htm

Scottish Information Commissioner

www.itspublicknowledge.info

Commissioner: Kevin Dunion

Kinburn Castle, Doubledykes Road, St Andrews, Fife KY16 9DS

Tel: 01334 464 610

Email: enquiries@itspublicknowledge.info

You can find a list of the Commissioner's cases under investigation at: www.itspublicknowledge.info/appealsdecisions/investigations/index.htm. A list of all his decisions is also available online and can be searched by public authority or the exemption used.

Scottish Public Services Ombudsman

www.scottishombudsman.org.uk

4 Melville Street, Edinburgh EH3 7NS

Tel: 0800 377 7330

Fax: 0800 377 7331

FOI Officer: Louise Davies, information analyst

Email: enquiries@spso.org.uk

Publication scheme: www.scottishombudsman.org.uk/foi/

Crown Office and Procurator Fiscal Service

www.crownoffice.gov.uk

Policy Group, Crown Office, 25 Chambers Street, Edinburgh EH1 1LA

Tel: 0131 226 2626

FOI Officer: Scott Pattison, Head of Policy Group

Tel: 0131 247 2650

Email: foi@copfs.gsi.gov.uk

Publication scheme: www.crownoffice.gov.uk/FOI/ReqInfo

Responsible for prosecuting crime in Scotland, the investigation of sudden or suspicious deaths and complaints against the police.

National Archives of Scotland

www.nas.gov.uk

HM General Register House, 2 Princes Street, Edinburgh EH1 3YY

Tel: 0131 535 1314/1371

Email: foi@nas.gov.uk

Publication scheme: www.nas.gov.uk/foi/publicationScheme1.asp

This is the Scottish equivalent of the National Archives in Kew. It preserves the public records of Scotland and advises on records management and archiving. The archive holds two types of information: about the daily administration of the NAS and that contained in the archives. The NAS states that anything in the collections is already made available to the public and is therefore exempt under section 25 of FOISA (already available). It advises that you should first consult the lists of archives available either at the NAS or online at the catalogues and indexes section. There are, however, some restrictions on archive data and this will be shown on the catalogue entry. In this case, you need to file an FOI request to the Freedom of Information Officer at the address above.

Her Majesty's Inspectorate of Education in Scotland
www.hmie.gov.uk
Dehholm House, Almondvale Business Park, Almondvale Way,
Livingston EH54 6GA
Tel: 01506 600 200 (enquiries)
Email: enquiries@hmie.gov.uk
Publication scheme: www.scotland.gov.uk/topics/government/foi
Disclosure log: www.hmie.gov.uk/foi_responses.asp

The Inspectorate is responsible to the Scottish Executive. It evaluates education in Scotland by reporting on all types of schools, colleges, community learning bodies, services for children, and local councils education function.

Scottish Water
www.scottishwater.co.uk
PO Box 8855, Edinburgh EH10 6YQ
Tel: 0845 601 8855 (customer service)
FOI Officer: Atholl Duncan, Freedom of Information Unit
Email: FOI@scottishwater.co.uk

Scottish Water was created in April 2002 from the merger of the three former water authorities – East, West and North of Scotland. Scottish Water is a publicly owned business, answerable to the Scottish Parliament and therefore the people of Scotland. It has nine PFI contracts – all waste water treatment works – that are scheduled to last for up to 40 years. Collectively these contracts cover 21 separate sites treating waste water from almost half the Scottish population.

Scottish Fisheries Protection Agency
www.sfpa.gov.uk
Pentland House, 47 Robb's Loan, Edinburgh EH14 1TY
Tel: 0131 244 6059

FOI Officer: Brian Henaghen, Head of Finance and Human Resources, Room 529
Tel: 0131 244 6456
Fax: 0131 244 6086
Email: brian.henaghen@scotland.gsi.gov.uk
Publication scheme: www.sfpa.gov.uk/foa.asp

Enforces fisheries legislation by upholding regulations, conducting marine surveillance and prosecuting illegal activity. An FOI request might help uncover the effectiveness of their enforcement.

Scottish Prison Service
www.sps.gov.uk
Headquarters, Carlton House, 5 Redheughs Rigg, Edinburgh EH12 9HW
Tel: 0131 244 8661/8745
Email: gaolinfo@sps.gov.uk

Audit Scotland
www.audit-scotland.gov.uk
110 George Street, Edinburgh EH2 4LH
Tel: 0131 477 1234
Email: info@audit-scot.gov.uk
FOI Officer: Mandy Gallacher, Communications Manager
Email: mgallacher@audit-scotland.gov.uk

Audit Scotland is the main body that conducts audits of public bodies in Scotland. It does this for both the Auditor General and the Audit Commission. The Auditor General examines NHS Boards, colleges, Scottish Water, Departments of the Scottish Executive, and quangos. Local councils and joint boards (such as fire and police) are examined by the Accounts Commission. The contact address is the same for all three bodies.

3
Laws of Access

'It will be of little avail to the people that the laws are made by men of their own choice if the laws be so voluminous that they cannot be read, or so incoherent that they cannot be understood.'

James Madison

The Freedom of Information Act 2000 is the primary law allowing access to information from public (and some private) bodies. It covers more than 100,000 organisations, from GPs to the Ministry of Defence. Its scope is broad in terms of who it covers, but it is not nearly as strong as it could and should have been. More on the Act shortly, but first it is worth mentioning that the FOIA is not the only law that gives a right of access.

A new set of Environmental Information Regulations allows greater access than the FOIA. Chapter 10 deals with accessing environmental information. Chapter 9 details laws specific to healthcare such as the Access to Medical Records Act 1990; Chapter 11 outlines laws that open up local authorities. Remaining chapters will mention other laws that affect public access to information.

The public also has a right to relevant information during the course of civil litigation, but this is a long and expensive process that most would choose to avoid. The rules for disclosure in litigation are greater than under the FOIA, as there are fewer exemptions and harsh penalties for failing to be candid. But any information you get can't be shared with others without the permission of the court unless it is presented in open court, and even then it could be restricted.

Article 10 of the Human Rights Act 1998 also grants a right to freedom of expression, while Article 8 gives a right to privacy. Article 10 states: 'Everyone has the right to freedom of expression. This right shall include freedom to hold opinions and *to receive and impart information and ideas without interference by public authority* and regardless of frontiers' (emphasis my own). Some news organisations have tried to use this argument to televise proceedings of the Hutton and Harold Shipman inquiries, but they were unsuccessful and the law has not been interpreted as giving a right of access.

Some kinds of individual privacy rights are enshrined in the Data Protection Act 1998. You'll find more about the Data Protection Act in Chapter 14. Don't feel, however, that you have to read up on every law before you make a request. All information can be requested using the sample letters (see Appendix); and a public agency is obliged to tell you (under section 16 of the FOIA) if you can get the information elsewhere or by means of other laws.

The basic law for requests

- Information about yourself – Data Protection Act 1998
- Information about a third party – Freedom of Information Act 2000
- Environmental information – Environmental Information Regulations 2004

HISTORY

The first Freedom of Information law was passed in Sweden in 1766 and was the result not so much of noble ideals but party politics – the new ruling party passed the law so it could access documents the previous government had kept secret. It took another 200 years before the next major FOI law was passed in 1966, after a 20-year campaign by newspapers. The strong act the US has today resulted from amendments made in 1974, passed in response to the Watergate scandal. Further amendments were made in 1996 to extend the law to electronic information. The US FOIA with its strong public right to know has been the most influential internationally and is a model for openness around the world. More than 70 countries have a Freedom of Information law; most were adopted in the last few decades, including countries with parliamentary systems such as Canada, Australia and New Zealand (1982) and more recently Ireland in 1997.

Meanwhile Britain continued along the path of secrecy and scandal. Successive public inquiries pointed to the same root cause: excessive secrecy had subverted the democratic processes. The Scott Inquiry investigated the government's secret export of arms to Saddam Hussein and concluded that there was 'consistent undervaluing by government of the public interest that full information should be made available to Parliament. In circumstances where disclosure might be politically or administratively inconvenient, the balance struck by the government comes down, time and time again, against full disclosure.'[1]

---

1. Rt. Hon Richard Scott V.C. *Report of the Inquiry into the Export of Defence Equipment and Dual-Use Goods to Iraq and related prosecutions* (1996).

Plans for a Freedom of Information law have been discussed since the 1970s only to be shelved. Finally, after a string of exceptionally embarrassing scandals, the Conservative government bowed to public pressure and introduced the Code of Practice on Access to Government Information on 4 April 1994. This was a precursor to an FOI law but with some important limitations: it was not legally enforceable and it only affected those agencies answerable to the Parliamentary Ombudsman (mostly central government bodies but ironically not Parliament itself). However, in some cases this code was more liberal than the current FOI law. For example, facts and analysis used in policy decisions were to be disclosed. Yet ultimately the code was unenforceable, so ministers could flout the Parliamentary Ombudsman's rulings, which they did on several occasions. The Cabinet Office twice failed to abide by the Ombudsman's rulings to release information in response to requests from the *Guardian*, forcing the paper to seek judicial review.

Why did it take so long for a law to be passed? The reality is that MPs in opposition are eager to champion the cause of freedom of information; once in power their eagerness fades dramatically. The Labour Party made passage of an FOI law part of its election Manifesto and published a very liberal White Paper soon after it was elected in 1997. The bill was not introduced, however, for two more years, during which time the new government came to dislike open government. Freedom of information benefits the people, but it does not always benefit politicians, and one embarrassing revelation followed another: large donations by Bernie Ecclestone to the Labour Party, the arrest of Jack Straw's son; the accidental publication of witness names in the Stephen Lawrence inquiry; press publication of Cabinet minutes on the failing Dome project, and Peter Mandelson's role in the provision of UK passports for the Labour-supporting Hinduja brothers.

The minister responsible for the White Paper was sacked and responsibility went to Jack Straw in the Home Office, a department not known for its liberal thinking. Soon the government had abandoned its 1997 Manifesto promises and Jack Straw fought successfully to weaken the 1997 White Paper. Specifically, the test for withholding information was changed from substantial harm to mere prejudice, and ministers were allowed to veto the rulings of the Information Commissioner. The number of exemptions also increased and the legislation swelled in size and complexity.

Lobbyists such as the Campaign for Freedom of Information and Liberty worked hard to salvage what they could from the bill and some important concessions were made in the final days. Debates in the House of Lords and Commons also committed the government to more liberal interpretations of the exemptions. But the government refused to budge on most of the bill, threatening to withdraw it altogether if substantial changes were made, and supporters of the original White Paper agreed that a weak FOI law was better than nothing. The law received Royal Assent on 30 November 2000, but as a further blow, full implementation was put off until January 2005, supposedly to give agencies the chance to 'prepare', but many agencies were not ready by the time the law came into force; fees regulations were issued just one month before and exemption guidance was still being written. So this extension was nothing more than putting off the inevitable.

A rolling schedule of publication schemes was phased in during the four years. There were continued hopes that the law might be amended, and in January 2004 this became a real possibility when the Independent Review of Government Communications made its final recommendations on how to rebuild trust between the government, the media and the public. It called on the government to abolish the ministerial veto, replace blanket exemptions with qualified ones, and commit to publishing more information about policy formulation. Despite the full backing of the Review Committee, which included senior Downing Street press officers, Tony Blair declined to change the law, preferring instead to see 'how the act bedded down'. This report could prove useful if the law is rewritten.

CURRENT LAW

Considering that the FOIA deals with the public's right to know, you would think that the drafters of this legislation would produce a document the public could understand. No such luck. This 80-page law is stuffed to bursting with legalese. It will get no awards for clear English. Follow the links at the end of the chapter to read the entire law for yourself. Below, I highlight the most relevant points.

A large percentage of the Freedom of Information law is taken up with a list of exemptions for keeping information secret. There's a whole grab-bag of exemptions for the secrecy-loving bureaucrat to choose from. First, though, let's first consider the main rights of access. The FOIA starts off well enough:

Any person making a request for information to a public authority
is entitled –

(a) to be informed in writing by the public authority whether it
holds information of the description specified in the request,
and

(b) if that is the case, to have that information communicated
to him.

The Act's fundamental strength is that it changes the balance of
power between the government and the governed in relation to
information disclosure. As Jack Straw said when he introduced the
bill, it would 'transform the default setting from "this should be kept
quiet unless" to "this should be published unless"' (HC 2R, 7 Dec
1999, col 714). The law creates what is called a 'duty to confirm or
deny', that is, the authority must inform the applicant in writing
whether or not it holds the information. Secondly, there is a duty to
disclose that information to the applicant.

Exemptions may allow an agency to withhold information (most,
though, are qualified by a public interest test). In addition, an agency
doesn't have to comply if the costs are too great or if the application
is considered 'vexatious' (for example, repeated identical requests
from the same person within a short space of time).

YOUR RIGHTS

Your main right is access to information from all public authorities.

What are public authorities?

This should be an easy question to answer. Common sense dictates
that any organisation providing a necessary public service or funded
primarily by public money ought to be accountable to the public
through the FOIA or EIR. In most American states, any organisation
that receives more than 50 per cent of its budget from public funds
is classed as a public authority under state FOI laws. In Britain, by
contrast, each organisation must be specifically identified. There are
broad categories such as 'any government department', local councils,
the NHS, maintained schools and the police, but the vast majority
of organisations (for example, quangos) must be included in the
Schedule 1 list found at the end of the law, for the Act to apply.
Organisations are constantly added and removed, so it is important
to have the most up-to-date Schedule 1 to know who is covered.

You can find this list on the Department for Constitutional Affairs website: www.foi.gov.uk/coverage-guide.htm

The situation is made even more problematic because while some of the new designations can be added easily when they meet certain criteria, others must be designated by a special Parliamentary order. As a result, by May 2006 there had not been a single order under section 5 of the Act despite promises by the Lord Chancellor that one would be forthcoming from 1 January 2005 onwards. Some of the organisations currently avoiding accountability because of this oversight are: city academies, harbour authorities, Network Rail, the Press Complaints Commission, private prisons, prison escorts, roads maintenance crews, PFI contractors for school building and operation, stock transfer housing associations, and leisure trusts.

What is information?

The definition of information outlined in section 84 is 'information recorded in any form', so that includes written material, photographs, plans, video and sound recordings, data on computer, and so on. As with the Data Protection Act, there is no requirement to disclose unrecorded information, so it's possible agencies could leave controversial items unrecorded, though this has not proven the case in other countries with a more advanced FOI regime. Recorded information is managed by agencies in a variety of ways. Most agencies used to have a central records office where all records were sorted and archived, but massive budget cuts severely reduced the staff in records offices at just about the time when the number of records began to escalate. The result is that record-keeping is probably not what it should be, and you may find that some agencies have no idea where or what records they keep. Some agencies have even transferred their records management to private companies, further confusing matters. As part of the FOIA, the Lord Chancellor has issued a Code of Practice on the Management of Records that is meant to improve the situation.

Basically, most agencies have a system of records management in which individual offices or departments keep those records they use most often. Problems arise when the records fall out of use. Should they be thrown away, stored in the office or sent to an archive? These decisions have been put off for years, but the prospect of having to hand over all documents in answer to an FOIA request is spurring departments to trawl through their records backlog.

The FOIA states that you are entitled to all information held 'at the time when the request is received'. The law is retrospective so you can also request information created at any time, not just since the law was passed. The only requirement is that the authority must currently hold it. The law makes it an offence to 'alter, destroy, hide or deface information' once an FOIA request has been made but it is not an offence to destroy records *before* a request is made. Cynics might suggest that the four-year run-up to the law was to allow agencies to 'clean house'.[2] But Whitehall officials insisted that any increase in shredding was solely to deal with mounting volumes of records.

Any request for information in writing (including email and fax) can be classed as a request under the FOIA even without mentioning the law specifically. This means all staff should be trained to recognise an FOI request when they see one. The Act states that once the agency has received your written request it has a duty to comply *promptly*. A limit of 20 business days is set, though the agency could be in breach of the law if the request could have been answered quickly yet they made you wait the full period. The time limit can be extended if:

- they need time to consult a third party
- they need to consider where the public interest lies (this does not apply in Scotland).

However, they must (under section 17(2)) give you an estimate of when they expect to make a decision and it must be reasonable and realistic. You have grounds for complaint if it is not.

Assistance

One of the most important parts of the Act is section 16, which directs agencies to provide an applicant with advice and assistance. This is an incredibly helpful directive as it means a public body has a statutory duty to help you formulate your request. Not all organisations will tell you about this duty, so know your rights. It means the organisation should provide detailed lists of catalogues and indexes so you can narrow your request. This may be especially pertinent if your initial request is refused on cost grounds.

2. A way round the potential problem of destroying documents would be to make an FOIA request asking whether records were destroyed in the past and what they were about, as it is possible that a current record exists detailing what other records have been destroyed in the past. Also see the link at the chapter's end for the Code of Practice related to records management.

The aim of section 16 is to provide you with help in making your application and is *not* an opportunity for the authority to find out why you are making the request. The authority has no right to enquire about your motivation or reasons for making the request and they must treat all requests fairly regardless of purpose. You could also get help to formulate your request from a local Citizens' Advice Bureau. I also post advice on the Your Right to Know website: www.yrtk.org

You have a right to see the information in 'one or more' of three specified formats:

- a copy of the information in permanent form
- a chance to inspect the record containing the information
- a digest summary of the information in permanent form.

Note: it's a good idea to use your right to one *or more* forms of the information and ask for a copy of the information as well as a chance to inspect the original document. You may find some other interesting information on the original that wasn't included in the summary. Inspecting the record is also a very good way to avoid incurring any fees that might result from photocopying. The authority must try and meet your specified preferences unless it is impractical to do so, but they must inform you in writing of the reason it is impractical.

All non-exempt information must be disclosed even if mixed with exempt information. For example, if a document has personal information that the agency thinks comes under an exemption, it can redact it but it must release the non-exempt information.

Who keeps information?

An authority cannot use the excuse that it is holding information for someone else (for example, a private company). The Information Commissioner has said he will be sceptical of authorities that withhold information on this basis. Public authorities don't have to consult affected third parties when releasing information, although good practice states they should. This is meant to stop public authorities relying on the excuse that they cannot release information because it concerns a third party even if the third party has no objection to disclosure. In some cases a third party may hold a copyright on a document. In this case, the FOIA trumps the copyright law, so the public authority can hand it over. However, the recipient does not have such immunity and must be mindful of the copyright.

What if some of the information you seek is held by another authority? The Code of Practice issued to public authorities states clearly that the authority to which you initially made your request must 'consider what would be the most helpful way of assisting the applicant with his or her request'. They should then tell you which authority they think has the information you need and provide you with contact details. They can also transfer your request directly, but they should confirm that the second authority has the information and consult you first.

The situation is a bit different when it comes to records transferred to archives. In these cases, the records authority decides whether an exemption is applicable and if it is an absolute exemption then the records are withheld. If it decides a qualified exemption or no exemption applies then the decision to release is transferred to the department most closely associated with the records known as the 'responsible authority'.

Historical records

Records are defined as 'historical' 30 years from the end of the year in which they were created. However, where records of different dates are grouped as in a file, the 30 years starts with the most recent document in the group. Once a record becomes historical, many of the FOIA exemptions fall away, so disclosure is more likely. Two other exemptions fall away at a later date:

- honours – the FOIA exemption lasts for 60 years
- law enforcement – the exemption lasts for 100 years.

The remaining exemptions can be applied whatever the age of the information. The transfer of historical records to the National Archives and other places of deposit is governed by the amended Public Records Act 1958 or the Public Records Act (Northern Ireland) 1923, but your right to access them is governed by the FOIA. It is hoped the FOIA will stop the 'extended closure' of historic records that led to many historic documents being withheld for much longer than the specified 30 years. Now, the majority of documents should be released after 30 years. Importantly, the FOIA also means that records can be requested long before they become historical, whether they have been transferred or remain with the department.

For example, records of important events such as the tragedy at Hillsborough football stadium, the miners' strike and the poll tax riots can be requested under the FOIA. Already the FOI law is prompting a continuous release of historical documents. The National Archives

released more than 50,000 files under the FOIA when the law came
into force – including papers on the history of the official Home Office
cat. More information about historical records is available at:

The National Archives (formerly the Public Record Office)
www.nationalarchives.gov.uk
Kew, Richmond, Surrey TW9 4DU
Tel: 020 8876 3444
Email: enquiry@nationalarchives.gov.uk
A list of key contacts is available at: www.nationalarchives.gov.uk/archon/
archondirectory.htm

For advice on the FOIA and how it affects records management and
archives contact Susan Healy in the Information Legislation section.
Tel: 020 8876 3444 (ext. 2305); email: susan.healy@nationalarchives.
gov.uk

Fees

Fees are always a contentious issue. Under the law, public authorities
are allowed to charge a reasonable fee for providing information,
but if too high, they will stifle the law's democratic ethos – that
everyone should have a right to hold their government accountable
regardless of wealth or status. In Ireland, the public's use of their
Freedom of Information Act plummeted by 75 per cent after the
government imposed restrictive fees. In 2004, a row erupted when
the government attempted to introduce excessive fees as a means of
restricting use of the FOIA. After public criticism, the government
decided (in secret) on a more liberal fee structure that set an upper
cost limit for requests at £600 for central government and £450 for
all other public bodies. This cost comprises time spent searching
and compiling and *not* consulting lawyers or third parties. If the fee
is within the limit, the public body can only charge for the cost of
supplying the information, though most have not bothered. If this
seems like an unusual freebie, just remember that the public have
already paid for the creation and maintenance of all this data through
taxes, so it really *ought* to be free to access it.

Fees are calculated by staff time at a rate of £25 an hour, equivalent
to an annual salary for a 40-hour week of £52,000-a-year! It's worth
noting that investigators at the UK Commissioner's Office were paid a
salary of just £15,000 a year.[3] If the request goes beyond the fee limit,

---

3. Evidence from Richard Thomas to the Constitutional Affairs Committee,
   14 March 2006.

it can be refused. Cost is one of the most common reasons cited for refusing information requests. A single large request may cost too much, but the Act defines many small requests at once as 'vexatious'. A solution may be to make small requests consecutively.

Also, under the duty to provide assistance, FOI officers should explore ways to help reduce the fee. For example, they could provide the information electronically instead of in hard copy or invite you to view the information and take your own notes, or to select the information you feel would be most useful to you.

You have three months to pay a fee and an authority doesn't have to give you the information until you pay. The 20-day time period is suspended from the date a fee notice is served until the fee is received, but if the authority serves a fee notice on you long after you made the request, any required fee should be waived. If you pay after the three-month period, the authority does not have to answer your request. If, after paying, you do not get the information, then the authority must return your fee.

You have a right to challenge a fee if you think it is unreasonable, even if it meets the published guidelines. Another way to overcome high fees would be to approach others who you think could benefit from the information, such as businesses, campaign groups or journalists. They may agree to split the cost.

A review of fees was under way in both the UK and Scotland. In 2006, the Department for Constitutional Affairs appeared to be laying the groundwork to impose fees again, and as before the discussions were held in secret without any public consultation. The good news is that both the UK and Scottish Information Commissioners are strongly opposed to the introduction of fees.

There is a different set of fee regulations under the Environmental Information Regulations, and Friends of the Earth reported problems with public authorities charging excessive amounts. The Tribunal decision, *Mr David Markinson* v. *Information Commissioner* (28 March 2006), ruled against such charges (see Chapter 1 for more details).

Publication schemes and disclosure logs

Under the FOIA, all agencies must have what is called a 'publication scheme'. This is a public register that lists information already available. The content of these schemes is left mostly to the discretion of the authority and you may find that some are nothing more than the usual information that you could find in a 'Your Council and What it Does' leaflet. Initially, the main goal was to get all agencies in compliance with the law. In 2006, the UK Commissioner said he would be reviewing the schemes and would be more demanding in selective cases.

At their most basic, the schemes must contain a list of publications available, what they cost (if anything), a description of what the agency does and a contact for information requests. Most authorities have done nothing to publicise these schemes, but some are becoming popular nevertheless. From December 2002 to the end of July 2003, the Department for Work and Pensions' scheme was one of the most viewed areas on its website. The schemes provide a central point for information and you'll find the majority are now online. Wherever possible in this book, I've included the address for an authority's publication scheme.

Disclosure logs are proving much more useful. They are not required by the Act, however, so not all public authorities have them. The logs can include a list of all FOI requests, answers (positive or negative) or just a list of disclosures the public authority decides are worth publishing. The BBC and Ministry of Defence have particularly good disclosure logs.

The Information Commissioner

Richard Thomas is the current Information Commissioner and his office is responsible for administration and enforcement of the FOIA as well as the Data Protection Act. The office is an expansion of the former Data Protection Commission and funding comes primarily from the Department for Constitutional Affairs.

The Information Tribunal

Formerly the Data Protection Tribunal, the Information Tribunal hears appeals concerning both the Data Protection and the Freedom of Information Acts. Members are appointed by the Lord Chancellor through the Department for Constitutional Affairs, so while technically independent, the government does seem to have an undue influence. However, based on early rulings it appears the Tribunal is not afraid to challenge the establishment. The chairman and deputy chairmen are legally qualified.

How to get information

1. Identify the agency you think is most likely to have the information you want. This may sound easy, but the British government is a meandering, chaotic structure, so you may have to do some investigation. You'll find an outline of the main

▶

agencies and the kind of information they hold in each chapter. Almost all public authorities now have a website, so you can also search online.

2. Look through the authority's **publication scheme** and **disclosure log** to see if it contains the information you need. You should be able to find this on their website, but if it's not obvious, do a search. If all else fails, ring up the agency and ask where you can get a copy (or they will mail you a copy).

3. No luck? Depending on your request, you may first want to make an informal request by phone or email. Although technically an email is considered a formal application under the FOIA, you may find that this informal approach will get you the information you seek quickly and without cost. If you encounter obstruction, or want to follow a more formal route, write a letter or send an email invoking the Act.

Making an FOIA request

1. The request must be in writing, although this includes emails so don't feel you have to compose a formal business letter. Include your name and an address for correspondence. Although not required, to speed things along you might want to state that you are making the request 'under the Freedom of Information Act 2000'.

2. Give as much detail as you can. A public authority can ask you for a more detailed description to locate the information you need. It doesn't have to give you anything until you have made it clear precisely what you seek. To avoid delay and unnecessary fees, be narrow and detailed in your request. A narrow time frame of a year, say, is easier to handle than several years, so keep the time frame limited to what you need. You can always extend your information request later. Also, you might like to add a gentle reminder that the information be supplied within the mandated 20 business days. Specify in which format you wish to receive the information.

3. The public authority has 20 working days from the time it receives your application to provide the information. It's worthwhile either sending your request by registered mail or including in your letter a phrase such as 'please could you confirm in writing that you have received this request'. Then if you don't hear anything in a few days, telephone to see what's happening. In some circumstances, the authority may need more than 20 days, but they must tell you why and give an estimated date for an answer.

4. The authority may ask you to pay a fee and you have three months to do this.

Tip: from the time you send your request, keep a diary of your dealings with the agency. If they deny your request, this will prove very helpful during an appeal process.

Appeals

What to do if your request is denied
(Parts IV (sections 50–6) and V (sections 57–61) deal respectively with enforcement and appeals)

▶

1. First, complain to the public authority that has denied your request. The authority has a statutory duty to provide you with reasonable assistance including details on how to complain. If the authority fails to review the case to your satisfaction the next step is to approach the Information Commissioner.

2. Write a letter to the Information Commissioner outlining the information you requested, the action (or inaction) taken by the authority and why the authority's decision should be reviewed. Don't wait to make your appeal as the IC can refuse if he thinks you've shown undue delay. The deadline for complaints is only two to three months. You should also state your efforts to resolve the situation with the authority and include any copies of correspondence as your request for appeal can be denied if you haven't exhausted all means of complaint within the agency.

3. The IC can issue several types of notice:

   - **an information notice** – requires the agency to hand over whatever information is necessary for the IC's enquiry, though the IC does not have to give this to the applicant
   - **a decision notice** – issued after the IC has reviewed a complaint. It states the IC's decision and, if the agency is found in violation of the Act, what steps the agency needs to take and the deadline for compliance
   - **an enforcement notice** – where there is no complainant but the IC has found an authority in violation of the act, he will issue this notice, which calls for the agency to remedy a violation.

4. These notices have a similar effect to a court order, so if the authority ignores or fails to answer them, then the court can enquire into the matter. It is then up to the court to decide if the authority has committed contempt of court. If found guilty, the authority can be fined, and if they refuse to pay, there is the threat of imprisonment.

5. The applicant or authority can appeal to the **Information Tribunal** against a decision notice. National Security certificates can be appealed by the applicant or Commissioner who must satisfy the tribunal on judicial review grounds that the certificate is unwarranted. If the Information Commissioner decides not to issue a notice, you can appeal by way of judicial review or complain to the Ombudsman. The public authority has an additional right to appeal against an enforcement notice. Even greater rights are accorded to certain government departments allowing an 'accountable person' (in most cases a Cabinet Minister) to certify there was no failure to comply with FOI duties, thus voiding the enforcement or decision notice. A copy of these certificates along with the reasons for issuance must be laid before each House of Parliament (in Wales, the National Assembly). This section in the law (section 53) severely limits the Information Commissioner's ability to enforce the FOIA as it leaves final judgement as to whether some exemptions apply up to a member of the government who may have a vested interest in keeping something secret. You can challenge the ministerial override certificate by making a court application for judicial review.

6. If you get an unfavourable ruling in the Information Tribunal, you can appeal to the High Court in England, Court of Session in Scotland or High Court in Northern Ireland – but only on a point of law. They will not review the case otherwise.

The good and bad of our FOIA

Good

- A broad and extensive definition of public authority.
- Creates an independent office of Information Commissioner.
- Makes it an offence to destroy or alter requested records. The absence of such a statute in Canada led to cases of deliberate destruction after requests were made and the Canadian act had to be amended in 1999 to stop the abuse.
- Retrospective (unlike Ireland).
- Includes operational activity of police and Parliament.

Bad

- Blanket exclusion of security services (US, Canada and New Zealand include these agencies).
- Number and vagueness of exemptions – particularly bad are section 29: information held for purpose of investigations or proceedings; section 35: information related to policy-making; and section 36: information which 'would in the reasonable opinion of a qualified person be likely to prejudice the effective conduct of public affairs'.
- Ministerial veto (New Zealand requires collective ministerial veto, other countries have no veto).
- There are still as many as 147 laws prohibiting disclosure including the odious Official Secrets Act (other countries have very few laws prohibiting disclosure (US) or have abolished them – New Zealand repealed its Official Secrets Act to move toward more open government).
- Easy to exclude based on 'excessive cost' and there is no fee waiver for requests that are proven to serve the public or for requests made by an educational institution or news media as in the US FOIA.

EXEMPTIONS

Exemptions to the FOI Act are *discretionary* – that is, public authorities do not have to use them. They could release *all* information if they wanted. The FOIA imposes (under section 17) a duty on authorities to explain the reason an exemption applies. They cannot make a blanket refusal (unless the exemption is one of the few absolute exemptions). They must also give reasons why the public interest is best served in withholding information unless, in typical *Yes, Minister* style, it's against the public interest to state the reasons why withholding the information is in the public interest!

There are 25 exemptions within the Freedom of Information Act (23 set out in Part II plus the exemptions for vexatious requests and those that go beyond the fee cap). The exemptions provide an excuse for *not* providing pretty much anything. Reading through the list, it soon becomes clear that the law is principally designed to protect politicians from public scrutiny. A strong FOI law has exemptions that are based on harm rather than blanket categories of information. The US FOIA, by contrast, has just nine exemptions and they are concisely and narrowly defined with a harm test not just 'prejudice'. Reporters and lobbyists in the UK often file FOI requests with the US government to glean information about the UK. Even under the new UK freedom of information law, this practice will probably continue.

All qualified exemptions require a public interest test and, with a forceful Information Commissioner and officials who believe in FOI, it is possible that the UK law could provide a strong right to know. One of the main faults in the law is that nowhere does it say exactly how to conduct such a test.

What is in the public interest?

Although the public interest test is not specified in the law its definition is a matter of common sense. A matter of public interest is one that furthers or benefits the interests of the community. The Commissioner has online guidance listing factors that affect the public interest. It could include such information that helps the public to:

- participate effectively in decisions affecting them
- adequately scrutinise the decision-making process
- hold authorities to account for spending public money
- see that authorities are doing their jobs properly
- maintain they are not deceived about the way public authorities operate
- stay informed about possible dangers to health and safety or the environment
- ensure they are treated fairly by authorities
- ensure any misconduct is exposed.

Factors that should not be considered relevant to the public interest test include:

- possible embarrassment of government or other public authority officials
- the seniority of those involved in the subject matter
- the risk of the applicant misinterpreting the information
- possible loss of confidence in government or other public authority.[4]

4. Scottish Ministers' Code of Practice on the Discharge of Functions by Public Authorities Under the Freedom of Information (Scotland) Act 2002. These factors are equally applicable to the UK.

The public interest test does not start with an even balance; the presumption is on disclosure. This is because openness is considered to be a fundamental principle of democracy. It promotes transparent government, and a more informed and active public combined with accountable politicians leads to better policy decisions and public confidence in government.

The public interest can also change over time. For example, while law enforcement information is exempt, the public interest in disclosing it changes with time. At the start of an investigation, it may be in the public interest to withhold information so the inquiry is not prejudiced, whereas later, as the investigation is winding down or complete, the public interest will be for disclosure. In these cases, if you are denied information at one time, try again later.

Qualified exemptions

How these exemptions are interpreted will be built up using decisions made by the Information Commissioner, the Information Tribunal and the courts. Check the Information Commissioner's website for the latest guidance and decisions. All the exemptions in this category are qualified by the public interest test.

- **Section 22 – information intended for future publication**. This could include results from a safety investigation or research conducted by a public authority. Note that the agency must have created the information and be holding it with a view to future publication. If they only make this claim after you've filed a request, then they are using the exemption improperly as a delaying tactic.
- **Section 24 – national security**. Similar to the absolute exemption in section 23, this applies to information other than from the twelve specified security bodies. A Minister of the Crown can sign a certificate stating any information meets this requirement. The only way to appeal is through the Tribunal.
- **Section 26 – information likely to prejudice defence of the UK, colonies, and armed forces of the Crown or cooperating forces**. This is a weaker test of harm than the original 'substantial prejudice' that exists in the Scottish Act.
- **Section 27 – likely to prejudice international relations**. Again the test is weaker than the original 'substantial prejudice'. However, the less significant the prejudice, the more likely the balance is in favour of disclosure.

- **Section 28 – likely to prejudice relations within the UK.**
  This includes relations between central government, devolved
  governments (Wales, Scotland, Northern Ireland), local
  governments and agencies.
- **Section 29 – likely to prejudice the economy.** This blanket
  exemption means any information that would be likely to
  prejudice the economic or financial interests of the UK (whole
  or in part) or any UK administration can be withheld. A local
  authority could use this to withhold anything that might
  prejudice a local concern. It is worth noting that minutes of
  monthly meetings between the Chancellor of the Exchequer
  (Monetary Policy Committee) and the Bank of England are
  published by statute without causing any damage to the economy
  – surely information that is more economically sensitive than
  how much a council spends on local art projects.
- **Section 30 – investigations and proceedings by public
  authorities.** Information held by an authority may be exempt
  if at any time it was held for any of the following reasons:
  - an investigation to determine whether a person should be
    charged with, or is guilty, of an offence
  - an investigation conducted by a public authority that may
    lead to criminal proceedings
  - criminal proceedings which the public authority has power
    to conduct.
  The second part of this exemption relates to information
  collected from confidential sources for the purpose of an
  investigation or civil proceedings.
- **Section 31 – likely to prejudice law enforcement functions.**
  This is another wide-ranging exemption that applies to
  information that relates to the prevention or detection of crime,
  catching and prosecuting offenders, the administration of justice
  and immigration controls. It also includes anything that might
  prejudice civil proceedings, including regulatory investigations
  relating to incompetence of company directors, investigations
  in regulated professions or those who require a licence (medical,
  financial, and so on); investigations into accidents and actions
  relating to health and safety. This would exclude exactly that
  information most useful to the public. For that reason it faced
  great opposition in the House of Lords during its passage, so
  keep in mind the assurances of Lord Falconer (who presented
  the bill in the House of Lords on behalf of the government): 'If

there were no criminal prosecution in the case, I am sure that the public interest in knowing of health risks or the causes of accidents would outweigh the public interest in maintaining exemption' (HL 3R, 24 Oct 2000, col 274). This is one of the exemptions where the public interest changes over time, so once an investigation is complete, it should no longer apply.

- **Section 33 – likely to prejudice the functions of auditing or assessing the effectiveness of other public authorities.** This means that some information could be withheld while an audit is ongoing, but once the final report is made, background papers should be released.

- **Section 35 – government policy.** This was one of the most controversial exemptions during passage of the bill and is everything that an FOI law should *not* be. It's purpose is to prohibit scrutiny of policy-making and is actually more restrictive than the previous Code of Practice on Access to Government Information that required bodies to publish facts and analysis considered relevant to decisions. Information about the formulation of policy, ministerial communication, advice by law officers, operation of ministerial private office, consultants' or research reports, evidence of health hazards, assumptions about wage or inflation levels, studies of overseas practice, advice given by private companies, supporting data showing whether official assertions are realistic or not – all fall under the exemption.

Some members of the House of Lords argued valiantly against this exemption and to include, at the very least, a harm test. Lord Lucas said: 'Here we have a government who say that they want much more openness in public affairs but when we reach the part of the Bill where their own affairs are concerned, they are quite clearly determined to stay rooted to the spot and even to go backwards' (HL 3R, 24 Oct 2000, col 279).

Lord Falconer asserted during debate that 'the government believe that factual information used to provide an informed background to decision-taking will normally be disclosed', so his words can be used to challenge the government when it withholds this type of information (HL 3R, 24 Oct 2000, col 297).

Also, section 35(2) states that any statistical information used must be released, but only after a decision is made. This leads to a strange situation of determining the difference between statistical information (which can be released) and specific facts (which can be withheld). Lord Goodhart showed what a ridiculous state of affairs this presents by giving the example of information about the Hatfield rail disaster, where the number of broken rails discovered on the rail track in the last twelve months is a statistic, but the discovery of a single broken rail at the site is a fact, and thus exempt. The only guidance given for determining the difference between a statistic and fact came from Lord Falconer: 'It is pretty easy to identify what is a statistic: you know a statistic when you see it' (col 299).

- **Section 36 – prejudicial to the effective conduct of public affairs**. This is the 'catch-all' exemption for anything the government may have forgotten about. The wording couldn't be more vague. During the Lords' debate, Lord Mackay wittily summed up the section's purpose: 'Obviously the draftsmen decided, just in case something escaped and there is one last fish in the sea, let us get it with a grenade; and this is the grenade' (HL 3R, 24 Oct 2000, col 311).

  Despite promises in Parliament that this exemption would be used infrequently, it has become a favourite along with section 35. The whole purpose of FOI is to give people a right to understand and participate in decisions that affect their lives. These exemptions make that impossible and must be repealed.

- **Section 37 – Honours and communication with the royal family**. The Honours system came in for a battering after a *Sunday Times* exposé in December 2003 revealing the political machinations behind selection. It only got worse in 2006 when the same paper broke the cash for peerages scandal that revealed how major party donors were being rewarded with peerages. The royal family includes not only the Queen, but all members of the royal family and the royal household.

- **Section 38 – likely to endanger an individual's health and safety**.

- **Section 39 – environment**. This simply reflects that environmental information is released under a different law and not the FOIA (see Chapter 10 for more details).

- **Section 42 – legal professional privilege**. This includes certain confidential documents passed between a lawyer and client, including legal advice to an authority.

- **Section 43 – trade secrets and information likely to prejudice commercial interests**. In order to use the exemption for commercial interest, a public body must first prove that a commercial interest would be harmed by the release of information, and then conduct a public interest test. An important point to note is that when conducting the public interest test, the authority should not take into account any harm that may be caused to a private firm by disclosure. That is a private interest rather than a public interest and so should not be taken into account. However, if the disclosure affects the public authority's ability to do business, then that will be relevant.

Absolute exemptions

Absolute exemptions mean there is no public interest test for withholding information, making them very difficult to counter and open to abuse. The government has already shown abuse by issuing Public Interest Immunity Certificates merely to cover up official embarrassments. Absolute exemptions also contradict recommendations made by government inquiries into disasters directly caused by withholding information. For example, the Macpherson Inquiry into the mishandling of the Stephen Lawrence murder stated specifically that there should be no 'class exemptions' for law enforcement services. Making a government authority accountable to no one but itself is always a bad idea.

Fortunately, there are not many absolute exemptions in the Act and several are absolute only because disclosure is governed by different laws (such as the Data Protection Act for personal information). But even a few is too many. The only grounds for appeal against an agency's decision to use an absolute exemption is to argue that the information requested does not fall into the exempted category. The absolute exemptions are:

- **Section 21 – information accessible by other means**. A public authority is not obliged to give you information if it is available elsewhere, but under the 'duty to assist' they should tell you where to obtain the information. The guidance states that 'there should be no possibility of applicants being left in any doubt as to how they can obtain the information which they want'. The applicant's location, means, ability to understand information and physical condition have a bearing on whether or not information can be considered accessible.

- Section 23 – information relating to or supplied by the
  security and intelligence services, GCHQ, the special forces,
  the National Criminal Intelligence Service and certain
  other specified bodies with security functions. A minister
  can issue a certificate to establish information is covered by
  this exemption, which the Commissioner cannot overturn.
  The Information Tribunal can set aside the certificate if it
  finds the information does not relate to and has not been
  supplied by the named bodies. These organisations are: the
  Security Service, the Secret Intelligence Service, Government
  Communications Headquarters, Special Forces, the Security
  Vetting Appeals Panel, the Security Commission, the National
  Criminal Intelligence Service, the Service Authority for the
  National Criminal Intelligence Service, and four tribunals set
  up under the Regulation of Investigatory Powers Act 2000, the
  Interception of Communications Act 1985, the Security Service
  Act and the Intelligence Services Act 1994 respectively.

  These institutions are not considered public bodies under the
  Act despite being funded entirely by the taxpayer – an example
  of the feudal attitude of allowing public involvement only by
  way of providing the cash.
- Section 32 – court records. The exemption for court records
  might be acceptable if the court system had its own adequate
  openness laws, but it does not. Time and again, judges in the
  UK have shown little regard for the importance of maintaining
  an open judicial system that satisfies the public's need to see
  justice being done. Court records do not have to be withheld,
  but unless an obliging lawyer deigns to honour the public with
  this vital information, it is secret for 30 years. This exemption
  is discussed in more detail in Chapter 5. The Information
  Tribunal's decision in the case *Alistair Mitchell* v. *Information
  Commissioner* (10 October 2005) clarified the definition of a
  court record (see Chapter 1).
- Section 34 – parliamentary privilege. A certificate signed
  by the Speaker of the Commons or Clerk of the Parliament
  (House of Lords) is enough evidence that this exemption is
  met and there is no recourse to appeal. More details are found
  in Chapter 4.
- Section 36 – information (held by either House of Parliament)
  likely to prejudice the effective conduct of public affairs in
  the opinion of the Speaker of the Commons or the Clerk of

the Parliaments. Section 36 is usually a qualified exemption except when the information concerned is held by the House of Commons or House of Lords.

- **Section 40 – data protection.** This complex exemption provides guidance on areas where the FOIA overlaps with the Data Protection Act. Some parts provide an absolute exemption while others are qualified. More information is found in Chapter 14.

- **Section 41 – breach of confidence.** Although this is an absolute exemption, there is a public interest test within the law of confidence. See Chapter 13 (Private Companies) for more about this topic. Section 41 only applies to information provided to a public authority where disclosure would be a *legal* breach of confidence. In the past, authorities have made liberal use of this term to exempt all manner of information. It has been difficult to challenge this secrecy because the legal principles involved in the doctrine of confidence are complex and uncertain. There is no statutory framework for confidence, only a collection of case law. If authorities are given discretion to determine what is confidential, they often favour those groups who have the greatest influence and lobbying power, such as companies, at the direct expense of the public who they are meant to be representing. The FOI law says authorities no longer have discretion and must confine this term to only that information defined as confidential in law.

- **Section 44 – prohibitions on disclosure.** Information is exempt if disclosure is prohibited by other laws such as the Contempt of Court law or the Official Secrets Act. Note that part of the FOIA (section 75) calls for the Lord Chancellor to review these laws and repeal or amend those that are unnecessarily secretive. Notably, section 118 of the Medicines Act 1968 has been repealed, allowing the release of some clinical trial information for drugs approved for sale to the public.

FURTHER INFORMATION

The Information Commissioner's Office
www.ico.gov.uk
Wycliffe House, Water Lane, Wilmslow, Cheshire SK9 5AF
Tel: 01625 545 745 (enquiries)
Email: mail@ico.gsi.gov.uk

The IC's office has online guidance on the law and how to interpret the many exemptions.

Information Tribunal

www.informationtribunal.gov.uk
Information Tribunal Secretariat, Arnhem House Support Centre,
PO Box 6987, Leicester LEI 6ZX
Tel: 0845 600 0877
Fax: 0116 249 4253
Email: informationtribunal@tribunals.gsi.gov.uk

Campaign for Freedom of Information

www.cfoi.org.uk
Suite 102, 16 Baldwins Gardens, London ECIN 7RJ
Tel: 020 7831 7477
Fax: 020 7831 7461
Email: admin@cfoi.demon.co.uk
Director: Maurice Frankel

The Campaign is the leading lobbying organisation for the public's right to know and was instrumental in getting a freedom of information bill passed. You can download the entire law from www.cfoi.org.uk and also a very useful user's guide that explains how to use the Act.

Codes of Practice

These are issued by the Department for Constitutional Affairs and offer guidance to public authorities. They are worth reading to find out what authorities *should* be doing and may help you if you have a complaint.

- Code of Practice on the discharge of public authorities' functions under Part I of the Freedom of Information Act: www.foi.gov.uk/codepafunc.htm
- Code of Practice on the Management of Records: www.foi.gov.uk/codemanrec.htm

Background information on the law can be found at www.foi.gov.uk/bkgrndact.htm

There are helpful, user-friendly books and websites about the Freedom of Information Act 2000:

Blackstone's Guide to the Freedom of Information Act 2000, by John Wadham, Jonathan Griffiths and Bethan Rigby (Blackstone Press, London, 2005)

Butterworths New Law Guides: The Freedom of Information Act 2000, by Michael Supperstone and Timothy Pitt-Payne (Butterworths Tolley, London, 2001)

Essential Law for Information Professionals, by Paul Pedley (Facet Publishing, 2003)

Your Right to Know website, www.yrtk.org – get updates for the book plus the latest contact information, guidance, laws, fees, news, tips and actual requests

UK Freedom of Information Act Blog, http://foia.blogspot.com – all the latest FOIA news

4
Central Government

Information drives government, and in the current administration all roads lead to the centre. That is why the brightest light of openness should be directed at the very heart of government, namely the Prime Minister and Cabinet Office. The laws, policy, research and guidelines that come from central government affect even the most local issue.

All central government departments must adhere to the Freedom of Information Act 2000, along with Parliament, which consists of the House of Commons and the House of Lords and the politically neutral permanent staff who oversee the daily running of the houses. This includes administration, finance, Hansard, the library, records management, public information, research and catering. The passing of the FOIA marks the first time the public have had a right to access information about the operation of Parliament, so if you've always wanted to know how much the wine is subsidised at The Terrace restaurant, now is the time to ask.

Essentially 'the government' comprises the Prime Minister and his chosen ministers who are collectively responsible for managing national affairs in the name of the sovereign. The United Kingdom is not a government 'of the people by the people' but rather a government of the Crown ruling over its subjects. It is *Her Majesty's* government, *Her Majesty's* Treasury, the *Crown* Prosecution Service. The Prime Minister's role is 'sovereign in Parliament' and his powers are those of royal prerogative, meaning they derive from the power of the monarch. The monarchy no longer plays an active role in government (although it still has more influence than most people think), but the Prime Minister's position as executive as well as leader of the majority party in the legislative Parliament means he is in a unique position to both make laws and implement them. In the British parliamentary system the separation between powers is not always clear. The executive is part of the legislature while the Lord Chancellor is part of the executive, the legislature *and* the judiciary!

THE EXECUTIVE

Prime Ministers have varying styles of leadership. Some seek consensus from Cabinet while others take a more autocratic approach. In the last few years, a new group has ingratiated itself into the cosy coterie of executive power – special advisors. These are unelected staff appointed by politicians and, unlike civil servants, they do not have obligations of objectivity, hence their more usual name, 'spin doctors'. The Prime Minister, his ministers and special advisors effectively comprise the 'executive' branch of government and this is where the majority of policy decisions are made. Traditionally the watchdog of the executive is Parliament, in particular the opposition party. But if the ruling party's majority is large, the opposition party has little chance of blocking or changing legislation. The House of Lords also acts as a check on government power, but although it can modify bills, it cannot block them indefinitely.

The public have just one chance every four or five years to make their voices heard. In the interim, the government can pretty much do what it likes and the UK is often described as an elected dictatorship. It's easy for the government to go beyond its democratically elected mandate in such a system, and the best way to prevent this from happening is to ensure that the public's right to scrutinise government does not stop the day after an election. This is what freedom of information is all about.

However, what you will find is that the closer you get to the power centre of government, the less likely your FOI requests will be answered positively. While the Prime Minister and Cabinet have been keen to force local governments to open up, they are equally keen on exempting themselves from the same requirements! Ironically, the department in charge of implementing FOI across government has consistently kept secret all discussion on freedom of information!

In the United States, politicians are so used to openness requirements that not only are their travel details made public, but you can even find out how many frequent flyer points they are awarded. The Scottish Parliament now publishes all detailed expense claims for its MSPs. In Westminster, public representatives are still struggling with the basics of public accountability.

Navigating through central government can be tricky. Bureaucracy loves nothing more than needless complexity, so what we have is a system of central government departments splitting off into numerous non-departmental public bodies, non-ministerial bodies and executive agencies. Effectively, these are all quangos, meaning their leaders are appointed by politicians rather than elected by the people. All the main departments are listed in this chapter with the relevant contacts, the type of information available as well as contacts (updates are available on the Your Right to Know website: www.yrtk.org). Some departments are covered in greater detail in other chapters, such as the Department of Health in Chapter 9, or the Department for Environment, Food and Rural Affairs (DEFRA) in Chapter 10.

Also, be aware that local authorities undertake many central government responsibilities. So if you want figures on benefit fraud specific to your area, you should contact your local Jobcentre rather than the Department for Work and Pensions, which holds national figures.

Secrecy at the top

FOI requests to the Prime Minister can be directed either to Number 10 Downing Street or, preferably, the Cabinet Office at the address below. If you want information about the Prime Minister in his capacity as an MP, e.g. information about his expenses or constituency staff, then the request should go to the House of Commons. As an MP, the Prime Minister is subject to the same rules as other MPs (described below) and so must update the register of interests and gifts, and follow the MP's Code of Conduct.

As leader of the majority party, the Prime Minister is able to formulate policy (usually done with the help of the Cabinet) and deliver it through Parliament. Not only does he appoint the Cabinet (about 20 ministers) but he also chairs all the meetings and allocates membership and duties for Cabinet Committees.

What exactly goes on in Cabinet meetings? No one knows because they're totally secret! Minutes are taken for these and other Cabinet Committee meetings but they are not publicly available; neither are the agendas or any background papers used to formulate decisions. Rhetoric about open government rings hollow when you discover the main decisions are still being made entirely behind closed doors with little, if any, public consultation and no public accountability.

Policy

There are many problems with making policy in a rarefied atmosphere of secrecy. Firstly, ministers are generalists, already under enormous pressure to deal with their own department's mountain of information. Should they be expected to fully understand the complexity of say, a Tube privatisation deal? There may be little chance for discussion as many policies come ready formed to Cabinet from Cabinet Committees. And because the PM has a major hand in setting the membership and agenda for these, he has great influence on how a policy is presented.

There is also a quaint tradition of collective responsibility in cabinet, which means all decisions are unanimous and any differences between ministers must be kept secret; speaking out often results in removal. Recently, this convention has extended to all junior ministers and even some parliamentary private secretaries. What we have then, is a system where the main people who scrutinise policy are appointed by the PM and who know that if they scrutinise too much they'll get the boot. This is not a system particularly conducive to the 'free and frank' discussion that secrecy is meant to protect.

Some policies don't even come under the scrutiny of the Cabinet. For example, Gordon Brown announced the decision to give the Bank of England the power to change interest rates to the media, without any discussion with the Cabinet. Tony Blair went to the media first again to announce his surprising U-turn on holding a European referendum, without consulting Parliament or the Cabinet.

Membership of Cabinet Committees and their responsibilities used to be a state secret. In 1946, Sir Norman Brook, the then Secretary of the Cabinet, confronted the editor of *The Times* about a brief in the paper that mentioned a Cabinet Committee by name and the minister in charge. 'Publication in the press of such details is a hindrance to the efficient discharge of public business,'[1] he claimed.

The general attitude toward public accountability has changed little since it was set down in a ministerial procedure book in 1949: 'The underlying principle is, of course, that the method adopted by Ministers for discussion among themselves of questions of policy is essentially a domestic matter, and is no concern of Parliament or the public.'

As one of the people who provides the money, through taxes, for all the government projects that result from these secret policy discussions, I wonder if you feel the same?

1. Public Record Office, PREM 8/156, 'Future of the Steel Industry: Leakage of Information', Brook to Attlee, 3 April 1946, as quoted in Peter Hennessy's essay 'The Long March', in *Open Government: What do we need to know?* (Canterbury Press, Norwich, 2003).

At least we know the Cabinet Committee structure, and you can thank John Major for that. He also decided to publish the remit and membership of ministerial Cabinet Committees and the ministerial rulebook *Questions of Procedure for Ministers.*

Appointments

Not only does the PM appoint his ministers, he also appoints life peers (Lords) and Tony Blair has set the record for the most peers appointed. By 2000 he had already appointed 99 new Labour peers since being elected, compared to 39 by the Tories and 30 by the Liberal Democrats in the same time period. In March 2006, the public got an insight into Tony's penchant for appointing peers when the *Sunday Times* revealed how political party donors were being rewarded with a peerage. The PM also appoints a range of top-level positions in the public sector such as the chairman of the BBC, archbishops, and even the Poet Laureate. Parliament cannot veto any of the choices. This politicisation of public bodies is cause for concern, for if public officials are beholden for their jobs on a politician rather than the public, it is easy to see whose interests they will work for. A better system would be for nominees and their qualifications to be made public and a cross-party committee charged with selecting candidates with finalists presented in an open hearing. In posts of national importance, such as chairman of the BBC, these hearings should be televised.

Increasingly there have been calls for greater transparency in the appointment system, and the Office of Commissioner for Public Appointments (www.ocpa.gov.uk) may well issue further recommendations to ensure that these jobs are going to the best-qualified people rather than to political supporters. Some well-placed FOI requests could be the tools needed to open up this system.

Office of the Commissioner for Public Appointments
www.ocpa.gov.uk
35 Great Smith Street, London SW1P 3BQ
Tel: 020 7276 2625

The office was created in 1995 in response to the Nolan Committee to increase public confidence in the appointments system. It regulates ministerial appointments to the boards of quangos, NHS bodies, public corporations, nationalised industries, and utility regulators. It is charged with investigating complaints about the way such appointments are made. The office publishes an annual report and code of practice.

Advisory Committee on Business Appointments
www.acoba.gov.uk
FOI Officer, Jan Ashton in the Committee secretariat
Tel: 020 7276 2610
Fax: 020 7276 2607

The committee provides advice to the Prime Minister and other ministers about senior civil servants wanting to leave the service and take up outside appointments within two years. This is where you can find evidence of a 'revolving door' between government and big business.

House of Lords Appointment Commission
Same address as above
Tel: 020 7276 2625

The Appointments Commission hit the front pages in 2006 when the 'Cash for peerages' scandal was revealed. It makes recommendations for non-political peers and vets all others.

Honours

The PM also makes recommendations to the Queen on who should receive honours and titles. The secret fortress within which honours decisions are made was breached by a spectacular leak to the *Sunday Times* in December 2003 that revealed the government hadn't been exactly truthful when it described the recommendation process as 'non-political'. Minutes from these top-secret meetings revealed that celebrities were chosen to add excitement to the list, and civil servants like nothing better than to dole out awards to their colleagues. And who is making these decisions? No one knows, not even the Parliamentary Select Committee instructed to investigate the honours system. When the members asked Sir Richard Mottram, the chair of one of the honours committees, who were the other members deciding on the nominees, they were given the unhelpful reply: 'We have six of the most distinguished people in the field on the committee, but you'll just have to take my word for it because I'm not allowed to disclose their names' (29 April 2004).

Why the need for such cagey behaviour? If an honour is worth having, we should know how someone was chosen. To conduct the process in such ridiculous secrecy lends weight to the public's impression that honours are doled out not so much on merit but on who a potential recipient knows and how much money they have given to a political party. Maybe there's a valid argument for waiting a few years to disclose the whole proceedings, so those who didn't succeed aren't embarrassed. But the present waiting time of 60 years is entirely unjustifiable. The FOIA won't help open up the process, either – section 37 of the FOIA exempts this information from disclosure, along with all communication with the royal family. However, it must still pass the public interest test and this could be the wedge that prises open the door of secrecy, as it seems public credibility is not a sufficiently strong incentive.

The civil service

Politicians may come and go, but civil servants remain, doing the day-to-day work of running the country. There are more than 560,000 civil servants working for the government[2] under the direction of the head of the civil service (also known as the Cabinet Secretary), who in turn answers to the Prime Minister. They are all bound by the new FOIA.

Whistleblowers

The Civil Service Code requires impartiality and allegiance to the government of the day. What is less acceptable is that all civil servants must sign a confidentiality agreement, which prevents them from revealing any information they learn during the course of their duties, even after they leave their jobs. Civil servants are an essential source of information as they do the bulk of the government's work, and as long as there is a deficit of meaningful official information, their leaks are often the only way the public discovers wrongdoing in the government. Civil servants blew the whistle on serious problems in the country's immigration system for Eastern European applicants and received the sack for their trouble. In the US, whistleblowers are treated as heroes who save the taxpayer money. In the UK, they are scorned and silenced.

Whistleblowers should be protected because they save the public a lot of money. In June 2004, a study by the charity Public Concern at Work documented how whistleblowers were preventing frauds worth £2.5 million a year in Whitehall and that since the Public Interest Disclosure Act came into force in 1998 the number of frauds

2. 43rd Civil Service Yearbook.

in Whitehall stopped by whistleblowers increased by 30 per cent. Yet rather than fixing the problems when they are exposed, the government often prefers to spend its energy investigating leaks. There is often little protection for the whistleblowers. If they believe they are being asked to do something illegal, unethical or improper their only recourse is to discuss the matter with their manager and as a last resort the Civil Service Commissioners (13 non-civil servants appointed by the Crown and charged with ensuring that the service is effective and impartial). If they are still not satisfied, their only option is to resign. They are not allowed to go to the press or any outside person with their complaint even if their manager has completely ignored their concerns. The government's treatment of Dr David Kelly, a scientific expert on Iraq's weapons of mass destruction, highlighted the danger whistleblowers face when they make information public. Dr Kelly committed suicide after he was named by the government as the source behind former BBC reporter Andrew Gilligan's report that the government had 'sexed up' a dossier on Iraq by including claims that the country could launch an attack on the UK in 45 minutes.

Hutton cleared the government of any wrongdoing and placed the blame on the BBC, a verdict that does little to improve the already fragile position of those who speak out. And in May 2004, John Scarlett, who had been chairman of the Joint Intelligence Committee and partly responsible for 'outing' David Kelly, was appointed the head of MI6 (in a totally secret selection process, of course).

Whistleblowers do have some protection from Section 43H of the Public Interest Disclosure Act 1998. The act, which only came into force in July 1999, gives workers who 'blow the whistle' some rights of protection from being dismissed. The legislation covers workers in the public sector, but there is a major exception – those who work in the security services who are covered by the Official Secrets Act. They are allowed no rights to disclose anything, even if the information is vitally in the public interest.

Copyrighting public information

You might think that documents created and produced on behalf of the taxpaying public would be free for public use, but you couldn't be more wrong. In Britain, all official documents are protected by some form of restrictive copyright. Crown Copyright is the most familiar as it covers most government documents. It is administered by the Office of Public Sector Information, formerly Her Majesty's Stationery Office, a section of the Cabinet Office. This means public documents are *not* free to use, reuse or distribute however you'd like. This applies even to information made available on publication schemes and in answer to FOIA requests. Crown Copyright stifles public access to information and has a chilling effect on its dissemination. Until the restriction is abolished, there can be no real freedom of information.

First the good news. A few years ago, the Campaign for Freedom of Information drew attention to the ridiculous state of affairs whereby even the laws under which we are supposed to live were copyrighted so the public could not view them without paying and asking the government's permission! A consultation was launched to review the copyright, and as a result, HMSO made a few concessions, agreeing to waive copyright on certain categories of material such as legislation and explanatory notes, ministerial speeches, consultation documents, documents featured on official websites (except where expressly indicated otherwise), headline statistics, government press notices, and unpublished public records. You can find a full list of the categories at: www.opsi.gov.uk/advice/crown-copyright/copyright-guidance

But now the bad news: 'For other types of material however, the supply of documents under the Freedom of Information Act does not give the person or organisation who receives them an automatic right to re-use the documents in a way that would infringe copyright, for example, by making multiple copies, publishing and issuing copies to the public.' All publication schemes have some variation of this copyright notice. This particular one is from the Foreign and Commonwealth Office's scheme.

If people go to the trouble of requesting information from the government they ought to be able to use it. An environmental group will want to use pollution data in campaign material. A historian will want to include official documents in a book. Why should they have to navigate a complex path of licensing and possibly hand over more money for information compiled by public officials at public expense?

Crown Copyright is also used as a method of last resort by the British government when it is desperate to suppress information. When the government's initial cases against former MI5 intelligence officer David Shayler failed, the government sued him and a London newspaper for breaching Crown Copyright. The Ministry of Defence warned the *Guardian*'s Rob Evans that if he quoted from a report released under the Open Government code without their permission, legal action would be taken for breach of Crown Copyright. Although this threat was unfounded, it might be enough to deter some members of the public from making information received from an FOIA request widely available.

To complicate matters further, Parliamentary Copyright is different from Crown Copyright while information from the Environment Agency has a different copyright again. All have unique licensing arrangements. You should also be aware that the publication of some public documents is contracted out to a private company called, confusingly enough, The Stationery Office.

To find out about reusing government documents call the OPSI licensing division. They handle licensing agreements for all the various copyrights (see below). But the reality is that unless you are using the information for commercial gain, Crown Copyright is not enforced. In the last ten years, OPSI/HMSO has not brought one case to the courts in their sole name, according to Licensing Manager Andrew Eeles. It is more common for departments to notify OPSI that they intend to launch legal proceedings, though this, too, happens relatively infrequently and only involves money-making concerns. From 1996 to 2005, there have been nine cases involving Ordnance Survey mapping data and six cases instigated by the UK Hydrographic Office. Most were settled out of court. 'But it obviously gives the wrong signal, especially to law-abiding citizens who will think they'll get in trouble if they use public information,' says Maurice Frankel, the director of the Campaign for Freedom of Information. For years, he has actively published government information and correspondence protected by Crown Copyright on the campaign's website and has never been prosecuted.

Even using information obviously in the public interest is fraught with difficulty. When software developer Francis Irving was building the pro-democracy website www.theyworkforyou.com that allows citizens to follow their MP's activities in Parliament, he was threatened with legal action by Parliament because the site used Hansard material – protected by Parliamentary Copyright. 'We had to take the risk of publishing without a license because we believe everyone has a right to reproduce what their MP has been saying in Parliament,' Irving says. 'Parliament very kindly did eventually give us a licence but one shouldn't have to rely on their kindness. It should be every citizen's right to reproduce that information without having to ask permission.'

Along with restrictive copyright comes hefty licence fees for the most important information such as mapping, addresses, and tidal charts. While it may seem sensible to charge for these resources, it costs the taxpayer far more in the long term. More than 50 per cent of national UK mapping data is actually sold back to government which means the taxpayer effectively pays not once but dozens, if not hundreds of times (through fees and/or council tax). The restricted availability of Ordnance Survey data is perhaps the most contentious, thwarting everyone from pro-democracy groups who need to discover electoral boundaries to private companies such as the AA who require mapping for road atlases.

In the United States, any information prepared by government employees as part of their official duties is entirely free from copyright, so anyone can use and reuse the information without having to gain permission or ask for a licence. This applies to data as well, even when given to a private publisher, and this is one of the main reasons the US is home to so many successful database services such as LexisNexis. If everyone starts out with the same public information, companies must provide more value-added material if they expect people to pay for their services. Private companies in the UK, on the other hand, are able to exact usurious rates while providing no value-added extras at all. The Stationery Office simply reprints official public documents (created at public expense) and then charges the public a small fortune to view them. A copy of the Bichard Inquiry report that examined police failings in the murder investigation of two Soham schoolgirls costs £26.50, while a list of products determined harmful to human health and/or the environment was retailing at £105.

PARLIAMENT

I took a tour of the New Zealand Parliament a few years ago and was struck by how much our guide wanted us to feel right at home in the building. 'Our aim is to make the public feel welcome,' he told us. We were a group of about 20, most of whom were New Zealanders. 'The public paid for all this, so we think it's essential they feel like it's their building. No one should feel like they don't belong here.' We went in all the committee rooms and were even allowed to sit on the green benches of the Commons chamber. Indeed, even if my taxes hadn't paid for the building, I felt right at home.

Contrast this with the UK Parliament where everything is designed to intimidate and exclude the public. You can't sit on the green benches here. What you can do is queue for a seat in the public gallery, but now even that level of participation has been obscured by a thick bulletproof screen and soon the public may be excluded altogether. The public are barred from most of Parliament's restaurants and bars unless they are the guests of a member, which is a shame as we subsidise the food and drink to the tune of almost £6 million a year.[3]

Politicians in Parliament ought to be at the vanguard of the campaign for the public's right to know; after all, they are the public's representatives. Instead many MPs and Lords view the public as an inconvenience. This attitude is best expressed in politicians' exemption of themselves from many of the terms of the Freedom of Information Act.

Setting a bad example

Section 34 – parliamentary privilege – allows any information to be withheld if the Speaker or Clerk signs a certificate saying the information is exempt. Unlike other exemptions, this one cannot be challenged. Section 36 allows any information 'likely to prejudice the effective conduct of public affairs' to be kept secret. This exemption normally requires a public interest test, but *not* when the information is held by either the Commons or the Lords. So the one body of government that is meant to represent the public has exempted itself from the public interest test that all other public authorities must face!

Votes

Amazingly, Parliament does not provide an easy means of viewing MPs' voting records. If you want to know how your MP voted on a particular issue, you would have to find all the relevant debates in Hansard and manually search all the full division lists where the votes are tallied. Fortunately, a group of activists have taken it upon themselves to remedy this problem and you can now easily access MPs' voting records on the website: www.publicwhip.org. The information is mined from Hansard and allows you to search votes and ministers' answers to written questions by MP, topic or your postcode. Voting data extends back to May 1997, although there are a few divisions (vote counts) missing in the 1997 Parliament. New votes appear a few days after they happen and accuracy is not guaranteed, so you should confirm figures with Hansard or the House of Commons Information Office. Written answers are indexed back to the start of 2003.

3. House of Commons Commission, *Annual Report 2002/03*.

Parliamentary questions

You can get a staggering amount of information from the questions asked verbally and in writing by MPs and Lords. About 40,000 questions are asked each year and only 3,000 are answered orally, so ministers answering written questions, which are published in Hansard, provide the vast majority of information. You can search Hansard's online index by subject or by the questioner's name. Answers to House of Commons parliamentary questions are available on the parliamentary website at www.publications.parliament.uk/pa/cm/cmpubns.htm, and for the House of Lords at www.publications.parliament.uk/pa/ld/ldvolume.htm. However, I would suggest heading to www.TheyWorkForYou.com, which presents the information in a much more user-friendly format that is easier to search.

Register of members' interests

This can sometimes be a good source of information about an MP's extra-curricular activities: how much an MP gets for an after-dinner speech, for writing a newspaper article or appearing on a television show. It also includes property income and other business interests. The main criticism is that money ranges are very broad. For example, Michael Portillo MP received 'up to £5,000' for writing an article for *The Times*. You can request the register from the information centre or look at it online: www.parliament.uk/about_commons/register_of_members__interests.cfm or on www.theyworkforyou.com

The other problem with the register is that not all MPs are as diligent as they should be about reporting their interests. David Blunkett was forced to resign a second time in November 2005 after newspapers revealed he held a series of outside business interests that included the directorship of DNA Bioscience, a company that was in the process of bidding for a contract from the very same government department Blunkett was leading!

All peers must register consultancies or any parliamentary lobbying on behalf of clients for payment or other reward. They must declare these interests before they speak about, vote on or lobby on any issue where there could be a conflict of interest, although they are sometimes caught out. Early in 2004, Lord Inge, a former Chief of the Defence Staff, argued against proposed cuts to military spending, conveniently forgetting that he was a paid consultant of the giant defence contractor BAE Systems and also of Alvis Vickers, the armoured vehicle manufacturer. You can get a copy of the Lords register of interests by calling the Lords information centre, or online at www.parliament.uk/about_lords/register_of_lords__interests.cfm

There is also a public register of interests for MPs' pass-holders and Westminster journalists that you can find online at the address above.

Gifts

The public now have access to a listing of gifts ministers receive during their official duties. This is the result of an Open Government request filed by the *Guardian*'s Rob Evans and David Hencke. It seemed like a simple request, as politicians in most democracies are obliged to disclose their gifts. Not in Britain, however, where the reporters received two years' delay and obstruction that only came to an end after the Parliamentary Ombudsman overruled Downing Street. Even then, the government tried to force the Ombudsman to change her recommendation. Finally, in March 2003, the Cabinet Office agreed to make public the first of an annual gift list. Reading through the list, you'll wonder why the government fought so adamantly to hide the fact that the PM had received a guitar from Bryan Adams and a nativity scene from Yasser Arafat.

The value of gifts that ministers must declare is set quite high – £140 and over – so there is surely a mountain of gifts of lesser value that go unreported. It is important to know who is giving and receiving gifts because gifts buy influence and the public have a right to know who is influencing their representatives. The gift list remained elusive even after the *Guardian*'s battle, but finally it is online: www.cabinetoffice.gov.uk/propriety_and_ethics/ministers/

Allowances and expenses

www.parliament.uk/site_information/allowances.cfm
Apart from their salary, MPs are eligible for a wide array of allowances and expenses that far exceeds their official remuneration. Currently, expenses are published each autumn in these categories: additional costs allowance and/or London supplement, incidental expenses provision, staffing allowance, members' and members' staff travel, centrally purchased stationery, central IT provision and other central budgets (such as the winding-up allowance or temporary secretarial allowance). The figures for members' travel covers travel on parliamentary business within the UK plus individual travel to designated European destinations. The problem is that a myriad of sins can be hidden in sum totals. When Scottish expense claims

were published, Brian Monteith was forced to pay back £250 after admitting he made false claims for taxis to return from various nights socialising in Edinburgh restaurants and bars. *The Scotsman* revealed how Alex Salmond claimed £8,500 to commute by taxi from his home in Linlithgow to the Scottish Parliament, and Keith Raffan, the former Liberal Democrat MSP, claimed mileage expenses for driving round his constituency – when he was out of the country.

If this is happening in Scotland, it's undoubtedly going on in Westminster to an even greater extent. After all, there are only 129 MSPs (compared to Westminster's 659) and they get roughly half (£61,240) the amount of their Whitehall compatriots. A number of cases challenging this secrecy are with the Information Commissioner.

A factsheet outlining the salaries, allowances and expenses that an MP can claim is available from the House of Commons Information Office or can be downloaded from the parliamentary website's section 'Publications and archive'.

Staff allowance

The names of MPs' staff are still kept secret, though this refusal was appealed to the UK Commissioner for judgment. For 2004/05 MPs were able to claim £66,458–£77,534 for staff costs. Staff are paid centrally from public funds on agreed pay scales and standard contracts, but are considered employees of MPs. The investigative reporter Michael Crick estimates that around 100 MPs employ members of their family, and while most work very hard, some may do nothing at all. The lack of oversight for these handouts was highlighted when the Parliamentary Standards Commissioner investigated Crick's allegations that the former Conservative leader Iain Duncan Smith's wife was not doing enough public work to warrant her public salary.

An MP's signature is all that is needed to draw money from the public purse, admitted Andrew Walker, the head of the Commons fees office in his evidence to the Standards Committee. He also described the boundaries between using public money for constituency work and party political campaigning as 'fuzzy'.

Housing and accommodation

This allowance is meant to help pay for London accommodation during parliamentary session for those MPs (or Lords) whose primary residence is outside London. In reality, some have used it to subsidise second homes in the country, a practice detailed in a *Sunday Times* article (11 January 2004). The total number of MPs and Lords who can claim this allowance has been a closely guarded secret, but under the FOIA these payments had to be disclosed from autumn 2004 onwards. If you want information about claims paid out before then, you might try filing an FOI request.

Standards

All ministers must abide by the Ministerial Code. You can download a copy of the staff handbook (also known as the Green Book) from the parliamentary publications page listed above. This is one of the documents made public for the first time by the FOIA.

The Lords did not have a written code of conduct until 2001. You can now download a copy from the parliamentary publications online page or request a copy from the Lords information centre.

Hansard

Hansard is the official journal of the House of Commons and the House of Lords, published daily and weekly when Parliament is in session. As the main public record of our government, it should be readily available to the public, but until 1996 it was virtually unobtainable. Even now it is only easily accessible if you're online. Despite being produced with public money, Hansard is prohibitively expensive for the public to access: an annual subscription to the daily version for both houses costs £1,185 for the paper version and £1,997 for a CD version. Even libraries cannot easily meet the costs from their meagre budgets, and gradually the daily records of Parliament are becoming unobtainable in hard copy. At least we now have a free and accessible online version. That is entirely due to the efforts of Ian Church, a former editor of Hansard who, in 1996, initiated the process of putting the record online and managed to persuade the government to forgo the revenue from the subscription fees in the name of open government. This feat earned him an award from the Campaign for Freedom of Information, and it is an example many other government departments could follow.

SOURCES FOR PARLIAMENTARY INFORMATION

The main portal for Parliament information on the internet is www. parliament.gov.uk. Parliament publish a number of informative factsheets, which you can access online or by contacting the House of Commons Information Office. Full audiovisual coverage of both chambers is now available online along with the proceedings of some Select Standing Committees from the website: www.parliamentlive. tv

House of Commons
www.parliament.uk
Westminster, London SW1A 0AA
Tel: 020 7219 3000

House of Commons Information Office
Westminster, London SW1A 0AA
Tel: 020 7219 4272
Fax: 020 7219 5839
Email: hcinfo@parliament.uk
FOI Officer: Bob Castle, Department of Finance and Administration
Tel: 020 7219 2032
Email: FOIcommons@parliament.uk
Publication scheme: www.parliament.uk/parliamentary_publications_and_ archives/commons_foi.cfm

FOIA requests for the Commons, Hansard, catering, security and records should be directed to the House of Commons Information Office. If you have questions about making an FOI request to the Commons, you should contact the Information Office in the first instance, followed by the FOI Officer if you need detailed guidance or feel your request is being ignored.

A lot of information is already public: reports, memoranda of evidence submitted to committees, minutes (for domestic committees, Standing Committees and Select Committees), bills, Hansard debates, annual reports and accounts. Other public documents of interest include the staff handbook, guidance for members, occupational health and safety policies and procurement information.

Official documents www.publications.parliament.uk/pa/cm/ cmpubns.htm

Research Papers www.parliament.uk/parliamentary_publications_ and_archives/research_papers.cfm

Members of Parliament
If your MP has an email address it will be listed on the parliamentary website's alphabetical directory of MPs: www.parliament.uk/ directories/hciolists/alms.cfm, but many MPs treat email with some

disdain. Your correspondence will carry more weight if sent by letter or fax. If you are righteous about communicating electronically, you might try the web service at www.writetothem.com, which provides a neat gateway into the paper-filled world of the House of Commons.

Parliamentary Archives

www.parliament.uk/parliamentary_publications_and_archives/parliamentary_archives.cfm

Tel: 020 7219 5315/3074

Email: hlro@parliament.uk

The records of both the House of Commons and the House of Lords are kept in Victoria Tower in the Palace of Westminster under care of the Clerk of Records. Lords' records go back to 1497, and Commons' records to 1547. You can visit the record office by making an appointment. There is no cost for the public to look at documents in the public search room, but you will have to pay for copying or despatching records or if you reproduce the records commercially. The records office can answer simple questions over the phone, but they prefer enquiries to be sent by post, fax or email. This is also where you will find plans and maps that have to be deposited by law (such as compulsory acquisition of land).

The Parliamentary Records Management Handbook is available online. It is a thorough guide and will help you determine where and how records are kept.

Hansard

www.parliament.uk/hansard/hansard.cfm

If you want to look up back issues or a hard copy, you can contact the House of Commons Information Office for details on which libraries in Britain and Ireland stock the publication. Also online are reports of committees, command papers and the daily proceedings. Hansard has a fully searchable online database so you can search by MP/peer or subject. The full text of Lords' Hansard is available online going back to 16 November 1994, and the Commons going back to 1988. Hansard is useful not only for its verbatim record of debates; it also includes vote counts and answers to written parliamentary questions.

The Electoral Commission

www.electoralcommission.gov.uk

Trevelyan House, Great Peter Street, London SWIP 2HW
Tel: 020 7271 0500
Fax: 020 7271 0505
Email: info@electoralcommission.org.uk

Money buys influence, so if you want to know who gave money to your local MP's election campaign, you can find out from the Electoral Commission. The Commission is an independent body that was set up in 2000 to increase public confidence in the electoral process. It also reviews local electoral boundaries. To access the registers, follow the links to 'Regulatory issues' then 'Registers'. You can index donors by how much they gave, to whom and when. There is also a register of campaign expenditure by political party and donations to registered third parties. This is where the cost of Cherie Blair's hairstylist was logged (£7,700) and Michael Howard's campaign makeup (£3,600).

House of Lords
www.parliament.uk/about_lords/about_lords.cfm
London SWIA 0PW
Main telephone number: 020 7219 3000. Messages for individual peers can be left by phoning 020 7219 5353.

The House of Lords has three functions: it makes law (legislature), it scrutinises the government and it is the final court of appeal. The judicial function of the House of Lords will end in September 2008 when a separate Supreme Court is set up. Reforming the Lords has been an issue since the early part of last century and will likely continue. In 2006, the Lords comprised 600 life peers, 30 lords of appeal (of which twelve are law lords), 92 hereditary peers and 26 Lords Spiritual (Church of England Archbishops, bishops and other clergy).

House of Lords Information Office
Tel: 020 7219 3107
Email: hlinfo@parliament.uk
FOI Officer: Frances Grey
Tel: 020 7219 0100
Email: Foilords@parliament.uk
Publication scheme: Available from the 'Publications' list on the main House of Lords website.

Register of Lords Interests www.publications.parliament.uk/pa/ld/ldreg.htm
House of Lords Library Enquiries Tel: 020 7219 5242

Scrutiny

Bad behaviour has led to the formation of several checks on government and parliamentary power. The following groups are an excellent source of information about the underbelly of government.

Committee on Standards in Public Life
www.public-standards.gov.uk

This committee was set up by John Major in 1994 to examine the standards of all those in public office, which includes civil servants, MPs, advisors, MEPs, councillors and senior officers of local government, members of executive agencies, quangos and other groups performing public functions. The committee's occasional reports are always worth reading and you can find them on their website. They have recommended a new civil service act, new rules for special advisors, and independent checks on ministers' conflicts of interest – but the current government ignored these.

Parliamentary Commissioner for Standards
www.parliament.uk/about_commons/pcfs.cfm
Office of the Parliamentary Commissioner for Standards
House of Commons, London SW1A 0AA
Tel: 020 7219 0311/3738
Fax: 020 7219 0490
Email: standardscommissioner@parliament.uk

The Commissioner advises MPs on standards and conducts investigations on alleged breaches. Diligence is questionable, though, as the position is appointed by the very people it is meant to scrutinise. Former Commissioner Elizabeth Filkin earned a reputation as an effective sleaze-buster for her thorough investigations of prominent Labour MPs John Prescott, Peter Mandelson, John Reid, Geoffrey Robinson and Keith Vaz. Unfortunately, this also earned her the sack! MPs like talking about the values of transparency and scrutiny, but what this episode showed is that they aren't keen to accept it themselves. The Commissioner is Sir Philip Mawer whose term will expire 25 June 2008. His reports can be found online: www.parliament.uk/about_commons/pcfs/annualreports.cfm

The Parliamentary and Health Service Ombudsman
www.ombudsman.org.uk
Millbank Tower, Millbank, London SW1P 4QP
Tel: 0845 015 4033; 020 7217 4163

Fax: 020 7217 4000

Email phso.enquiries@ombudsman.org.uk

The Ombudsman investigates complaints of maladministration from the public about government departments and some public bodies (but note, *not* about Parliament itself). You can get a good idea about how open a department is by reading the Ombudsman's annual reports, in particular the section about compliance with the old 'Open Government' code. The Ombudsman's rulings are not enforceable and the Cabinet Office and Downing Street have frequently thumbed their noses at the Ombudsman's rulings for greater disclosure.

Public Administration Select Committee

Clerk of the Public Administration Select Committee, Committee Office, First Floor, 7 Millbank, House of Commons, London SW1P 3JA

Tel: 020 7219 3284

Email: pubadmincom@parliament.uk

This committee examines the quality and standards of services administered by civil service departments. It frequently examines issues of government openness and its reports are a source of inside information about the running of government. The list of reports is available at www.parliament.uk/parliamentary_committees/public_ administration_select_committee.cfm

Commons Public Accounts Committee

www.parliament.uk/parliamentary_committees/committee_of_public_ accounts.cfm

Committee Office, House of Commons, 7 Millbank, London SW1P 3JA

Tel: 020 7219 5708

Email: pubaccom@parliament.uk

This committee examines how well government departments and some agencies are carrying out their functions.

National Audit Office

www.nao.gov.uk

157–197 Buckingham Palace Road, London SW1W 9SP

Tel: 020 7798 7000

Fax: 020 7828 3774

Email: enquiries@nao.gsi.gov.uk

The NAO is an independent body that reports to the Commons Public Accounts Committee. It audits the accounts of all government departments and some public bodies. It also conducts value-for-money audits reviewing the cost-effectiveness and efficiency of these bodies. For the latest audit reports you can contact the NAO or visit the webpage: www.nao.gov.uk/publications/vfmsublist/index.asp

Audit Commission

www.audit-commission.gov.uk
1 Vincent Square, London SW1P 2PN
Tel: 020 7828 1212

The Audit Commissioner is an independent body (itself audited by the National Audit Office) that audits more than 15,000 organisations in local government, the National Health Service, housing and criminal justice system in England and Wales (together these groups account for £125 billion annual spending). Reports are available on the website.

SOURCES FOR GOVERNMENT INFORMATION

A great deal of government information is now available online. The primary sources of government information are:

Directgov
www.direct.gov.uk

Directgov is the third generation of a government portal to public information. This latest version launched in 2004 aims to answer 90 per cent of queries within the site. It is a directory and also a storehouse for information across all departments.

Office of National Statistics

www.statistics.gov.uk
London Headquarters, Drummond Gate, London SW1V 2QQ
Enquiries: 020 7533 5888
Email: Info@statistics.gov.uk
Family Records Centre
1 Myddelton Street, London EC1R 1UW
Tel: 020 7233 9233; 020 8392 5300
General Register Office
www.gro.gov.uk

This agency collects, compiles and analyses a broad range of statistical information about the population and state of the UK. It also conducts research for government departments and conducts the decennial census. As the ONS is part of the government, there is an obvious conflict of interest with presenting statistics that may show the flaws of future or existing government policies. FOI requests for the raw stages of data collection would help ensure the objectivity and accuracy of the statistics collected to ensure they are free from political spin. The Registrar General keeps a central register of all those on GPs' lists for the National Health Service. The Family Records Centre houses the Public Search Room, a central search facility for finding birth, marriage, death and adoption certificates, and wills.

Information asset register

Most central government departments have an information asset register, which is a register of unpublished information held either electronically or in hard copy. You can search these registers online, though they don't provide direct access to the information holdings themselves, rather they just let you know what's available and where. Unfortunately many departments fail to keep their register up to date.

Prime Minister's Office

www.number-10.gov.uk
10 Downing Street, London SW1A 2AA
Tel: 020 7270 3000
Fax: 020 7925 0918

The PM's official residence is 10 Downing Street, and although the house is closed to the public, the website offers a virtual tour with information on the history and furnishings of each room. The Cabinet Office (see below) handles all FOIA requests related to the Prime Minister.

Civil Service

www.civil-service.gov.uk

The head of the civil service is usually also the Cabinet Secretary. FOI requests about the civil service should be directed to the Cabinet Office. *The Civil Service Yearbook* is published annually and lists all civil service contacts for departments throughout the UK, making it very useful for finding out the name of exactly who is dealing with a project or policy. There is an online version – www.civil-service.co.uk – where you can search for departmental addresses and telephone numbers; however, it does not provide names (the whole point of a directory!). The version with names costs £70 for a hard copy or £110 for an annual online subscription (another example of the excessive fees charged for copyrighted public information). You may find a copy at your local library.

DEPARTMENTS

Ministers may make the big policy decisions, but it is up to the departments, staffed by civil servants, to implement them. There are more than 60 departments and 100 executive agencies that deliver government services. Most of the departments contacted for this chapter have adopted a decentralised approach to FOI, so you should send requests directly to the division or person you think holds the information. The FOI officers listed here are the central advisors who offer guidance to staff and to the public, but you should try the department's main enquiry line first in most cases. If you encounter difficulty or obstruction, then the FOI officer may be able to help you and speed things along.

Office of the Attorney General

www.lslo.gov.uk
Attorney General's Chambers, 9 Buckingham Gate, London SW1E 6JP
Tel: 020 7271 2400
Email: lslo@gtnet.gov.uk
Private Office, Tel: 020 7271 2405

The chief legal advisor to the government and responsible for all Crown litigation. Currently Lord Goldsmith QC.

Cabinet Office

www.cabinet-office.gov.uk
70 Whitehall, London SW1A 2AS
Direct FOI requests to: The Openness Team, Histories, Openness and Records Unit, Cabinet Office, Admiralty Arch, North Entrance, The Mall, London SW1A 2WH
Tel: 020 7276 6334/6352/6335
FOI Officer: Dennis Morris
Tel: 020 7276 6333
Email: dennis.morris@cabinet-office.x.gsi.gov.uk, but send requests to: openness.team@cabinet-office.x.gsi.gov.uk
Publication scheme: Follow the button on the 'Main links' section of the homepage.

The Cabinet supports the Prime Minister in formulating policy and coordinates its implementation across government. You can find the latest Cabinet Committee membership information on the website: www.cabinetoffice.gov.uk/secretariats/cabinet_committee_business/general_guide/types.asp

Government Car and Despatch Agency
www.gcda.gov.uk
46 Ponton Rd, London SW8 5AX
Tel: 020 7217 3839
Fax: 020 7217 3840
Email: info@gcda.gsi.gov.uk

This is a division under the Cabinet Office responsible for providing chauffeur-driven cars to central government workers, and a secure mail and despatch service. The chief executive, Nick Matheson, stated in the 2001–02 annual report that, 'Culturally, we have become far more open in our management style.' I tested this out in 2005 by filing an FOI for the cost of ministers' cars. You can read the annual reports at www.gcda.gov.uk/information_report_accounts.htm

COI Communications
www.coi.gov.uk
Hercules House, Hercules Road, London SE1 7DU
Tel: 020 7928 2345 / 020 7261 8409 (general enquiries)
Fax: 020 7928 5037

Formerly the Central Office of Information, this Cabinet Office division employs 441 people whose job is to publicise and advertise for the government and give media advice to ministers. The government has complained about the costs of complying with the Freedom of Information Act, so bear in mind that this department spends £330 million a year on government publicity![4]

Office of Public Sector Information (formerly Her Majesty's Stationery Office)
www.opsi.gov.uk
St Clements House, 2–16 Colegate, Norwich NR3 1BQ
General enquiries: 01603 723 011
FOI Officer: Alan Pawsey, Head of Publishing Services
Publication scheme: www.hmso.gov.uk/information/pub_scheme.htm

4. Central Office of Information Annual Report 2004/05.

OPSI is responsible for implementing the EU directive on access and reuse of official information that became UK law on 1 July 2005. It also has responsibility for the publication of legislation and manages Crown Copyright.

Department for Constitutional Affairs (see Chapter 7 for more detail)
www.dca.gov.uk
5th Floor, 30 Millbank, London SW1P 4XB
Tel: 020 7210 8500 (switchboard), 020 7217 4879 Information Access Unit
FOI Officer: Kevin Fraser, Information Access Unit
Tel: 020 7217 4844
Email: Kevin.fraser@dca.gsi.gov.uk but send FOI requests to: dca.foi@dca.gsi.gov.uk
Publication scheme: www.dca.gov.uk/rights/dca/pubscheme.htm
Disclosure log: www.dca.gov.uk/rights/dca/disclosure.htm

This was formerly the Lord Chancellor's Department and deals predominantly with legal matters and constitutional issues such as House of Lords reform. The DCA is also responsible for the Freedom of Information and Data Protection Acts and works closely with the Information Commissioner. Its legal and court functions are outlined in Chapter 7. The DCA also has responsibility for human rights, the Electoral Commission, referendums and party funding. The following two public authorities are responsible to the DCA:

HM Land Registry
www.landreg.gov.uk
32 Lincoln's Inn Fields, London WC2A 3PH
Tel: 020 7917 8888
Email: enquiries.pic@landregistry.gsi.gov.uk
FOI Officer: Allison Bradbury, Land Registry, Nottingham West Office, Chalfont Drive, Nottingham NG8 3RN
Tel: 0115 906 5375
Allison.bradbury@landregistry.gsi.gov.uk
Publication scheme: www.landregistry.gov.uk/foi/pub_scheme/

The Land Registry is responsible for land registration in England and Wales. You can now access the register for England and Wales online and search by postcode or address but not owner. The record includes a description of the property, who owns it and any charges such as mortgages that may affect the property. You can also get a title plan showing the location and boundaries of a property. Another source of information available online is the Residential Property Price Report, containing the average selling price of property by county based on the latest housing transactions lodged with the Registry. Not all land is registered, notably the Crown Estate and other aristocratic holdings. Each title search costs £2, which might sound reasonable but if you are trying to do any kind of academic or campaigning research on land ownership then this price makes the database inaccessible as there are over 20 million title records. The Land Registry had received about 185 FOI requests as of May 2006.

National Archives (formerly the Public Record Office) – see Chapter 3

Department for Culture, Media and Sport
www.culture.gov.uk
2–4 Cockspur Street, London SW1Y 5DH
Tel: 020 7211 6200 (general enquiries)
FOI Officer: Joanne Othick, Information Manager
Tel: 020 7211 2024/2026
Email: FOI@culture.gsi.gov.uk
Online FOI request form: www.culture.gov.uk/foi/6_foi_requests
Publication scheme: www.culture.gov.uk/foi/pub_scheme.htm

This department has a rag-bag of responsibilities: architecture, arts policy, broadcasting and media, crafts and creative industries, libraries, cultural education, archives, museums, galleries, historic environment, sport (including the 2012 Olympics), tourism, gambling and gaming licences, and that great cultural institution, the National Lottery. It also oversees the Government Art Collection. This department has always been one of the most open and oversees a number of the country's landmark institutions such as the BBC, English Heritage, the British Library and the British Museum. It is also in charge of listing buildings of historical or architectural significance.

British Library
www.bl.uk
96 Euston Road, London NW1 2DB
Tel: 020 7412 7000 (London); Tel: 01937 546 000 (Boston Spa)
Publication scheme: www.bl.uk/about/policies/freedom2.html
Disclosure log: www.bl.uk/about/policies/freedomdisclosurelog.html

British Museum
www.thebritishmuseum.ac.uk
Great Russell Street, London WC1B 3DG

Tel: 020 7323 8000 (switchboard); 020 7323 8299 (information desk)
Email: information@thebritishmuseum.ac.uk
Publication scheme: www.thebritishmuseum.ac.uk/corporate/

Olympics Games Unit
DCMS address as above
Email: Olympics@culture.gsi.gov.uk
Tel: 020 7211 6446

The London Olympics in 2012 will consume a huge amount of public funds – already the estimate is £2.375 billion – so it's worth putting in a few requests to ensure that the money is properly and well spent.

Government Art Collection
www.gac.culture.gov.uk
DCMS address as above
Tel: 020 7211 6200
Email: gac@culture.gov.uk

With 12,000 works of art, the GAC is one the most extensive art collections in the country, but despite being paid for by the public, few of us will ever get to see the displays. They are housed in government buildings, British embassies, residences and consulates. Find out what's in the collection and ask for access.

Foreign and Commonwealth Office
www.fco.gov.uk
King Charles Street, London SW1A 2AH
Tel: 020 7008 1500 (general enquiries)
FOI Officer: Rosaleen Wotton
Freedom of Information Team, Information Management Group,
Old Admiralty Building, Whitehall, London SW1A 2PA
Tel: 020 7008 0414
Email: dp-foi.img@fco.gov.uk
Publication scheme and disclosure log: follow the links at www.fco.gov.uk/foi

The FCO covers all matters dealing with international relations such as diplomacy, promoting British business overseas and protecting UK citizens abroad. The FCO is an old-style secrecy stronghold with little regard for the public's right to know. It was criticised by the Parliamentary Ombudsman in 2003 and 2004 for withholding and obstructing the release of information about seconded employees of private companies working in the department. The FOI section has overall responsibility for information access and coordinates a network of open government liaison officers covering each FCO department and each overseas post. The liaison officers are your first point of contact for FOI issues, and if you need help identifying who this person is, contact either the enquiry line or the FOI section. The Consular Directorate deals directly with Britons in distress overseas and queries about the action (or inaction) taken by the FCO to help these people should be directed to: the Consular Assistance Group, Old Admiralty Building, London SW1A 2PA; Tel: 020 7008 0223. The FCO also has a few attached quangos, none of which hold public meetings or conduct public consultation exercises. My favourite of these is the:

Government Hospitality Advisory Committee for the Purchase of Wine
Government Hospitality, Lancaster House, Stable Yard, London SW1A 1BB
Tel: 020 7008 8517
Fax: 020 7008 8526
Chairman: Sir David Wright; Head: Robert Alexander
Email: robert.alexander@cvg.gov.uk

I just couldn't resist throwing this funny little quango into the mix. It advises the government on purchasing wine – nice work if you can get it! Why not send some FOIs to see their tipples of choice courtesy of your taxes.

Home Office
www.homeoffice.gov.uk
For initial enquiries contact the Direct Communications Unit,
2 Marsham Street, London SW1P 4DF
FOI Officer: Jane Sigley, Information Access Manager
Tel: 020 7035 1306
Email: public.enquiries@homeoffice.gsi.gov.uk (state 'FOI request')
Publication scheme: www.homeoffice.gov.uk/about-us/freedom-of-information/publications-scheme/
Disclosure log: www.homeoffice.gov.uk/about-us/freedom-of-information/released-information/

Prisons and probation
National Offender Management Service. Write to:
Open Government Unit, National Offender Management Service, Room 410, Abell House, John Islip Street, London SW1P 4LH
Tel: 020 7217 2125
Fax: 020 7217 5150
Email: opengovernment@hmps.gsi.gov.uk

The Home Office deals with the internal affairs of England and Wales. Its primary function is to ensure a safe society and it is responsible for all that goes along with crime reduction: police, criminal policy, criminal justice and law reform, security, anti-terrorism, fighting organised crime, prisons and probation. This is covered in more detail in Chapter 8. The Home Office is also charged with building strong communities, and this involves civic renewal, citizenship, immigration and asylum, and race equality.

To locate the Home Office division that deals with your topic of interest, read this webpage – www.homeoffice.gov.uk/about-us/freedom-of-information/asking-for-info – or contact the Direct Communications Unit who can provide enlightenment on the ins and outs of this vast government department. There are also several units that are responsible for major Home Office services, including the Passport Service and the Immigration and Nationality Directorate.

Immigration and Nationality Directorate

Central Freedom of Information Team, 5th Floor East, Whitgift Centre, Wellesley Road, Croydon CR9 1AT
Tel: 020 8760 3085
Fax: 020 8760 3085 FOIs
Email: freedom.informationteam@homeoffice.gsi.gov.uk

The most interesting information available here is the Quarterly Asylum Statistics that include figures on asylum seekers entering the country, percentages of appeals rejected, the number of seekers deported and the number claiming benefits: www.homeoffice.gov.uk/rds/immigration1.html. An FOIA request could be used to request more detailed information about the asylum system.

The Criminal Records Bureau, Forensic Science Service and HM Prison Service are covered in Chapter 8.

Identity and Passport Service

www.ips.gov.uk
Globe House, 89 Eccleston Square, London SW1V 1PN
Tel: 020 7901 2452
Fax: 020 7901 2459
FOI Officer: Denis O'Brien, Open Government Coordinator, IPS
Email: Denis.O'Brien@ukpa.gsi.gov.uk but send FOI requests to: infoaccess@ukpa.gsi.gov.uk
Publication scheme: www.passport.gov.uk/news_publications.asp

When the highly controversial identity card scheme was finally pushed through Parliament, the UK Passport Service was quickly renamed to incorporate their new role providing ID cards. This will now be the place to direct any FOIs you might like to make about this scheme such as its total cost, contracts, correspondence between government and private companies, its Gateway review, etc. You can find a list of their publications at the link above. Mr O'Brien said the Service plans to publish as much information as possible online.

Forensic Science Service – see Chapter 8

HM Treasury
www.hm-treasury.gov.uk
Correspondence & Enquiry Unit, Freedom of Information Section, 2/W1,
HM Treasury, 1 Horse Guards Road, London SW1A 2HQ
Tel: 020 7270 5000 (switchboard); 020 7270 4558 (public enquiries)
Fax: 020 7270 4861
Email: public.enquiries@hm-treasury.gsi.gov.uk
Publication scheme: available under the 'About' section of the website
Disclosure log: www.hm-treasury.gov.uk/about/information/foi_disclosures/
foi_disclosures_index.cfm

The Treasury is one of the oldest government departments, founded in the eleventh century. It raises taxes, plans public spending in the form of the budget, and deals with all monetary issues. The FOIA section 29 exemption for information that could prejudice the economy will have particular relevance to requests made to the Treasury. Several major organisations are attached to HM Treasury, the most notable being HM Revenue and Customs, the product of a merger between the Inland Revenue and HM Customs and Excise. The Treasury has the worst record among central government departments for its poor response to FOI requests. It responds in time to requests in only 43 per cent of cases, according to the DCA's quarterly statistics.

HM Revenue and Customs – see Chapter 8

The Valuation Office Agency
www.voa.gov.uk
New Court, 48 Carey Street, London WC2A 2JE
Tel: 020 7506 1700
Email: custserv.voa@gtnet.gov.uk

Values land and buildings for taxes administered by HM Revenue and Customs and council tax.

Office of Government Commerce – see Chapter 13

Royal Mint
www.royalmint.com
Royal Mint, Llantrisant, Pontyclun CF72 8YT
Tel: 01443 222 111
Fax: 01443 623 148

Produces coins for the UK and other countries along with medals and official/royal seals. There's an interesting leaflet on modern money manufacturing processes available along with more general information from the annual report.

Bank of England
www.bankofengland.co.uk
Threadneedle Street, London EC2R 8AH
Tel: 020 7601 4444
Email: enquiries@bankofengland.co.uk
Publication scheme: www.bankofengland.co.uk/publications/foi/index.htm
Disclosure log: www.bankofengland.co.uk/publications/foi/disclosurelog.htm

This is the central bank of the UK and is responsible for setting interest rates, issuing banknotes and maintaining a stable economy.

Department for Communities and Local Government (formerly Office of the Deputy Prime Minister)
www.communities.gov.uk
Email: enquiryodpm@communities.gsi.gov.uk
Tel: 020 7944 4400 (general enquiries)
FOI Officer: Richard Smith, Information Management Division,
Ashdown House, Victoria Street, London SW1E 6DE
Tel: 020 7944 3146
Email: richard.smith@communities.gsi.gov.uk
Publication scheme: Under the 'Freedom of Information' online section

A mixed bag of responsibilities that fall into three main categories: local and regional government (including the fire service and civil resilience); regeneration and regional development, and planning (urban policy, the Dome, Thames Gateway, London, building regulations). A searchable database of all publications is available online at www.publications.odpm.gov.uk. The DCLG has begun to open up its policy-making process by holding public consultations on issues such as regional assemblies. It is also one of the departments with a large percentage of new material on its publication scheme – about 50 per cent was not previously publicly available, according to FOI Officer Richard Smith. The website has a directory that outlines the responsibilities of each division. In addition, a number of quangos answer to the DCLG:

Ordnance Survey
www.ordnancesurvey.co.uk
Romsey Road, Southampton, Hampshire SO16 4GU
Send FOI requests to: Freepost FOI, Customer Service Centre FPN 1399, Ordnance Survey, Romsey Road, Southampton SO16 4GU
Email: foi@ordnancesurvey.co.uk
Publication scheme: www.ordnancesurvey.co.uk/oswebsite/aboutus/foi

Official topographic surveying and mapping authority of Britain.

Queen Elizabeth II Conference Centre
www.qeiicc.co.uk
Broad Sanctuary Westminster, London SW1P 3EE
Tel: 020 7222 5000
Fax: 020 7798 4200
Email: info@qeiicc.co.uk

Conference and banquet facilities.

Planning Inspectorate
www.planning-inspectorate.gov.uk
Customer Support Unit, 3/15 Eagle Wing, Temple Quay House,
2 The Square, Temple Quay, Bristol BS1 6PN
Tel: 0117 372 6372
Fax: 0117 372 8128
Email: enquiries@planning-inspectorate.gsi.gov.uk
Publication scheme: available from 'Publications' section online

The Inspectorate holds local inquiries when there are objections to local authority plans and hears appeals and casework on issues relating to planning, the environment, highways, housing and transport.

Department for Education and Skills – see Chapter 12

Department for Environment, Food and Rural Affairs (DEFRA)
www.defra.gov.uk
3–8 Whitehall Place, London SW1A 2HH
Tel: 020 7238 6000

FOI Officer: Lewis Baker
Tel: 020 7238 6591
Email: lewis.baker@defra.gsi.gov.uk but send requests to: accesstoinfo@
defra.gsi.gov.uk
Publication scheme: www.defra.gov.uk/corporate/opengov/pubscheme/
index.htm
Disclosure log: www.defra.gov.uk/corporate/opengov/inforelease/index.htm

DEFRA has a huge remit and a huge staff – 10,400 people work for
this department. For a full listing of information available from this
department see Chapter 10.

Department of Health (NHS) – see Chapter 9

Department for International Development
www.dfid.gov.uk
1 Palace Street, London SW1E 5HE
Tel: 020 7023 0000 (switchboard)
Frank Rankin, Head of Open Government Unit
FOI Officer: Russell Banks, Open Government Unit, Information and Civil
Society Department, DFID, Room 504, Abercrombie House, Eaglesham
Road, East Kilbride, Glasgow G75 8EA
Tel: 0135 584 3549
Fax: 0135 584 3632
Email: R-Banks@dfid.gov.uk, but send requests to: foi@dfid.gov.uk
Publication scheme: www.dfid.gov.uk/aboutdfid/foi/foiclasses.asp
Disclosure log: www.dfid.gov.uk/aboutdfid/foi/foidisclosures.asp

This department's remit includes promoting sustainable development,
universal education and gender equality, and eliminating world
poverty. It is one of the most open departments in central government
and a worthy example for the rest to emulate. The DFID publishes
a detailed directory of internal contacts, minutes and agendas for
meetings and policy consultations. It also makes public an extensive
range of data on international development such as indicators of
development progress (poverty, education, gender equality and
health), figures of public spending on aid, aid by income group and
region, debt relief, and a list of the top 20 recipient countries.

Department of Trade and Industry – see Chapter 13

Department for Transport – see Chapter 6

Department for Work and Pensions
www.dwp.gov.uk
Tel: 020 7712 2171 (general enquiries)
FOI Officer: Charles Cushing, Adjudication and Constitutional Issues
DP/FOI, 2nd Floor, Adelphi, 1–11 John Adam Street, London WC2N 6HT
Tel: 0207 962 8581
Fax: 0207 962 8725
Email: charles.cushing@dwp.gsi.gov.uk, but send requests to: freedom-of-information-request@dwp.gsi.gov.uk
Publication scheme: www.dwp.gov.uk/pub_scheme

This central government department works closely with local authorities to distribute a range of social welfare benefits. Benefit fraud is a major problem, and estimates given to the National Audit Office for 2002–03 show £3 billion was lost (2.7 per cent of gross benefits spending). Income Support and Jobseeker's Allowance are the most vulnerable to fraud. In the year ending 30 September 2002, almost 6 per cent of total Income Support spending and more than 11 per cent of Jobseeker's Allowance went missing. Housing Benefit is also being abused with an estimated £750 million (or 6.2 per cent) overpaid.[5]

Jobcentre Plus, despite being in operation only since 2002, already employs nearly 77,000 civil servants according to the 43rd Civil Service Yearbook for 2005/06. Such a huge amount of publicly funded resources deserves some closer scrutiny courtesy of FOI. The DWP holds information about national policy and fraud; for more specific data you should contact your local office. The DWP oversees the Benefits Agency, the Child Support Agency, the Employment Service and the Appeals Service.

Other bodies

Charity Commission for England and Wales
www.charity-commission.gov.uk
13–15 Bouverie Street, London EC4Y 8DP
FOI Officer: Ted Baker, Information Centre
Tel: 020 7674 2409
Fax: 020 7674 2300
Email: ted.baker@charitycommission.gsi.gov.uk
Publication scheme: www.charity-commission.gov.uk/spr/pubscheme.asp

5. 'NAO Qualifies DWP's Accounts for the 14th Year in a Row', *Public Finance*, 19 December 2003–8 January 2004, p. 6.

The Commission regulates and monitors charities. You can search the register of charities online and also view charity accounts. Some charities have a poor record of submitting accounts and there is concern that enforcement is not rigorous enough. For example, the Commission waited almost a year before removing Abu Hamza from Finsbury Park mosque after it suspended him.

British Broadcasting Corporation

www.bbc.co.uk/foi/
BBC Freedom of Information, PO Box 48339, London W12 7XH
FOI Officer: James Leaton Gray, Head of Information Policy and Compliance
Tel: 020 8008 2883
Fax: 020 8008 2398
Email: foi@bbc.co.uk
Publication scheme: www.bbc.co.uk/foi/contents.shtml
Disclosure log: On the front page of the FOI homepage

The BBC, along with Channel 4 and S4C are only covered by the FOIA 'for purposes other than those of journalism, art or literature'. So while you might be able to find out about expenses, salaries and other administrative issues, you are unlikely to uncover much about why certain shows are commissioned and others axed. The *Press Gazette* reported in April 2006 that the BBC had used the journalistic exclusion to reject more than 400 FOI requests. A test case related to the BBC's refusal to make public a report on its coverage of the Israeli–Palestinian conflict by citing this exclusion was scheduled to be heard by the Information Tribunal in summer 2006.

In 2005 the BBC received 971 FOI requests, according to written evidence the corporation submitted in March 2006 to a parliamentary committee. The Information Policy and Compliance Team coordinates FOIA requests, provides policy advice and approves every FOI response. The BBC report that five members of the team work on FOIA and the team reports to the General Legal Counsel and the Director of Strategy. It works closely with the BBC's Regulatory Legal Department and a network of divisional representatives across 13 Divisions and the Nations and Regions. While the Board of Governors agreed to publish minutes of its meetings on the internet from May 2005, those from the controversial meeting in January 2004 in which Greg Dyke resigned are still secret. This case was awaiting a judgment by the Information Tribunal at the time this book went to press.

Channel 4

www.channel4.com/microsites/F/foia/
The Corporation Secretary, c/o Freedom of Information Team,
Channel 4 Television Corporation, 124 Horseferry Rd, London SW1P 2TX
Tel: 020 7306 8777
FOI Officer: Paola Tedaldi, Corporation Secretary
Email: foiadmin@channel4.co.uk
Online request form: www.channel4.com/microsites/F/foia/request.html
Publication scheme: www.channel4.com/microsites/F/foia/three.html

People often forget that Channel 4 is covered by the FOIA and direct all their TV queries to the BBC. Don't pick on the BBC – send a few questions round here! The *Sunday Telegraph* uncovered an interesting story using FOI that showed how Channel 4 consistently broke the 20 minutes of TV to one ad break rule and on occasion exceeded the 12 minutes of advertising in any one hour rule. The disclosures of correspondence between Channel 4 and Ofcom also highlighted the regulator's failure to do anything about the breaches.

Welsh broadcaster S4C

Parc Ty Glas, Llanishen, Cardiff CF14 5DU
FOI Officer: Pamela Forte
Email: pamela.forte@s4c.co.uk
Tel: 02920 741 412
Publication scheme: www.s4c.co.uk/e_index.html

Ofcom

Riverside House, 2a Southwark Bridge Road, London SE1 9HA
Tel: 0845 456 3000 or 020 7981 3040
Fax: 020 7981 3333
Email: information.requests@ofcom.org.uk

Ofcom regulates the UK communications industries including TV, radio, telecommunications and wireless services.

Royal Mail/Post Office

www.royalmailgroup.com
Freedom of Information Unit, Royal Mail Holdings Plc, Company Secretary's Office, 5th Floor, 148 Old Street, London EC1V 9HQ
Tel: 020 7250 2888 (possibly the worst switchboard on earth)
FOI Officer: Colin Young
Email: colin.young@royalmail.com, but send requests to: foi@royalmail.com
Publication scheme: Now available under the heading 'Who are we'

NB – Official advice is to 'Clearly mark across the top of the letter and on the envelope that your letter is for the "Freedom of Information Unit" – this will make sure it gets dealt with properly and quickly.' (After all, they're experts in mail going astray!)

The government (i.e. the taxpayer) is the main shareholder of Royal Mail Holdings Plc. If you only make one FOI in your life, make it to the Royal Mail/Post Office – there is no more deserving candidate, replacing last edition's favourite, Transport for London. Royal Mail has shown possibly the worst arrogance toward the public of any public authority included in this book (tied with the Highways Agency). Royal Mail operates Parcelforce and the Post Office Services. It is licensed by the Postal Services Commission to provide postal service in the UK. A full list of post office closures was revealed for the first time using FOI. The law is also bringing to light the scope of lost and stolen mail. The *South Wales Echo* found that Royal Mail was forced to pay £200,000 compensation to 17,000 people in South Wales because of postal errors. The paper was also able to identify the areas with the most complaints.

Postcomm
www.psc.gov.uk
Hercules House, 6 Hercules Road, London SE1 7DB
Tel: 020 7593 2100
Fax: 020 7593 2142
Email: info@psc.gov.uk
FOI Officer: Chris Webb
Tel: 020 7593 2114
Email: info@psc.gov.uk

If we had a strong FOI law, regulators such as this would not be needed. Until the public can easily access information directly, however, Postcomm serves an important role as a consumer watchdog on postal services.

Church of England
www.cofe.anglican.org
Tel: 020 7898 1000 (switchboard of national church institutions)

Church Commissioners
www.churchcommissioners.org.uk
1 Millbank, London SW1P 3JZ
Tel: 020 7898 1000
Email: commissioners.enquiry@c-of-e.org.uk

The Church of England is not considered a public body under the FOIA, but Church spokesman Ben Wilson says it will nevertheless 'seek to follow the principles of the Freedom of Information Act as far as possible,' though he adds, 'much of the Church's work is naturally involved in pastoral and confidential areas and therefore some topics are not open for disclosure'.

The Church Commissioners deals specifically with the Church's assets.

THE MONARCHY

Love them or hate them, the monarchy are publicly funded and should therefore be publicly accountable. However, they are not covered under the Freedom of Information Act and communication with the royal family is exempt from the Act. The main way to investigate the royals is through their interaction with public bodies; for example, go to the Treasury for information on the tax breaks Prince Charles receives for the Duchy of Cornwall. The royal household's policy is to 'provide information as freely as possible... and to account openly for all its use of public money,' the Queen's press secretary Penny Russell-Smith told me. In some instances the Queen has adopted a greater level of openness than Parliament. For example, all royal travel above £500 is reported, whereas MPs have consistently refused to release this information. In other cases, however, the royal family is becoming less accountable to the public. In 2004 the Queen imposed lifelong gagging orders on all staff who work for the monarchy. The public picked up the cost via the civil list for £125,000 in legal bills for drawing up the new contracts. In the absence of official information, leaks from staff are often the only way the public can find out the truth about the monarchy, so these bans on servants' free speech are cause for concern.

Meetings with the Queen

The Prime Minister holds a weekly meeting with the Queen to keep her up to date on government activity; after all it is Her Majesty's government. The contents of these meetings are secret, so unless the PM decides to reveal their contents in a memoir (and few do) the public have little idea of the influence the reigning monarch has on its elected representatives, though MPs are required to list visits with the royal family in the register of members' interests.

Royal finances

The estimated cost of keeping the Queen as head of state was £36.7 million in 2005, according to the Keeper of the Privy Purse, Alan Reid, who is in charge of the royal finances. The royal family receives parliamentary funding from several sources. The primary one is the Civil List, which provided £10.6 million in 2005. The Queen receives this annually as part of an agreement with the Treasury to turn over the income from the Crown Estate. The current amounts were set in 2000 and were unchanged from 1990 except for a £45,000 increase for the Earl of Wessex upon his marriage. The allowances will be reviewed in December 2010. Since 1993, the Queen has reimbursed the Treasury for payments to all Royal family members except the Duke of Edinburgh. According to Palace information, most of the money is spent on staff who support the royals on public engagements and correspondence. The royals also have a number of other sources of capital including art, antiques, jewellery, land and investments. The royal family's private art collection contains more than 500,000 pieces of art – a collection that would likely rival the Louvre, though its exact extent is unknown as there is no publicly accessible inventory. The public is a 'stakeholder' in the collection – much of the work was purchased with public funds and the Queen holds the collection in trust for the nation – but public access is extremely limited. The royal family also receive a number of lucrative tax breaks (for example, the Duchy of Cornwall does not pay corporation tax). The exact amount of these resources is unknown as the royals are under no obligation to account for themselves to their subjects. The increasing cost of security is also not included in the accounts, making it difficult to identify the true cost of running the monarchy.

Royal salaries

The Duke of Edinburgh – £359,000
HRH The Duke of York – £249,000
HRH The Earl of Wessex – £141,000
HRH The Princess Royal – £228,000
HRH Princess Alice, Duchess of Gloucester – £87,000
TRH The Duke and Duchess of Gloucester – £175,000
TRH The Duke and Duchess of Kent – £236,000
HRH Princess Alexandra – £225,000

Information about the royals

The Queen
Buckingham Palace, London SW1A 1AA
Tel: 020 7930 4832
Finances: www.royal.gov.uk/output/page308.asp

Duchy of Cornwall
10 Buckingham Gate, London SW1E 6LA
Tel: 020 7834 7346
Email: london@duchyofcornwall.gov.uk

The estates of HRH the Prince of Wales are mainly agricultural located in southwest England and a small area in London.

Duchy of Lancaster
Duchy Office, 1 Lancaster Place, Strand, London WC2E 7ED
Tel: 020 269 1700

A landed inheritance belonging to the Sovereign.

The Crown Estate
www.crownestate.co.uk
The Crown Estate, 16 New Burlington Place, London W1S 2HX
Tel: 020 7210 4377
FOI Officers: Tim Riley, Librarian, and Geoff Barlow
Tel: 020 7851 5037/5053
Email: tim.riley@crownestate.co.uk, but send requests to:
enquiries@thecrownestate.co.uk
Publication scheme: www.thecrownestate.co.uk/freedom

Unlike the monarchy, the Crown Estate *is* a public authority under the terms of the Freedom of Information Act 2000. Profits to the Treasury from the estate for the year ending 31 March 2005 were £185 million. The Crown Estate includes major London real estate such as Regent Street, Regent's Park and St James's; almost 120,000 hectares of agricultural land, as well as almost half the foreshore and the seabed (out to twelve nautical miles to sea) along the UK coast. The Crown Estate is part of the hereditary possessions of the Sovereign. The profits are paid back to the Treasury each year.

Annual Reports www.thecrownestate.co.uk/102_financial_information.htm

Map of the estate – an excellent clickable map is available at: www.thecrownestate.co.uk/interactive_maps.htm

Art collection – an inventory of the works of art and antiques owned by the Crown Estate is available by contacting Tim Riley.

INFORMATION SOURCES

Books about central government

Essential Central Government by Ron Fenney (LGC Information, London). As a recommended textbook for the National Council for the Training of Journalists, this comprehensive and detailed book, published every two years, does a good job of making central government understandable for non-politicos.

Hilaire Bennet's *Britain Unwrapped: Government and Constitution Explained* (Penguin Books, London, 2002) is another reader-friendly book that also includes local and EU governments.

Directories

You should be able to find at least one of the following directories at your local library.

The Stationery Office annually publishes *The Whitehall Companion*, which provides a listing of the relevant people and contact details for UK parliamentary offices, UK government departments, regulatory organisations, public bodies (quangos), executive agencies and devolved governments. Listings contain some historical information, the number of staff and a helpful guide of responsibilities and associated agencies or offices along with biographies of the main players.

Dod's Parliamentary Companion – published annually, the standard reference book for serious politicos with biographies of Lords and MPs.

Directory of Political Websites by Iain Dale – a comprehensive listing of all manner of political websites from government and parties to think tanks, media, lobbying groups and political sites around the world.

Carlton Publishing and Printing publishes guides for all the main political groups: Whitehall, House of Commons, House of Lords and so on. *The Guide to the House of Lords* has an alphabetical listing of Lords, women peers, and committees, along with interesting biographical lists of peers' publications, memberships, political organisations, directorships, and even what foreign languages the peers speak.

Get involved

BBC Action Network www.bbc.co.uk/dna/actionnetwork, the BBC's new interactive site gives you the opportunity to learn about government, take place in forums, start your own campaigns and lobby for change.

www.yougov.com – the leading e-consultation and public opinion research company in the UK. You can register your opinions on a variety of subjects and many government departments and councils use their research to gauge public opinion and formulate policy.

www.writetothem.com – contact councillors, MP, MEPs, MSPs, or Welsh and London Assembly Members for free.

www.TheyWorkForYou.com – find out everything there is to know about your MP with a report page that includes summary information about their attendance, recent speeches, voting records, expenses, register of members interests, ministerial career. Also links to other biographical and constituency information on external sites. Provides a free service that emails you every time an MP speaks or when a certain word is said in Parliament.

5
Intelligence, Security and Defence

'They that can give up essential liberties to obtain a little temporary safety deserve neither liberty nor safety.'

Benjamin Franklin

BBC reporter Kate Adie tells a story about a time she was stopped by authorities for filming the entrance to the Atomic Energy Research Establishment at Harwell. They informed her that filming was forbidden. The reason: national security – a Soviet spy might see the report on TV. Why would the Soviets need to watch TV?, Adie asked. The name of the agency was on a large noticeboard next to the main gate that anyone could see from the road! This pertinent information did not persuade the officials.[1]

I've used this example to illustrate the way 'national security' has become a completely devalued term, trotted out whenever someone in authority wants to avoid potentially embarrassing material reaching the public. But resorting to such drastic measures for every minor embarrassment makes it difficult to determine when something actually *is* a matter of national security.

Without public scrutiny of the intelligence and security services we are unable to judge their competence until a catastrophe occurs as happened in the London tube and bus bombings of 2005. As the 9/11 Commission in the United States made clear, the real danger comes not from transparency but from secrecy. The 9/11 hijackers were able to carry out their plan because intelligence officials failed to share information with each other and with outside organisations. The same problems may be occurring in the UK, but we have no way of knowing.

Too often our civil liberties are invaded on the basis of 'protecting national security' even before the most cursory protections are made. For example, while cement barricades have been erected around the Houses of Parliament and a barrier put up between the public gallery and House of Commons, nearly 7,000 Westminster security passes

---

1. 'No – I Haven't Got News for You' by Kate Adie in *Open Government: What do we need to know?* (Canterbury Press, Norwich, 2003).

are being lost or stolen each year.[2] GCHQ is spying on thousands of citizens in order to prevent organised crime; meanwhile, criminal gangs are entering the country thanks to a disorganised and ineffective immigration system.

The FOIA may help to curb this abuse because it adds a public interest test to the national security exemption. The Ministry of Defence and Special Branch are covered by the Act, but any information they received from the security services is not. Section 23 of the FOIA provides an absolute exemption for information about or from the following security bodies: the Security Service (MI5), the Secret Intelligence Service (MI6), Government Communications Headquarters (GCHQ), Special Forces, the Security Vetting Appeals Panel, the Security Commission, the National Criminal Intelligence Service, the Service Authority for the National Criminal Intelligence Service and the four tribunals set up under the Regulation of Investigatory Powers Act (RIPA) 2000. A certificate from a minister is all that is needed for the exemption to apply. This is exactly the kind of class exemption that William Macpherson warned against in his inquiry into the Stephen Lawrence murder investigation.

The Hutton Inquiry provided one of the only glimpses into the secretive world of government intelligence. Initially the government claimed internal documents could not be released due to – you guessed it – 'national security'. Even parliamentary committees could not be trusted with these 'top secret' documents, and without access to the main evidence or witnesses they were unable to properly scrutinise the government's decision to go to war in Iraq. All this information was later released to Lord Hutton.

The release included 900 memos, letters and emails that ran to around 9,000 pages. The evidence was published on the Hutton Inquiry website, and for the first time the public were able to see inside the dark heart of government. What they found were not state secrets that jeopardised the safety of the country, but rather a catalogue of political manoeuvrings between government officials and spin doctors as they struggled to defend themselves against allegations that the government had 'sexed up' the dossier that was used as the basis for going to war in Iraq.

Without Hutton, these documents would never have come to light, and we would never have known that they didn't actually

2. Answers to written questions by Rt Hon. Mark Oaten, 12–14 January 2004.

affect national security at all. The 9/11 Commission report released a similar amount of information that had previously remained secret due to 'national security'. These documents showed a similar use of the term as a means of holding back information that contradicted government policies, such as intelligence reports that cast doubt over the government's claim that Saddam Hussein was involved with al-Qaeda.

The total exclusion for security services is particularly bad considering that many of the major scandals that led to enactment of FOIA involved these same services. One of the worst abuses came to light during the Matrix Churchill arms-to-Iraq case in 1992 when the government showed it was willing to see innocent people go to jail rather than disclose documents that proved it had secretly reversed its policy of denying arms sales to Saddam Hussein.

There is an inherent danger in letting those people who have a vested interest in suppressing information for political convenience make the decision about what is a matter of national security. The only way to ensure that the exemption is not used for political gain is to have an objective mediator to judge whether the disclosure is in the public interest and if it will produce any actual harm to the nation (rather than to a politician's career).

When the *Guardian*'s Rob Evans tried to find out whether ships deployed in the Falklands War carried nuclear weapons, the Ministry of Defence refused to confirm or deny the information, saying that to do so would endanger national security. One might think that firing torpedoes at a ship with nuclear weapons on board was a more obvious and immediate threat than releasing information to a reporter after the fact, yet it took six years and an investigation by the Parliamentary Ombudsman before the MoD released the documents – which revealed that there *were* nuclear weapons on board ships sent to the Falklands. However, they still refuse to say whether nuclear weapons were on board HMS *Sheffield* when it sank.

LACK OF SCRUTINY

Until the late 1980s, even the existence of MI5 and MI6 was a state secret. It wasn't until critical rulings came down from the European Court of Human Rights that the UK finally was forced to define the agencies in law and set up a regulatory framework. Those regulations are today codified in the Security Service Act 1989 (amended in 1996), the Intelligence Services Act 1994 which established the Intelligence and Security Committee, and the Regulation of Investigatory Powers Act 2000 (RIPA) – the 'wiretapping' law that regulates communications interception, the use of informants and other types of intrusive surveillance. RIPA also governs the Commissioner for Interception, the Commissioner for the Intelligence Services, the Chief Surveillance Commissioner and a tribunal to examine complaints and hear proceedings under section 7 of the Human Rights Act 1998. This might sound like a lot of oversight, but all are renowned for doing very little. Privacy International has dubbed the three commissioners 'The Three Blind Mice' for their failure to issue sanctions against the police or security services despite numerous findings that the wrong telephone numbers are often tapped and authorisations are issued on skimpy evidence. The Commissioners also refuse to release the number of national security intercepts authorised, claiming that to do so would endanger national security, even though the United States, Canada and New Zealand make this information publicly available.

Secondary legislation passed in 2003 expanded the number of government bodies that can access private telephone records, mail and internet activity, so it now includes not only the police, the intelligence services, Revenue and Customs, but also a raft of other organisations such as local government. There is concern that some organisations lack the necessary checks and audits to prevent secret material being misused against a person. During parliamentary debate, Baroness Blatch argued that 'the issue of oversight of the system is particularly crucial, and the Interception Commissioner has been particularly silent on his methods of oversight' (HL 13, Nov 2003, col 1538).

In order to conduct surveillance on citizens, an organisation has to declare that the actions are needed to protect national security, the economic wellbeing of the UK, public safety, or for assessing or collecting tax, and so on. The definitions are purposely vague and open to interpretation, so it is important that if the public are to have confidence that organisations are using their powers properly, there should be a system in place to objectively scrutinise how they conduct surveillance. RIPA created several tribunals to do this. However, these tribunals are not covered by the FOIA. The Anti-Terrorism, Crime and Security Act 2001 also requires communications providers to keep records of their users' activities for national security purposes. Again, the oversight of these powers is far below what is required to ensure public confidence that they are not being abused.

Until May 2004, a blanket ban prevented anyone from saying anything officially about the activities of Britain's Special Forces (the SAS and its naval equivalent, the SBS). Rear Admiral Nick Wilkinson, Secretary of the Defence Advisory Committee, said Britain's policy of total secrecy about the forces had become impossible when American and Australian allies were providing much more information to the media and public. The public still do not have a statutory right to this information – it is given out only at the discretion of the Ministry of Defence.

Overall scrutiny of the intelligence services is shared between several groups. The parliamentary committee that scrutinises MI5, MI6 and GCHQ is the Intelligence and Security Committee but this is a watchdog with few teeth. The Prime Minister appoints members of the Committee and all their reports are submitted to him for approval before being sent to Parliament. The Committee's hearings are held in secret and no minutes are published. As a government committee it does fall within the scope of the FOIA, but it would be difficult to access information because so much of it comes from the agencies covered by section 23. The ISC has no power to command witnesses or evidence, and was denied access to ministers, civil servants and documents during its investigation into the Iraq war dossier allegations. After Lord Hutton was given access to all this information, the ISC demanded that it have greater powers to scrutinise the government and security services. So far, though, they have not been given such powers.

That intelligence failures come to light in America is no surprise. The United States operates a dramatically different system where bipartisan congressional committees have the power to demand evidence and witness statements from those in the security services. They are even able to question the executive on certain issues. Except in rare instances, the proceedings are public, unlike the secretive British 'public' inquiries, which the public actually have no right to attend. The US does not have an Official Secrets Act, so Richard Clarke, President Bush's former top aide on counter-terrorism strategy at the CIA, was perfectly within his rights to tell the American people: 'Your government failed you, those entrusted with protecting you failed you...' in relation to the threat of al-Qaeda before September 11. The British public have no idea if they have been failed by their government, and if a former intelligence employee told them so, that person would be charged with violating the Official Secrets Act. The head of MI6 is under no pressure to answer to the public or even to Parliament. If he answers questions at all it is either in secret hearings or, as in the Hutton Inquiry, by telephone. And while the director of the CIA, George Tenet, resigned over intelligence failings, no one at Britain's intelligence agencies took responsibility for similar failings, even though much of the intelligence on weapons of mass destruction and Saddam Hussein's involvement with al-Qaeda came from UK security services.

The security services in the United States manage to operate within the confines of their (much stronger) FOI law. That is not to say they have welcomed such openness, but at least the public have some means of discovering whether these agencies are abusing their vast powers. The CIA is consistently the agency that refuses the most requests,[3] although now the Department of Homeland Security is taking the lead.

The only way to ensure a just system is through greater transparency. In a democratic country there must be a balance between citizens' rights (to privacy and freedom) and an effective defence against terrorist threats and criminal activity. The security and intelligence services must better account for themselves to Parliament and to the people.

OFFICIAL SECRECY

All employees of the security and intelligence service have to sign the Official Secrets Act. This imposes a lifelong ban on revealing any details of their work or information gathered during the course of their employment. The penalties are severe and the law protecting whistleblowers specifically excludes security and intelligence workers.

'It does have a heavy influence over them. They're frightened,' Richard Norton-Taylor, the *Guardian*'s security and intelligence reporter told me. 'They are constantly being told about it and what will happen to them if they say anything to anybody.'

The Official Secrets Act provides no protection for people who disclose information that is in the public interest. Nor does the Freedom of Information Act override these existing prohibitions. Conscientious workers who expose serious wrongdoing are treated the same as spies who commit treachery. In the absence of official

3. *The Secrecy Wars: National security, privacy, and the public's right to know* by Philip H. Malanson (Brassey's Inc., Washington DC, 2001), p. xii.

information and oversight, leaks and whistleblowers are the only sources of information about the effectiveness and legitimacy of the intelligence and security services.

It was a 1975 *New York Times* exposé on the use of secret surveillance to monitor American student groups that prompted the first congressional review of the CIA, which uncovered the CIA's numerous attempts to assassinate or overthrow foreign leaders. If the UK security services have been involved in similar abuses, our own elected representatives would struggle to find out about them.

WHERE TO GET SECURITY AND DEFENCE INFORMATION

Ministry of Defence
www.mod.uk
Info Access, 6th Floor, Zone E, Main Building, Whitehall,
London SW1A 2HW
Tel: 0870 607 6645; 020 7218 9000 (general enquiries)
FOI Operations Manager: Rod Belcher
Email: info-access-office@mod.uk
Online request form: www.forums.mod.uk/foi/foirequest.htm
Publication scheme: www.mod.uk/DefenceInternet/FreedomOfInformation/
PublicationScheme
Disclosure log: www.mod.uk/DefenceInternet/FreedomOfInformation/
DisclosureLog

Unlike the intelligence services, the MoD comes under the FOIA. The Ministry has overall responsibility for the administration and command of all the UK's armed forces including more than 200,000 service personnel in the Royal Navy, Army and Royal Air Force along with 88,430 civilian staff. Back in 2004, Simon Murphy, then FOI Programme Manager, told me the MoD was intent on changing its image: 'Of course everyone sees us as intensely secretive, but we are trying to put more information into the public arena.' This is one case where the reality lived up to the rhetoric. A huge trove of UFO information known as the 'Rendlesham file' was made public in July 2003. Since then, the MoD has surprised applicants by the quality and professionalism of its FOI responses. It has one of the most comprehensive disclosure logs and seems willing to challenge traditional secrecy. Documents released in April 2006 under FOI revealed the frequency and cost of government ministers' use of the Royal Squadron aircraft. It took more than a year for the answer to come through, but eventually it did, and the publicly funded use of these aircraft is now more accountable and less open to abuse.

But the MoD has found one novel way of avoiding the FOIA. Officials say thousands of documents stored in an area of the old War Office building in Whitehall may have been contaminated by asbestos and requests for documents are refused on health and safety grounds. The contents will eventually be released, officials say, but not before summer 2007 at the earliest. About 63,000 files, containing around 10 million pages, are affected.

One area in particular need of public scrutiny is how the MoD spends the public's money – and we're talking about a lot of money! The MoD's proposed spending for 2005/06 was almost £32 billion. The MoD has a woeful record of money management, with its top 20 major projects running 18 months late and £3.1 billion over budget at the end of 2003, according to the National Audit Office. The troops in Iraq were nicknamed 'the borrowers' for their reliance on American spares to get them by. The MoD's failure to deal openly and forthrightly with problems means they get shoved under the carpet until the lump is too big to hide. It was only after a critical All-Party Commons Defence Committee report that the MoD finally agreed that 'large quantities of equipment, store and supplies were "lost" in theatre'. And only then did they begin the process of overhauling the logistics tracking system. Secrecy in MoD policy-making also has an enormous effect on the use (or more accurately misuse) of public funds. For example, some have claimed that the £20 billion Eurofighter programme is a complete waste of money and only in place for the politically popular reason of creating jobs in key voting areas. Unless these big-budget policy decisions are conducted in public, the country is in danger of funding 'defence' projects that serve politicians rather than the country's best interests.

The National Audit Office reported that the MoD paid out £97 million for claims of personal injury and loss resulting from negligence, and this excludes all incidents resulting from combat or internal security operations. One of the biggest factors for the sky-rocketing claims was based on the MoD's refusal to offer apologies or explanations.

Getting the details of these contracts is not always easy. Invitations to tender for public contracts (usually around £100,000) must be advertised in the EU and you can search these on the Tenders Electronic Daily website http://ted.publications.eu.int. Contracts already awarded may be available from the MoD Defence Contracts

Bulletin (www.contracts.mod.uk) but this site is set up specifically for vendors and suppliers; you'll notice an important person missing from the list – the public who pays for all these projects! Contrast the profiteering MoD site with the US Department of Defense, which is required by law to list all contracts above a certain amount on a freely accessible website. You do not need to register, pay money or be an arms company to access any of the data at www.defenselink.mil/contracts/, which updates contracts daily.

The FOIA is already proving useful in getting these contracts. The MoD is a huge department, so knowing where to direct your query is half the battle. There are more than 40 different agencies and organisations operating under the Ministry of Defence. You can contact the MoD's FOI team for advice or look online where you will find a comprehensive publication scheme and guidance.

Arms trade

Activist groups often conduct useful research on arms trading and the Campaign Against the Arms Trade (www.caat.org.uk, 020 7281 0297) is an excellent source as it keeps research files on country, company and issues as well as government statistics and yearbooks. When the government failed to release the names of invited countries to London's Defence Systems and Equipment International Exhibition in 2005, CAAT conducted its own research revealing countries such

---

Where to find defence information

- General information – the National Audit Office is one of the best places to look for detailed analysis of the MoD. Although their reports are not done with great frequency, they are sufficiently rigorous and detailed to make the front pages of most newspapers.
- Financial information – MoD annual reports, National Audit Commission.
- Defence contracts – National Audit Office, MoD annual reports, but primarily the Defence Procurement Agency www.mod.uk/dpa
- Historic information – National Archives.
- National Service records – Home Office.
- Military personnel – the Stationery Office www.tso.org.uk publishes annual directories of military personnel: *The Army List, The Navy List, The Air Force List*, and so on.
- General equipment information – *Jane's Information Group* www.janes.com publishes a wide range of surveys and assessments of the world's military hardware. You can order books online or ask at your local library. *Whitaker's Almanac* and *Statesman's Yearbook* have statistics on the world's air forces, armies and navies. Whitaker's is more detailed on UK defence composition, giving the number and type of aircraft and number of officers, while Statesman's focuses on other foreign countries.

as Saudi Arabia, China and Colombia on the guest list. To do this yourself, contact the embassies and defence attaché offices of foreign countries – they often view such invitations as a source of pride.

The Security Service (MI5)
www.mi5.gov.uk
Enquiries Desk, PO Box 3255, London SW1P 1AE
Tel: 020 7930 9000

The Security Service is overseen by the Home Office and is charged with internal security. Agents are assisted by Special Branch officers. The only public information available about MI5 is found on their website or from Intelligence and Security Committee reports.

The service is largely unanswerable to the public. You can access general information from the website or write to the enquiries desk at the above address, and I've also added a telephone number I managed to dig up. You're not guaranteed an answer if you take the time to write: 'We read every letter we receive but unfortunately with limited staff and resources we simply cannot reply to everyone who writes to us.' MI5 certainly has no problem taking your money, however. In 2004, the agency received a 50 per cent budget increase, bringing the total amount of public money it receives to £300 million, in recognition of its role in fighting terrorism.

MI5 does not even bother with the pretence of being accountable to the public. There is no MI5 press or public information office. Instead just one person is assigned to answer all press queries, and even then only sufficiently 'vetted' reporters are given this person's contact details. The likelihood of collusion in such a 'boys' club' atmosphere is great – after all, reporters are unlikely to print anything that jeopardises their relationship with their special source. The public are not well served by this system and MI5 ought to make a greater effort to account for itself to the public who provide its budget.

Is there a file on you?

MI5 holds about 440,000 files, 290,000 of which are on individuals. Not all are active, but you might want to know if you're on the list, especially if you're an activist. No one, it seems, is immune from the spying eyes (and ears) of the Security Service. Former MI5 agent David Shayler revealed that MI5 had files on Jack Straw and Peter Mandelson. Jack Straw was president of the National Union of Students from 1969 to 1971 (deemed to be a stronghold of communists) and Mr Mandelson joined the Young Communist

League while at grammar school (though his file was still active even in 1992, according to former MI5 agent David Shayler).

Until October 2001, MI5 refused all applications for personal information made under the Data Protection Act without consideration. Then Norman Baker MP, with the help of Liberty, decided to challenge the policy. On 1 October 2001, the Information Tribunal (National Security Appeals) ruled that the Home Secretary had acted unreasonably in allowing MI5 to refuse all requests for information via a blanket exemption from the Data Protection Act. Baker's case set a precedent and now applications must be handled on an individual basis.

To find out if MI5 holds a file on you, write to: The Data Controller, The Security Service, PO Box 3255, London SW1P 1AE.

Although you have a right to access information about yourself, section 28 of the DPA exempts data required for the purpose of safeguarding national security. So it's not likely the system will become dramatically more transparent. When Mr Baker received his file from MI5, all it contained were his letters asking for his file!

In order to use this exemption, MI5 has to get a signed certificate from the Home Secretary, and you can appeal this decision by writing to: The Secretary, The Information Tribunal, Room 916, Home Office, 50 Queen Anne's Gate, London SW1H 9AT.

General Communications Headquarters (GCHQ)
www.gchq.gov.uk
Hubble Road, Cheltenham, Gloucestershire GL51 0EX
Tel: 01242 221 491

GCHQ is the government's listening centre responsible for telephone interceptions and bugging. Its functions are set out, albeit in abstract terms, in the Intelligence Services Act 1994. GCHQ is the largest employer in Gloucestershire and the largest of the security agencies in terms of personnel with 4,500 staff spread across three locations. Until 1994, however, its existence was a state secret! It often works in cooperation with the US National Security Agency. Former employee Katherine Gun's exposure of the joint operation between the NSA and GCHQ to bug the offices of the UN's National Security Council pointed out some of the dubious practices that go on here.

Complaints about unlawful surveillance are made to the Investigatory Powers Tribunal, but until January 2003 all hearings were held in secret, excluding even the complainant. A case brought by Liberty changed the rules so that now the tribunal will be able to hear some parts of cases in public. However, as with the other tribunals set up by the RIPA law, it is not subject to the Freedom of Information Act.

Secret Intelligence Service (MI6)
PO Box 1300, London SE1 1BD

The Secret Intelligence Service, headed by John Scarlett, is responsible for intelligence abroad and is formally under the control of the Foreign and Commonwealth Office. It is the agency of spies and subterfuge and as such has been the last government agency to see the benefits of openness. Since MI6 provided most of the information that led to the notorious September 2002 dossier on Iraq's readiness for war, its operating structure has come in for questioning. There's no point in giving you any false hope – your chances of getting any information out of this secrecy stronghold are close to zero. However, in a possible sign that the service was entering the modern age, it began openly advertising for staff in the British press in 2006.

The Investigatory Powers Tribunal
PO Box 33220, London SW1H 9ZQ
Tel: 020 7035 3711 / 020 7273 4514

Although not covered by the FOIA, you can make data protection requests to this tribunal at the address above. The tribunal is responsible for dealing with complaints about the conduct by or on behalf of the security and intelligence agencies and those public authorities which have powers given to them by the Regulation of Investigatory Powers Act 2000. Any individual or organisation can make a complaint either about individual treatment, or treatment of property or communications.

Intelligence and Security Committee (ISC)
www.cabinetoffice.gov.uk/intelligence

The ISC exercises parliamentary oversight of MI5, MI6 and GCHQ. The committee examines the spending, administration and policy of the three agencies, but as discussed earlier it does not have the power to compel witnesses to testify before it. The public have no way of knowing how well the committee is doing its job as the minutes from ISC meetings are not made public. I asked for a clear statement on the ISC's policy for publishing minutes and received only the unhelpful reply that the ISC 'does not comment on how it carries out its functions'. The only information publicly available is the ISC's published reports which have been submitted to the Prime Minister for editing – hardly the kind of non-political, objective analysis that is required to inspire public confidence. These reports are available from the Cabinet Office website: www.cabinetoffice.gov. uk/publicationscheme/published_information/3/index.asp

Joint Intelligence Committee
www.cabinet-office.gov.uk/intelligence

The members of this committee include the directors of the intelligence agencies and staff on secondment from the Foreign Office and Ministry of Defence. Requests for information relating to the ISC and JIC should be submitted to: The Openness Team; Histories, Openness and Records Unit; Cabinet Office; Admiralty Arch; North Entrance; London SW1A 2WH. Email: openness.team@cabinet-office. x.gsi.gov.uk

The Interception Communications Commissioner

The Interception Communications Commissioner submits an annual report to the Prime Minister, which is subsequently laid before Parliament and published. He will include in this report a review of the interception processes and a summary of the value of the intercepts and, in a closed annexe which is not published, accounts of the operational successes achieved as a result of the interception warrants he has reviewed. The commissioner also oversees arrangements for access to communications data by interested parties. This report is a step in the right direction, but it should be far more detailed and published in its entirety.

The Intelligence Services Commissioner

The Intelligence Services Commissioner reviews the issue of warrants by the Secretary of State who authorises intrusive surveillance or interference with property. He also oversees the use of covert surveillance and use of agents to ensure that these activities are legal. The agencies are legally obliged to provide him with any documents he requires during his investigations. He also provides the Prime Minister with an annual report for presentation to Parliament. Again, this is a sign of progress, but most of the information is not made public.

Office of Surveillance Commissioners
www.surveillancecommissioners.gov.uk

Sir Andrew Leggatt, Chief Surveillance Commissioner
Office of Surveillance Commissioners, PO Box 29105, London SW1V 1ZU
Tel: 020 7828 3421
Fax: 020 7592 1788

These commissioners review authorisations, renewals or cancellations for property interference and intrusive surveillance by the police and other law enforcement bodies. The commissioners are appointed by the Prime Minister, so you will not be surprised to hear that even when they find examples of unwarranted surveillance they merely issue a chummy warning to try harder instead of enforcing any sanctions that would actually protect the public.

6
Transport

Transport is one of the areas most affected by the new access laws for two reasons. Firstly, until the Freedom of Information Act the public had few legal rights to information from transport authorities. Many, such as Transport for London, were not covered by the previous Open Government code, ensuring almost complete secrecy. Until 2005, the contracts between London Underground and the two private companies running parts of the Tube were secret, and the public were never consulted on whether or not they thought this public-private partnership was the right way to run the Tube.

Secondly, because transport is an issue of such great public importance, most of the exemptions will be outweighed by the public interest. So even where data may be exempt perhaps because of commercial interests, the public interest test will ensure disclosure. The law is also retrospective, meaning all documents from the railway privatisation onwards are fair game.

Some of the disclosures that came to light using the FOIA and Environmental Information Regulations:

- The first-ever comprehensive list of all London minicab firms and the results of their safety compliance inspections. More than 40 per cent failed their inspection!
- A list of all the railway stations unmanned at night, leading to a rail safety campaign in the *Evening Standard* that was taken up by Parliament.
- The number of times police have accessed Oyster card data (London's travel card).
- Documents about British Airways' decision to scrap Concorde including correspondence between BA and Virgin Airways.
- Details of franchise payments for rail companies such as ONE railway and GNER.

The immense cost of *not* having a freedom of information law is best illustrated by the transport sector. An examination by the National Audit Office found that the secretive public-private partnership of London's Tube cost taxpayers £455 million, and while there is no guarantee that this unscrutinised spending will result in better service for the public, private engineering companies stand to make profits of 18–20 per cent per year. Surprisingly, the government still has not learned that openness is the best way of ensuring that public funds are spent wisely.

The other obstacle to efficient transport services is the needlessly complex operational structures that have evolved. Spared the need to justify themselves to the public, bureaucracies have multiplied like bacteria in a petri dish. The end result that is no one knows what the other is doing and no one is ultimately responsible. Excessive complexity combined with secrecy is a surefire way of wasting the public's money while producing shoddy projects that don't work.

RAILWAYS

First, a potted recent history of the railways. British Rail was privatised hurriedly in 1996/97. Railtrack was set up as a profit-making company overseeing the rail infrastructure but in 2002 the company was replaced with the non-profit Network Rail, and in October 2003 the company stopped using private contractors and took repairs back in-house. Cynics may point out that the government has effectively gone full circle while spending billions of pounds of public money. The Strategic Rail Authority (SRA) worked with private train operators to coordinate use of the tracks and award franchises but in a far from transparent way. In August 2005 the SRA ceased to exist and its functions were taken over by the Department for Transport and the Office of Rail Regulation. The Office of Rail Regulation is charged with determining how much of Network Rail's request the government must provide. Amazingly, until July 2004 the government had to pay the amount ORR determined without question. The other principal public bodies involved in the railways are the Health and Safety Executive and the Rail Passengers Council.

This bizarre system has never worked well. Privatisation created a mutant hybrid of private companies controlled by the state yet largely unaccountable to the public, even though the public pays the bills when things go wrong. New layers of bureaucratic regulation have sprung up like weeds on tracks, making the system so convoluted that even those involved are unclear about who is in charge. But for years, ministers preferred sticking with the status quo for all its faults, rather than risk radical reforms. However, as the state of the railways spiralled downwards and public discontent increased, the case for reform grew.

No matter who ends up running the railways, the two main areas where openness is needed is the awarding of train operator franchises and the formulation of policy.

Network Rail

www.networkrail.co.uk
40 Melton Street, London NW1 2EE
Tel: 020 7557 8000
Fax: 020 7557 9000

Network Rail is a private engineering company, charged with improving and upgrading the railway infrastructure. This includes maintenance work on tracks, bridges, viaducts, tunnels, level crossings and stations. Network Rail's only shareholder is the government and its liabilities are underwritten by the taxpayer – yet it remains completely unaccountable to the public! And shockingly this will not change under the FOIA because as a 'private' company it does not come under the Act. The Lord Chancellor does have the power under the FOI law to designate some private companies providing public services as 'public', but this had yet to happen in 2006. Until the designation, the only information available on Network Rail is similar to any other private company: annual reports, audits, business plans, and so on.

Office of Rail Regulation

www.rail-reg.gov.uk/
1 Kemble Street, London WC2B 4AN
Tel: 020 7282 2000
Fax: 020 7282 2040
FOI Officer: Peter Clarke
Tel: 020 7282 2162
Email: contact.cct@orr.gsi.gov.uk
Publication scheme: www.rail-reg.gov.uk/upload/pdf/Publication_scheme.pdf
Disclosure log: www.rail-reg.gov.uk/server/show/nav.73

All train companies must have a licence to operate trains and the Office of Rail Regulation (until July 2004 called the Office of the Rail Regulator) regulates these. 'If you can control the licences then you control the railway companies,' says Mike Hewitson, policy research manager for the passenger advocacy group, the Rail Passengers Council. The Office's enormous power is due to its licensing responsibilities but also to its role as the economic regulator of the rail monopoly (Network Rail). Until July 2004, the rail regulator could order the government to pay whatever amount he saw fit to Network Rail. The huge sums involved prompted the Commons Transport Committee to denounce the regulator Tom Winsor as a 'high-handed rail czar' and a government decree ordered the reorganisation and operational change of the Office for July 2004.

The Railways Act 1993 already requires the ORR to publish many documents. These include official records relating to the regulation of passenger and rail freight such as licences (their granting, modifications, exemptions and revocation); track, station and depot access agreements (including contracts between an operator and facility owner); access directions and amendments; enforcement orders; and the financial penalties imposed on licence holders. You can find these listed on the ORR's publication scheme, although there is a substantial section detailing all the exemptions that the ORR may use. Remember, even in instances where an authority claims it cannot release 'commercially sensitive' data, it must still conduct a public interest test before it can withhold information.

Public register index – this online index lists all the items that are available electronically. New contracts and licences are added to the website, but a decision was made not to scan older material for reasons of cost. You can search all the registers at the office but only by making an appointment. The index is accessed from the link 'Public register' on the homepage.

Rail Passengers Council

www.railpassengers.org.uk
Whittles House, 14 Pentonville Road, London N1 9HF
Tel: 020 7713 2700
Fax: 020 7713 2729
FOI Officer: Kafil Badar, Business Planning Manager
Email: Kafil.badar@passengerfocus.org.uk
Tel: 0870 336 6005
Publication scheme: www.railpassengers.co.uk/Council/News

The Rail Passengers Council is the passenger advocate for the railways and is a public authority under the FOIA. Council members have a right to attend railway board and committee meetings and have a 'right to ask' under existing law, although how much the railway authorities listen to their concerns is debatable. They may be able to help you locate the information you seek and may even have it themselves. The council publishes its own research and reports which you can find on their website.

Rail Safety and Standards Board
www.rssb.co.uk
Evergreen House, 160 Euston Road, London NW1 2DX
Tel: 020 7904 7777
Fax: 020 7557 9072
Email: enquiries@rssb.co.uk
Safety reports: www.rssb.co.uk/spreports.asp

This is a non-profit limited company and therefore not subject to the FOIA, but I've mentioned it here because it holds a huge amount of information about the overall safety of the railways and makes this easily available online. There are several types of safety reports, the most comprehensive is the aptly named *Safety Performance Report* that comes out annually.

LONDON

Seeing the disasters caused by the public-private arrangement of the railways, many Londoners were against the same system being foisted on London's Tube network. Yet the government pushed through the public-private partnerships despite public protest led by the London Mayor, Ken Livingstone, and the capital's then Transport Commissioner, Bob Kiley.

The system is run by three operators: London Underground (a public authority), and two private companies, Metronet and Tube Lines. The private companies are charged with maintaining and upgrading the Underground's infrastructure, but responsibility for safety remains with London Underground, as do stations, train operations and signalling. Transport for London oversees the entire system along with all other transport networks in London. Such unneeded complexity costs money: the City law firm Freshfields was paid almost £30 million for providing legal advice and in total, external consultants collected £109 million for their services.

In the past, it's been nigh impossible to get detailed information from Transport for London as they were not covered by the previous Open Access code. In the first edition, I stated that 'if you only make one FOI request in your lifetime, there is no more deserving recipient than Transport for London'. TfL still has a way to go, but their efforts in the first few years of FOI have been encouraging.

Transport for London
www.tfl.gov.uk
Windsor House, 42–50 Victoria Street, London SW1H 0TL
Tel: 020 7941 4500
Email: enquire@tfl.gov.uk
FOI Officer: Richard Bevins, Information Access and Compliance Manager
Email: RichardBevins@Tfl.gov.uk, but send requests to: foi@tfl.gov.uk
Tel: 020 7126 3222
Publication scheme: www.tfl.gov.uk/tfl/foi/publicationschemes.shtml

One of the first successes using FOIA came when TfL was forced to publish its contracts with Tube Lines and Metronet. You can now find these mammoth documents on the TfL publication scheme, though some pricing information is redacted. TfL has also disclosed Tube safety statistics for the past three years and a detailed log of bendy bus accidents. It is one of the few major public bodies without a disclosure log, though Mr Bevins says one shoud be online by autumn 2006. Transport for London holds information on:

- London buses and bus services
- Docklands Light Railway
- London River Services
- London Underground
- Victoria Coach Station
- Regulation of taxis and minicabs
- Major London roads and traffic lights
- Transport Trading (including London's Transport Museum, lost property, ticketing systems and travel information).

Additional information about London's taxis and minicabs is held by:

The Public Carriage Office
www.tfl.gov.uk/pco
15 Penton Street, London N1 9PU
Tel: 0845 602 7000 / 020 7941 7941
FOI Officer: Darren Crowson, Information and Marketing Manager
Email: Darren.Crowson@pco.org.uk
Tel: 020 7126 1872

This is a subsidiary organisation of TfL and under the Private Hire Vehicles (London) Act 1998 holds the:

- Register of Licensed Private Hire Operators – www.tfl.gov.uk/ pco/php_safecabs.asp
- Register of Licensed Private Hire Drivers – www.tfl.gov.uk/pco/ ph_drivers_list.asp
- Register of Licensed Private Hire Vehicles – www.tfl.gov.uk/pco/ ph_vehicles_list.asp

You can search for licensed operators by service and locality at: www. tfl.gov.uk/pco/findaride (this does not list all of the licensed operators in London as some do not offer their services to the general public). The taxi cost calculations for the 2005/06 taxi fares and tariffs can be found at: http://origin.tfl.gov.uk/pco/abt_pco_report_library.shtml

Congestion charging

The Capita Group PLC runs central London's Congestion Charging Scheme on behalf of Transport for London. You can contact them at:

The Capita Group PLC
www.capita.co.uk
71 Victoria Street, Westminster, London SW1H 0XA
Tel: 020 7799 1525

London TravelWatch (formerly London Transport Users Committee)
www.londontravelwatch.org.uk
6 Middle Street, London EC1A 7JA
Tel: 020 7505 9000
Fax: 020 7505 9003
Email: enquiries@londontravelwatch.org.uk

London TravelWatch describes itself as the 'official watchdog organisation representing the interests of transport users in and around the capital'. It is a public authority and subject to the FOIA. The London Assembly appoints its members and provides funding so that it can help scrutinise mayoral transport strategy and delivery. It is a useful ally if you are having trouble getting the information you need from any of the transport authorities in London.

OTHER SOURCES FOR TRANSPORT INFORMATION

Health and Safety Executive
www.hse.gov.uk

Redgrave Court, Merton Road, Bootle, Merseyside L20 7HS
Tel: 0845 345 0055 (information line)
FOI Officer: Elaine Dearden
Tel: 0151 523 3807
Publication scheme: www.hse.gov.uk/foi/pubscheme.htm
Disclosure log: www.hse.gov.uk/foi/latest.htm

The HSE is covered in greater detail in Chapter 13, but this section relates to the HSE's work monitoring the safety of transport. On 1 April 2006, the Office of Rail Regulation (ORR) took over HSE's work of monitoring and enforcing health and safety on the railways. This transfer affects railways and other guided transport systems, including metros and light rail systems. HSE maintains responsibility for guided buses and trolley buses.

Department for Transport
www.dft.gov.uk
Southside, 105 Victoria Street, London SW1 E6DT
FOI Officer: Mike Carty, Head of Information Rights
Tel: 020 7944 5825
Fax: 020 7944 6248
Email: mike.carty@dft.gsi.gov.uk
Publication scheme: follow links 'Freedom of information' > 'Publication scheme'
Disclosure log: follow links 'Freedom of information' > 'DfT responses to FOI Requests'
Publications database: www.publications.dft.gov.uk/pubcategories.asp

The Department for Transport covers a huge range of topics, though many responsibilities have been farmed out to numerous agencies, which are listed below. They are all ultimately responsible to the DfT and you will find more information about them on the DfT publication scheme.

FOI Officer Mike Carty says the department holds such a vast number of records that the information contained in them may come as a surprise, even to people in the DfT. His advice for making FOI requests is to identify the department section or agency most likely to hold the data and apply directly. 'The closer you can send it to the right part of the business, the better it will be for all parties,' he said. His office primarily offers advice to in-house staff when they receive a particularly complex request. He is also consulted whenever an employee wants to refuse a request. 'We expect people will be hesitant at first to release information, so it's important they have a central place they can go for advice.'

The DfT has done an excellent job opening up new sources of information and making it widely available through a comprehensive disclosure log. Detailed reports are available online for investigations by the Air Accidents Investigation Branch (www.aaib.gov.uk), Marine Accident Investigation Branch (www.maib.gov.uk) and Rail Accident Investigation Branch (www.raib.gov.uk). The DfT also holds information about aviation, crime and public transport, local transport, roads and vehicles, shipping and ports, transport statistics and transport policy.

Airline safety

Airlines from outside the European Economic Area who set down or pick up passengers or cargo in the UK must get a permit from the DfT, which requires that they meet international safety standards. If the DfT believes an airline fails to meet these standards or if the airline has committed other offences, permits are denied. You can get a list of foreign airlines banned since 1 January 2000 from the DfT website by following the links: 'Aviation' > 'Aviation safety' > 'Foreign airline permits'.

There is concern that political considerations (such as not wanting to offend a particular country) have an undue influence on the permit process. This would be an area where an FOIA request could provide more detailed information about the reasoning behind a decision to issue or refuse a permit to a foreign airline. In the event of a crash, this information would be even more pertinent.

DfT executive agencies

Driver and Vehicle Licensing Agency
www.dvla.gov.uk
Vehicles Policy Group, DVLA, Swansea Vale 2, Swansea SA6 7JL
FOI Officer: Jean O'Donovan
Tel: 01792 765 195
Publication scheme: www.dvla.gov.uk/public/pub_scheme.htm
Disclosure log: www.dvla.gov.uk/disclosure.htm

Registration and licensing of British drivers and vehicles and collection and enforcement of road tax.

Driving Standards Agency

www.dsa.gov.uk
Stanley House, 56 Talbot Street, Nottingham NG1 5GU
FOI Compliance Manager: Debra Wilson
Tel: 0115 901 2706
Fax: 0115 901 2964
Email: foi@dsa.gsi.gov.uk
Publication scheme: follow links to Department for Transport
Disclosure log: follow links 'Freedom of Information' > 'Disclosure log'

The DSA tests drivers of all vehicles and maintains a registry of approved driving instructors. In 2003, the Ombudsman ruled that the DSA was wrong to refuse a request for information about driving test routes, made under the previous Open Government code. The ruling led to a change in policy and now test route details are routinely made available at test centres throughout the country.

Vehicle and Operator Services Agency

www.vosa.gov.uk
Room G9, Berkeley House, Bristol BS5 0DA
Tel: 0870 606 0440 (general enquiries)
FOI Officer: Beverley Whittle
Tel: 0117 954 3430
Fax: 0117 954 3303
Email: Inform@vosa.gov.uk
Publication scheme: www.vosa.gov.uk/vosa/publications/publications.htm
Disclosure log: follow links 'Freedom of information' > 'Disclosures'

This agency is mainly of interest for its work investigating serious vehicle accidents and vehicle defects and recall campaigns. It also holds applications for licences to operate lorries and buses, registers bus services, administers and enforces vehicle testing (such as MOT testing). VOSA was created in March 2004 after a merger of the Vehicle Inspectorate and the Traffic Area Network.

Highways Agency

www.highways.gov.uk
Freedom of Information, Highways Agency, 3 Ridgeway,
Quinton Business Park, Quinton Expressway, Birmingham B32 1AF
Tel: 08457 50 40 30
Email requests: ha_info@highways.gsi.gov.uk
FOI Officer: refused to give a name or direct line
Disclosure log: www.highways.gov.uk/aboutus/2296.aspx

Manages and maintains the national trunk roads and motorways of England. The Highways Agency is good at telling the public *what* is happening in relation to roads. It is less forthcoming about *why* things are happening and this is where the FOIA may help. For example, if there are severe delays and cost overruns on a road project, the Agency won't try and hide the fact, but it will be difficult to delve into why the delays occurred and who was at fault. The Agency is also responsible for clearing litter from the national trunk roads and motorways. It contracts this out to agents who look after the roads in certain areas. You can request a map of the areas and agents responsible from the Agency. Local authorities are responsible for picking up the rubbish on other roads.

Road projects – you can get a range of information about the building, maintenance and future tenders for roads under the 'Contracts' heading on the website.

Maritime and Coastguard Agency

www.mcga.gov.uk
Bay 3/5 Spring Place, 105 Commercial Road, Southampton SO15 1EG
Tel: 0870 600 6505 (information line)
FOI Officer: Kiernan Maguire, Technical Assurance Manager
Tel: 02380 329 287
Email: Kiernan.Maguire@mcga.gov.uk

This agency runs the Coastguard, checks that ships meet UK and international safety rules and works to prevent coastal pollution.

7

The Justice System

'Publicity is the very soul of justice. It is the keenest spur to exertion and the surest of all guards against improbity. It keeps the judge himself while trying under trial.'

Lord Shaw of Dunfermline
in *Scott* v. *Scott* [1913] AC 417 at 477

There is a well-known saying that justice must not only be done, it must be *seen* to be done. That is why it's surprising to discover just how difficult it is in the UK to see justice being done. There are reporting restrictions preventing journalists from publishing information presented in open court, postponement orders stopping the publication of hearings for years, contempt of court law which stifles discussion of cases, public interest immunity certificates that suppress vital evidence even from the accused, and judgments that are never published. Laws introduced to combat terrorism have reduced the standard of justice and allow for even greater secrecy in the name of protecting national security. Fundamental rights, such as trial by jury and the right to appeal, are threatened by political pressure to reduce the burgeoning costs of the justice system.

The Freedom of Information Act will not remedy these problems as courts and tribunals are not bound by its obligations. Section 32 of the Act allows an absolute exemption for all court records. The public's 'right to know' extends only to court administration, and not always even then. Lawyers have argued that courts are exempt from the FOIA because they have their own openness regimes, but these do not give the public a statutory right to court information. The good news is that some organisations are trying to make the legal process more accessible to the public. The British and Irish Legal Information Institute is a non-profit organisation that collects hundreds of court decisions from across the country. The Crown Prosecution Service is committed to greater transparency and is now releasing evidence used in trials. Yet the biggest changes need to come from inside the courts. Unfortunately, those who work in the system are resistant to change.

NOT SO OPEN JUSTICE

A century ago, the courthouse was a public gathering place where citizens came as much to be entertained as to see justice done. You can still go along to any local court today and watch a selection of cases being tried. But what if you work all day as most of us do? Public awareness comes primarily through media reports, but increasingly journalists are stifled about what they can report. Secrecy in the courts extends to court documents being routinely withheld from the public, cases conducted in secret and whole sections of the justice system hidden from public view (such as family court). Yet the biggest problem is access. Even when courts are open, they are only open if you have nothing else to do but spend all day in a courthouse and don't mind leaving behind your mobile phone. As our ability to attend court has decreased, the UK court system has done nothing to provide alternative means for the public to see what is going on in the courtroom. Cameras are not allowed in most courts and neither are sound-recording devices.

Instead, the courts have effectively become secret cloisters for barristers, court staff and those involved in a case because the courts refuse to allow recording (film or sound) of proceedings except in rare instances. And no photographs or sketches can be made anywhere in the court room. Some courts actually issue maps so court sketchers know when they have officially left court premises and can begin drawing! Not only is it ludicrous, but the many rules restricting access to the courts create an atmosphere of totalitarianism on all those in court who are afraid to do anything (such as use a tape recorder or doodle in a notebook) in case they get into trouble. Either a court is open to the public or it is not. If a person can sit in the courtroom and see and hear a case, there is no reason why others who cannot get to the courtroom should be forbidden from knowing what went on. There is an ongoing consultation to allow cameras in the courtroom, but in 2006 any changes to the present system seemed remote. Even if cameras were allowed, current proposals would only allow them to film appeals cases.

Many times the reason given for secrecy is to ensure a fair trial, but just as often the defendants lose out from closed justice. In the United States, minority groups such as the National Association for the Advancement of Colored People have actively lobbied for allowing cameras into the courtroom. Their reasoning is that the more people can see *how* justice is being done, the better it *will* be done. Transparency is a valuable way of ensuring legal proceedings are free from racial and other types of prejudice.

Public confidence also requires that the evidence and documents used in those proceedings should be made public. Yet again the British public have no legal right to examine these, even if there is a strong public interest in knowing the contents. This is the case even for defendants who may want the documents so they can get an independent expert to review them. One group of defendants in the UK who have been particularly disadvantaged by the closed system are the hundreds of parents whose children have been taken away in secret care hearings. The default position for all court proceedings and records should always be for openness. This does not strip judges of their powers to seal those records which they deem would be detrimental (such as a witness address) and there are already restrictions in place to prevent the identification of minors. But it does require that if judges decide to impose restrictions, they only do so as a last resort and give clear, written justification for such closure.

GETTING COURT LISTS AND COURT DECISIONS

The public also has no statutory right to see the listing of cases up for trial or the register of judgments. The Home Office has issued guidance to justices' clerks to meet reasonable requests by the media for copies of court lists. At the very least court lists should be available to the media and public in court on the day of the hearings, and if they are prepared in advance then copies should be made available on request. Registers are harder to obtain. After lobbying by the Newspaper Society, most magistrates' courts now provide copies of lists and judgment registers but they can charge you to make copies.

Registers are important because they reveal patterns in the way judges dispense justice and can highlight trends in crime and injustice. It's a nice idea that judges base their interpretation of the law solely on principles of logic and reasoning, but of course, being human, it is inevitable that personal views about justice, culture and beliefs influence thinking. In that regard, the public should have a right to know what any good lawyer knows – what are a judge's leanings? In the United States, it is very easy to compile just such a database of judges' rulings that reveals any latent prejudices. Such a system in the UK would highlight those judges with archaic and sexist beliefs about women or ethnic minorities.

You can try getting both the court lists and the registers of the major courts by contacting either the Court Service or the individual court directly. There is no uniformity of access. Some courts may make you show up in person to view the list and register; others may provide a hard copy, and a few may have them online. Magistrates' courts are particularly problematic as no formal transcript of the proceedings is kept and the press rarely cover these cases. Only in the past 20 years have the magistrates' courts even agreed to make their court list and register available to the public. It is usually only available in person at the court, though hopefully these documents will become more widely accessible online once the magistrates' new computer system is fully functional.

Keep in mind that the disclosure of court lists and the register is still entirely voluntary, a fact that says a lot about the UK courts' attitude toward the public's right to know.

REPORTING RESTRICTIONS – JUSTICE SEEN BUT NOT HEARD

Even in open court, there are many restrictions on what is made public. Judges have power over the procedure in their court, and they can exclude the public if the law permits. Problems arise when judges are overzealous in their use of this power and close court or make restrictions without giving a clear legal reason. There is an ongoing problem with courts placing a ban on reporting even the most basic information such as names and addresses. In an attempt to remedy this, the Information Commissioner has confirmed that the release of this information does not violate the Data Protection Act 1998. The disclosure of basic personal information such as the defendant's name and address ensures that those on trial are accurately identified and not confused with other people in the community with a similar name. 'Yet on a day to day level, courts do misinterpret their powers and unnecessarily ban reporters from publishing full reports of court proceedings,' says Santha Rasaiah of the Newspaper Society. The Judicial Studies Board, the Newspaper Society and the Society of Editors produced a guide for the Crown and magistrates' courts and media to help stop this. You can get a free copy of this guidance online at www.newspapersoc.org.uk

I experienced this myself while sitting in on the Abu Hamza trial. The court had produced transcripts of Hamza's sermons that were shown on video. For journalists, these were useful to record accurately what was said. But at some point the judge announced that transcripts could not leave the courtroom. This is wholly ridiculous. The public was paying not just for production of the transcripts but for the prosecution *and* the defence teams (through legal aid). Yet the public was refused access to the evidence produced in open court.

Reporting restrictions are unnecessary in many instances because automatic restrictions are already in place to protect the identity of victims of sexual offences and children under 18 in Youth Court. And courts often impose orders verbally, without reference to any statutory or legal basis, leaving reporters in an uncertain position regarding what they are allowed to reveal. Inevitably, court reporters who wish to avoid legal censure will err on the side of secrecy. The end result of all this is that you, the public, no longer know what is going on in the courtrooms. If we accept the principle of open justice then this system is patently wrong.

One of the most nefarious restrictions is to impose a postponement order. This prevents any information about a case being made public if the court decides it would cause substantial prejudice to the administration of justice, not just for the current case but for *any* future criminal proceedings. The danger is that without a defined time period when the information can be made public, secrecy can stretch out for years. The investigative journalist Paul Lashmar covered a 'supergrass case' that he was unable to report for five years. The rationale was that secrecy was necessary to ensure the safety of a witness until he had testified in the trials of 15 defendants. But what if there had been injustices in the trial? There was no public scrutiny to ensure justice was carried out. Other countries such as the United States manage to protect their witnesses and prosecute successive criminals while maintaining an open courtroom, so there is no reason why the UK can't do the same.

National security is another reason given for court secrecy and is often used to restrict reporting about people charged under anti-terrorism laws. One man who was arrested under the Terrorism, Crime and Security Act could only be identified as 'G'. Until it was overturned in December 2004 by the UK's highest court, the Act allowed police to detain foreigners indefinitely without charge or trial. Parliament then passed a law in 2006 allowing the police to hold people for up to 60 days without charge. In such a system, people can now effectively 'disappear' and neither the public nor the person's family would have any way of knowing what had happened to them.

Shutting the doors of justice should only ever be a remedy of last resort after all other measures have been taken. Instead, closing the courts and prohibiting the release of information to the public is more often the first reaction of police, judges and those in the legal profession to difficult cases.

In the UK, secret trials and evidence blackouts mean the public cannot be confident that the police are not abusing their powers in the collection of evidence and use of informants. Where there are concerns about the protection of witnesses, then it might be better to improve the way police deal with witnesses and improve the effectiveness of the witness protection programme. The Department for Constitutional Affairs found that 40 per cent of witnesses would be unwilling to attend court again and the main reasons were wasted time, repeated adjournments and lack of information. Only 54 per cent of witnesses gave evidence on the day they were called. The police are just as likely to endanger witnesses as open justice. In April 2004, Ken Ralphs and his partner were awarded £134,000 in compensation after the Greater Manchester Police mistakenly gave his name to the suspect's lawyers. Mr Ralphs was forced to enter the witness protection programme, adopt a new identity and leave his Stockport home after receiving death threats written in blood and a petrol bomb attack on his business.

COURT DOCUMENTS

What is most shocking about the British justice system is that the public have absolutely no right to see the majority of court documents. You might think that open court equals open records, but this is not the case in the UK. The US operates on the opposite principle. The default position is that all court records are open by fact that they are used in open court and their release is in the public interest. Only in exceptional cases will a judge seal records, and this should only be done after considering the public's interest in open justice. Even then, usually the bulk of documents used in evidence will remain open, with only the most sensitive ones sealed.

Lawyers in the UK argue that the public don't need to see documents because the evidence is presented orally. But increasingly, both sides rely on non-oral evidence such as written statements, expert testimony, electronic records, hard copies of documentary evidence and statistical and scientific analysis. For example, a vital piece of evidence in a murder trial may be a DNA analysis report, yet the public have no right to see this and judge its accuracy. They can only rely on what lawyers say about the report in court.

The mass of written documents is known as 'the bundle', and while barristers and QCs may spend a good portion of their time in court perusing this vital information, it remains hidden from public view. This begs the question: how can we know for certain that the evidence being presented is a true representation of the facts if it's not made public in its original form?

In autumn 2005, Ken Macdonald QC, Director of Public Prosecutions announced a new policy to end the secrecy shrouding evidence used in open court. The policy, agreed to by the CPS, Association for Chief Police Officers and the Society of Editors, guarantees a presumption of disclosure for prosecution material used in court. 'We are determined to provide an open and accountable prosecution process by ensuring that, wherever possible, we give the media access to all relevant prosecution material,' says Mr Macdonald.

Family courts

It doesn't seem likely that this new policy will extend to family courts. Not only are family courts closed but also, because records cannot be disclosed without permission of the judge, many parents find themselves unable to get justice. Almost 300 cases of child deaths had to be reviewed after several mothers successfully appealed their wrongful convictions based almost entirely on testimony from expert witness Professor Roy Meadows, who has since been discredited. There are also more than 5,000 children who have been taken into care or adopted in the past 15 years based on his theories. Parents were unable to challenge the testimony of the witness because as a 'court record' it could not be disclosed to anyone outside the case without the judge's permission.

Secrecy allows bad practice to carry on unchecked, which is why it took so many years for Professor Meadows' theories to be challenged. If these cases had been tried in open court with publicly available transcripts and documents, it is likely that the injustice would have been discovered much sooner and hundreds of parents would not be in jail or their children taken into care. Secrecy has also fuelled mistrust in the system by divorced fathers, parents accused of child abuse and victims of domestic violence who claim their cases are mishandled behind closed doors. Stories abound of the courts removing children from their families on flimsy medical evidence, and that miscarriages of justice are widespread.

If the courts are concerned about privacy, then a judge already has the power to impose naming restrictions; there is no need for an entire branch of the justice system to be hidden from public view. Public confidence in the justice system can only be assured if the courts and the evidence used in those courts are fully open to the public.

A public consultation was drawing to a close in 2006 and it looked as though the family courts would be opened up. There was widespread support from parents and judges. The only group not keen on openness was social workers – the very people facing the harshest criticism. Perhaps because they deal with vulnerable people, many social workers seem to have an inherent phobia for openness, especially when it concerns their professional conduct. In April 2006, the first-ever disciplinary hearing by the General Social Care Council was held in secret with press and public excluded, after Yvonne Doyle, from County Durham, told the board she would refuse to attend or give evidence if it was in public. Social workers are not above the law, and for too long the closed family court system has allowed them to exercise great power without adequate public accountability.

EXEMPTION (SECTION 32)

Section 32 of the Freedom of Information Act means that courts and public inquiries are not considered 'public authorities' under the FOIA. It also exempts court records from disclosure without the need for a public interest test. So even if all parties in the case are in favour, and disclosure would be in the public interest, a judge can seal the records, hiding them from public view for decades to come. The definition of a court record was narrowed slightly by an Information Tribunal case *Alistair Mitchell* v. *Information Commissioner* (10 October 2005). The decision specified that a 'court record' for the purpose of the Act applied to:

(i)   'documents created by a court' which meant the judge himself
(ii) documents created by the administrative staff of a court.

So if a document was recorded by an outside agency, it did not fall within either of these two categories, and was not exempt under this provision.

PUBLIC INTEREST IMMUNITY CERTIFICATES

Of course, the government cannot always rely on judges to keep secrets. So it has its own courthouse weapon in the form of public interest immunity certificates. These prohibit the release of evidence not only to the public but also the accused. When Labour came to power in 1997, politicians promised to halt the abuse of PII certificates to hide embarrassment and wrongdoing that was prevalent under the previous Conservative administration. However, the BBC's *File on 4* obtained lists showing that Tony Blair's government issued 100 PII certificates during its first five full years in power, compared to 70 in the last five years of the Tories – an increase of 40 per cent. And these gagging orders aren't just used by government to hide information from the courts. The prosecution in criminal cases uses them to withhold evidence about police surveillance methods and informants. Police have misused PIIs to cover up illegal surveillance, and prisoners have been blocked from accessing their own medical records when they attempted to prove abuse by guards. A string of cases involving the former Customs and Excise collapsed when a judge finally asked to see the evidence behind a PII certificate and found that the primary informant was completely unreliable. Many of these cases are going to the European Court. In 2003 the European Court of Human Rights ruled that Britain had breached two defendants' human rights by issuing PII certificates that prevented them from seeing the evidence against them.

CONTEMPT OF COURT

The contempt of court laws prohibit the publication of any information that could be judged to seriously impede or prejudice judicial proceedings while those proceedings are active. They also prevent publication of a suspect's background or previous convictions. This gag on freedom of expression is bad for two reasons. Firstly it assumes that juries (and the public) are incapable of rational thought once exposed to the media. It should be noted that this type of contempt only refers to trial by jury because a judge is deemed to be sufficiently intelligent to discount media coverage. This belief is just that – a belief without the backing of substantive evidence. Almost no research has been done in the UK on juries, how they reach their decisions and their courtroom experiences. Where empirical studies have been done – in the US and New Zealand for instance,[1] where there are no such contempt of court laws – the evidence is overwhelming and all points in one direction: media exposure has no effect on a juror's decision and in fact jurors are remarkably able to put aside what they have seen or heard about a case and judge it based on the evidence presented in court. Even the most publicised cases in the US have more often led to acquittals than convictions, debunking the myth that pre-trial publicity biases a jury against the defendant.

Secondly, contempt laws often hinder the rights of the accused. For example, an innocent person may have been framed by enemies or the police. A witness knows the police have the wrong man and tries to tell the press, but the press cannot print this information because it could prejudice the defendant's trial. Even the accused is instructed by police not to talk to the media. The law is so far-reaching it also prevents MPs from taking up care and custody cases involving children on behalf of their constituents. The Solicitor-General, Harriet Harman, found herself in trouble for contempt of court when she tried to have a case reviewed in which a child was taken away from her mother based on testimony that the parent suffered from 'Munchausen by proxy' syndrome.

The contempt law has another insidious effect. It is a convenient way for authorities to avoid public scrutiny and hide wrongdoing. For example, the Metropolitan Police are able to refuse all questions about the shooting of an innocent Brazilian on London's Underground and the botched raid by 250 officers at an East London home simply by citing the contempt law. Public debate is thus stifled on the most critical issues for years, sometimes decades, while official investigations are ongoing.

The public have a right to be kept informed in a timely manner as events happen, not years after the fact. Other countries manage to balance the rights of defendants with the rights of society to be kept informed. It is time to acknowledge that the contempt of court laws in this country produce far more harm than good. They are based

1. Steele and Thornborough, 'Jury Instructions: A persistant failure to communicate' (1988) 67 North Carolina L.R. 77, as discussed in William Young's 'Summing-up to Juries in Criminal Cases – what jury research says about current rules and practice', *Criminal Law Review*, October 2003, p. 665. Also, a summation of studies conducted by numerous American states on cameras and the courts is available on the court TV website: www.courttv. com/archive/legaldocs/misc/cameras/brochure.html

on inherently paternalistic and unproven perceptions that show a remarkable lack of respect for the public.

ACCESSING THE LAW

You might assume that as we live in a society governed by the 'rule of law', somewhere there is a big stack of books where you could find all the laws of the land. This is not true. The public have no means of accessing the vast majority of the laws that govern this country. In countries such as the United States, it is relatively easy to look up the law and judge for yourself what you can and cannot do. That is because their laws are codified. In the UK, the law is divided between common law (based on judges' decisions over centuries) and laws enacted by Parliament. The public's access to both types of law is severely limited, which affects not only the public but also less wealthy lawyers, charities and many vital public services such as the police, coroners and local authorities. In his review of the Terrorism Act 2000, Lord Carlile of Berriew QC said it was essential that the Home Office provide an updated version of the Terrorism Act 2000 on their website because even those who used the law frequently, such as lawyers and the police, could not keep up with all the changes.

Case law

Published decisions of the courts are called law reports and they are vital in determining precedent. It is precedent – the past decisions of judges – that makes up common law. The vast majority of these reports are not publicly available and the 'official' series of law reports covering the courts of England and Wales runs nine months behind.

The 'official' reports of the courts of England and Wales are called simply 'The Law Reports' and they are published by the Incorporated Council of Law Reporting, a body run by the Law Society and Bar Council. The Law Reports include cases selected by the editors as having jurisprudential value or value to other lawyers, not the public. The ICLR also publishes 'Weekly Law Reports' which include basic details from many more cases, though most of these don't make it into the official series. A mishmash of about 50 private companies also publish law reports, but the cases published are again decided on commercial factors, that is, which group of lawyers has the most money to spend on law reports. No consideration is given to making the Law Reports cheaply and easily accessible to the public who are deemed to 'know the law'.

Of the 200,000-plus cases heard in court in England and Wales alone, only about 2,500 are published. New initiatives to publish online mean that most House of Lords and Court of Appeal (Civil Division) cases are now reported. But this number decreases to just 20–30 per cent of High Court cases and 10 per cent for cases at the Court of Appeal (Criminal Division). Only a handful of tribunals are reported, and the figure plummets at Crown and county court level, with only one or two out of every 10,000 cases reported. The rest are either unpublished transcripts or are not recorded at all.

Even the definition of what constitutes an 'authoritative' report is up for debate, with some Law Reports accorded more respect than others. The 'official' Law Reports have the greatest authority but they only cover about 175 (or 7 per cent) of the 2,500 reported cases, so the amount of case law that is published *and* authoritative is a fraction of a fraction of case law. Shortened versions of decisions are often published in *The Times*, the *Solicitors' Journal* or the *New Law Journal*, but not all of these cases may be selected for full reporting. This means that even lawyers suffer from the lack of available case law, for if all they have to rely on is one of these briefs then they may find their argument weakened. In a House of Lords judgment, it was concluded that a case only reported in brief in the *Solicitors' Journal* was 'virtually unreported'.[2] This means that unless it was recorded and recorded in full (hopefully by an 'authoritative' journal) it is as if the law never existed!

Parliamentary law

Laws passed by Parliament are easier to find. Acts passed after 1988, and private acts passed after 1991 are available from the Office of Public Sector Information, along with a few important older acts. But be aware that the acts on the OPSI do not incorporate later changes such as amendments or appeals, making it difficult to know what's in force. Other laws passed before these dates are harder to find without access to a law library.

Local councils, police officers, and various professionals are all required to keep abreast of the latest changes in the law so a statute law database is essential. The Department for Constitutional Affairs

2. Lord Roskill in a House of Lords Judgment, *Export Credits Guarantee Department* v. *Universal Oil Products Co.* (1983) 1 WLR 399.

currently holds the raw data needed to build the database but has steadfastly refused to release it, preferring instead to delay the process ten years so it can oversee the construction itself at taxpayers' expense. The latest in a series of missed deadlines, puts the start date for the database at September 2006.

Tired of waiting for a government-funded solution, the designers of www.TheyWorkForYou.com made a Freedom of Information request for the raw data in 2005 with the intention of building a site similar to the Legal Information Unit built by Cornell University in the United States. But whereas Cornell was able to obtain the entire collection of American law and Supreme Court decisions freely from the US government using FOI, the UK government refused to release any data. 'Initially, the DCA said it would cost too much to provide the electronic data,' says Francis Irving. He tried to contact the DCA's IT department but was rebuffed. Then the department changed its reason for refusal, citing instead an exemption for data contained in future publications.

HOW TO FIND THE LAW

Case law

Approved judgments from the High Court and Court of Appeal are available immediately and you can find these on Her Majesty's Court Service website (www.hmcourts-service.gov.uk). Unapproved judgments can only be obtained by the parties involved in the case.

LexisNexis is the most comprehensive database containing all decisions of the High Court, Court of Appeal, Lords and EU. Major public libraries have a subscription. Full case summaries can be found on Lawtel, another commercial database. You can find summaries and digests of recent case decisions in law journals and newspapers with a good legal section such as *The Times* and *Independent*, or listen to *Law in Action* on BBC Radio 4.

British and Irish Legal Information Institute (BAILII)
www.bailii.org
Charles Clore House, 17 Russell Square, London WC1B 5DR
Tel: 020 7862 5806
Fax: 020 7862 5770

This non-profit organisation went online in 2000 and provides free access to the most comprehensive set of British and Irish law available on the internet. BAILII is founded on the premise that all citizens have the fundamental right to free access to laws in a clear and comprehensive form. Eventually, it could make researching the law as simple a process as it is in Australia, from where the inspiration for the BAILII project came.

The Incorporated Council of Law Reporting for England and Wales
www.lawreports.co.uk

You need to buy a subscription to access the official series of Law Reports and they do not come out until about nine months after the case. The Weekly Law Reports provide helpful summaries of the most important cases from the Lords, Privy Council, Court of Appeal and all divisions of the High Court. You can find these on the website.

European Court of Human Rights
www.echr.coe.int

Some important precedents are set here that impact UK legislation. The website contains a searchable site of full-text judgments.

It is sometimes possible to listen to tapes of court cases, but it is quite difficult and you need the permission of the judge. Another way of finding out what happened in a case is to get a transcript. Transcripts are not always produced, but if one party is rich or an appeal is likely, you may be in luck. You still need the court's permission to buy these from the agencies that produce them, and they are expensive. The investigative reporter Michael Crick paid £40 a day for the 2001 Jeffrey Archer trial, for example, which worked out at a total of over £1,000 for the whole case.

Parliamentary law

Office of Public Sector Information, www.opsi.gov.uk, is the main repository for parliamentary law.

- Laws made by the Welsh National Assembly are available in English and Welsh from www.wales-legislation.hmso.gov.uk
- The Scottish equivalent is www.scotland-legislation.hmso.gov.uk
- Northern Ireland is www.northernireland-legislation.hmso.gov.uk

- Current bills moving through Parliament (which could become future laws) can be found on the Parliament website: www.parliament.uk/bills/bills.cfm
- Some, but not all, draft bills moving through the Welsh Assembly are available from www.wales.gov.uk
- Draft legislation going through the Scottish Parliament can be found at www.scottish.parliament.uk/parl_bus/legis.htlm
- Northern Ireland, www.ni-assembly.gov.uk/legislation

Halsbury's Statutes of England – I mention this because it is the source used by all practising lawyers, although it is only accessible if you have access to a law library. Halsbury's is authoritative and kept thoroughly up to date. To give you an idea of the vastness of English parliamentary law, consider that this is a seven-part work. The first part comprises 52 volumes; the first 50 are the laws of England and Wales arranged by subject, with the last two for European Communities. A law librarian can help you find the laws you are looking for. Supplements take note of any new changes.

There are many other sources for law, but they are all expensive. Until the public have a statutory right to court information, we are left in a position where justice is open in name only.

The following books offer a good introduction to conducting more detailed legal research:

Legal Information: What it is and where to find it, Peter Clinch (Aslib, London, 2000), www.aslib.com

Using a Law Library, Peter Clinch (Blackstone Press Ltd, London, 2001)

COURT ADMINISTRATION

The Freedom of Information Act provides a right of access to information relating to the administration of the courts. The court system is the responsibility of the Department for Constitutional Affairs, a central government authority. As well as looking after all courts except the magistrates' courts (which are funded by the DCA but run by local authorities), the DCA is responsible for appointing and overseeing most judges, setting out legal policies and funding the courts. As part of its constitutional duties it looked after the preparation and implementation of the FOIA across central government and also oversees the Information Commissioner's office, which is in charge of enforcing the Act.

The actual running of the courts and tribunals in England and Wales (Crown, County, Appeals) was farmed out to an executive agency called Her Majesty's Court Service in 1995. The DCA and its two executive agencies (the Court Service and the Public Guardianship Service) are all public authorities under the FOIA and therefore have publication schemes. These list their publicly available records and are therefore your first stop for information about administration of the courts and justice system.

Department for Constitutional Affairs

www.dca.gov.uk
5th Floor, 30 Millbank, London SW1P 4XB
Tel: 020 7210 8500 (switchboard); 020 7217 4879 (Information Access Unit)
FOI Officer: Kevin Fraser, Information Access Unit
Tel: 020 7217 4844
Email: Kevin.fraser@dca.gsi.gov.uk, but send FOI requests to: dca.foi@dca.gsi.gov.uk
Publication scheme: www.dca.gov.uk/rights/dca/pubscheme.htm
Disclosure log: www.dca.gov.uk/rights/dca/disclosure.htm

The DCA holds the most information about the justice system, so look at its publication scheme and disclosure log to see if the information you seek is already published. Most new publications will be put on the department's website and the web team will contact the Information Access Rights unit so they can quickly add it to the publication scheme. At least this is the theory. If you want to find out details about court IT projects such as the Libra computer system for magistrates' courts – described by the Commons Public Accounts Committee as one of the worst public projects ever seen – then the DCA should be only too happy to help you with your enquiries!

Other interesting facts about the justice system are available on the statistical publications page: www.dca.gov.uk/statistics/statpub.htm. This includes statistics on waiting times at magistrates' courts, user satisfaction surveys, mortgage possession statistics and figures on the number of companies winding up or going bankrupt.

The DCA is also the place to go if you want data about how the FOIA is being enforced. You can send requests to either the Information Access Unit or to the individual member of staff or section that deals with the information you seek. The FOI Officer can help if you have questions about filing a request or feel your request is being ignored.

Information about judges

In a society based on the rule of law, judges should also reflect the nature of the society they are judging. An updated breakdown of judges by gender and ethnicity is available on the DCA website under 'Judicial statistics'. You can also obtain a list of all judges, when they were appointed and for what circuit, at www.judiciary.gov.uk or by contacting the DCA. The site also has details of judges' salary scales. The DCA's policy on judicial appointments can be found online by following the links on the DCA website, 'Judges' > 'Appointments'. On 3 April 2006 the appointment of judges was taken over by the Judicial Appointments Commission set up by the Constitutional Reform Act in 2005:

Judicial Appointments Commission
Steel House, 11 Tothill Street, London SW1H 9LJ
Tel: 020 7210 1453 (general enquiries)
Email: enquiries@jac.gsi.gov.uk

The commission is independent but sponsored by the DCA.

The Office of Judicial Complaints within the DCA monitors complaints about the personal conduct of judges:

Office for Judicial Complaints
www.judicialcomplaints.gov.uk
4th Floor, Clive House, Petty France, London SW1H 9HD
Tel: 020 7189 2937
Fax: 020 7189 2936
Email: customer@ojc.gsi.gov.uk

The Judicial Appointments and Conduct Ombudsman Office
www.judicialombudsman.gov.uk
8th floor, Millbank Tower, Millbank, London SW1 4RD
Tel: 020 7217 4470
Email: enquiries@ja-comm.gsi.gov.uk

The commission investigates complaints of discrimination, unfairness or maladministration in judicial and Queen's Counsel appointments. The commission has limited resources and scrutinises just three or four of the 1,000–3,000 appointments made annually by the DCA. Each year, it publishes a report about its activities that you can get by contacting the commission.

Her Majesty's Court Service
www.hmcourts-service.gov.uk

6th Floor, Clive House, 70 Petty France, London SW1H 9HD
Tel: 020 7189 2000
Email: customerserviceCSHQ@hmcourts-service.gsi.gov.uk
FOI Officer: Kevin Fraser, Access Rights Unit
Publication scheme: www.hmcourts-service.gov.uk/publications/misc/foi/
pub_scheme_1.htm

This is an executive agency of the DCA and administers the courts of England and Wales. The website is very good and you can get some remarkably candid views of the court system from documents which are now public and available on the website. The most useful to the general observer are found under the section 'About us' > 'Our performance'. The Scottish equivalent is www.scotcourts.gov.uk

Annual reports – you can find these on all the major courts: Supreme Court, Crown Court, Court of Appeal, High Court. The reports contain statements from the judge in charge of each court and the resident manager, and their comments are compelling for their honesty. For instance, in the County Courts annual report 2002–03, you can read about high staff turnover (as high as 50 per cent in some courts), erratic heating systems and vivid descriptions of courts such as Shoreditch 'like a Victorian prison' and Willesden 'like a run-down social security office'. It seems that judges don't hold back on their criticism of the courts in which they work. Underinvestment and neglect are common themes.

Daily case lists – details of cases for the next working day are available on the Court Service's website after 3.30 p.m. Magistrates' and lower courts are not included.

Selected judgments – you can find these online under the section 'Judgments'. House of Lords judgments delivered since 14 November 1996 are available on the parliamentary website.

Courts charter – each type of court has its own charter, outlining standards of services and what you can do if you feel the courts have not met these. You can find the charters on the website in the section 'Forms and guidance'.

Statistics on throughput – each year the Master of the Rolls (the overall presiding judge of the court system) analyses the amount of cases put through the system each year.

Tribunals – the decisions from many tribunals are accessed from the Court Service website. You can also get documents outlining the organisation structure and independence of various tribunals. Remember only the administration of tribunals is covered by the

FOIA, though some have their own openness requirements. The main tribunals overseen by the DCA and HM Court Service are:

Pensions Appeal Tribunals
www.pensionsappealtribunals.gov.uk
Procession House, 55 Ludgate Hill, London EC4M 7JW
Tel: 020 7029 9800
Fax: 020 7029 9818
Email: pensions.appeal@tribunals.gsi.gov.uk

Lands Tribunal
www.landstribunal.gov.uk
Procession House, 55 Ludgate Hill, London EC4M 7JW
Tel: 020 7029 9780
Fax: 020 7029 9781
Email: lands@dca.gsi.gov.uk

Adjudicator to the Land Registry
www.landregistry.gov.uk
Procession House, 55 Ludgate Hill, London, EC4M 7JW
Tel: 020 7029 9860
Fax: 020 7029 9801
Email: alr@dca.gsi.gov.uk
Publication scheme: www.landregistry.gov.uk/foi/pub_scheme/

Transport Tribunal
www.transporttribunal.gov.uk
Procession House, 55 Ludgate Hill, London EC4M 7JW
Tel: 020 7029 9790
Fax: 020 7029 9782
Email: transport@dca.gsi.gov.uk

Unclaimed suitors cash lists – these list all money received by the county courts that has remained unclaimed and paid to the Accountant-General. Sadly these are not currently available online, so the only way to find out if you're due any money is to ask for a hard copy from the Court Service.

Vexatious litigants – this is a handy list of those people for whom the phrase 'I'll see you in court' has become something of an addiction: www.hmcourts-service.gov.uk/infoabout/vexatious_litigant/index.htm

Record retention and disposition schedules – you might find these useful if you are filing an FOIA request and trying to track down a particular document. The schedules identify and describe record series, collections or systems of records and give guidance on the length of time records must be held. These are only available by hard copy, or you could try talking to someone in Records Management at the Court Service or DCA.

COURTS

Although the courts themselves are not subject to the FOIA, there are a number of organisations associated with them that are affected. Also, courts have their own laws and policies that govern openness. To find out what information is available from the different courts it is worthwhile to briefly outline the structure of courts and the types of cases each court hears. The first major division is between criminal and civil cases. Crimes against the state are prosecuted in criminal courts with the aim being to punish the criminal. They include theft, robbery, assault or murder and because they are deemed crimes against society, the state can prosecute the alleged offender regardless of the victim. The burden of proof is 'beyond a reasonable doubt' in order to counteract the greater personal restrictions if found guilty.

Civil courts deal with relations between private individuals or organisations where protection of private rights or interests is sought and where the state has no interest in suing. For example, even though a publisher may not be breaking a criminal law by failing to pay my invoice, I still want to protect my own interests and so would pursue a civil case against them. The burden of proof in civil cases is 'on the balance of probability'. Chances are that at some point in your life you will come into contact with the justice system, so it's worthwhile knowing what information is available and how to get it. Apart from the county courts that deal only with civil cases, all the other courts deal with both types of cases.

Complaints

Complaints about courts are usually made to the court manager of the specific court, and the courts' annual reports increasingly contain information about complaints and customer satisfaction. Those complaints which are not resolved at court level go to: HM Court Service Customer Service Unit, 6th Floor, Clive House, 70 Petty France, London SW1H 9HD.

Magistrates' courts

About 97 per cent of criminal cases in Britain are heard in a magistrates' court. The bulk of cases are traffic infractions – people driving without insurance, failure to have an MOT certificate of roadworthiness, driving over the limit, and so on. But there are also more serious family cases and youth crimes. You might also be interested in requesting information about magistrates' other duties:

- Issuing licences for betting shops and casinos
- Granting search and arrest warrants (how many does your local magistrate issue? Are they too lenient in allowing the police to search people's homes?)
- Applications for bail (do they set overly high bail, or too low?)

Although like all courts, magistrates' courts are not technically covered by the FOIA, they are managed by Magistrates' Courts Committees (MCCs) and these are subject to the Act. There are 42 MCCs in England and Wales and each one comprises magistrates (who are unpaid), their paid support staff, and a chief executive to head the committee. Overall, the MCCs run 394 courthouses, 1,510 courtrooms with 10,712 full-time equivalent staff. There are 24,419 magistrates who sit in the courts along with 105 district judges and 150 deputy district judges. MCCs get 20 per cent of their funding from local authorities and 80 per cent from central government.

Directory of Magistrates' Court Committees – you can get a listing and contact details for the 42 Magistrates' Courts Committees on the DCA website: www.dca.gov.uk/magist/links.htm

List of magistrates – the public and press have a right to know who their local magistrates are and this right was upheld in a court case, *Regina* v. *Felixstowe Magistrates' Court ex parte Leigh and the Observer Ltd* (1986). You can get this list from any magistrates' court and if withheld you have every right to challenge the court's unlawful secrecy.

Magistrates' Courts Annual Report – for the first time in 2003, the collected annual returns from all 42 MCC areas were made available to the public. The reports provide statistics on the gender and ethnic makeup of magistrates, the outcome of cases, how long witnesses had to wait to give evidence and the cost-effectiveness of the courts. It is available on the DCA website under the section 'Magistrates'.

Case lists and judgments – currently the only way to get this information is to contact each individual magistrates' court.

Her Majesty's Inspectorate of Court Administration

www.hmica.gov.uk
General enquiries: General Office, 8th Floor Millbank Tower, Millbank,
London SW1P 4QP
Tel: 020 7217 4355
Fax: 020 7217 4357

This is an independent office of the DCA and is covered by the FOIA. It inspects the court administration in Crown, county and magistrates' courts and the Children and Family Court Advisory and Support Service (CAFCASS). You can the get reports or view the most recent inspections online by following the links to 'Publications'.

Magistrates Association

www.magistrates-association.org.uk
28 Fitzroy Square, London W1T 6DD
Tel: 020 7387 2353
Fax: 020 7383 4020

This is the voluntary professional organisation for magistrates, so the FOIA does not apply. However, the association provides some useful public information about how to become a magistrate and sentencing guidelines and training.

Youth and family proceedings

The Audit Commission (www.audit-commission.gov.uk) audits the youth justice system, and its most recent report issued in 2004 is available on the website or you can order a copy by phoning 0800 502 030. The family proceedings court deals with issues such as care orders and finalising adoptions. Both these courts are closed to the public and documents can only be released with the judge's approval. However, youths can be identified if they are given anti-social behaviour orders.

Crown court

Crown courts try the more serious criminal offences at one of 78 centres across England and Wales. They may also deal with some High Court civil cases and family work. Many now have their own websites where you can get daily court lists and other information such as a virtual tour. For an overall round-up of the Crown courts and their performance, read the Crown courts latest annual report available on the Court Service website. The best-known Crown court is the Central Criminal Court in London, otherwise known as the Old Bailey.

The High Court

Directors Office, Room TM 8.10, Royal Courts of Justice, Strand, London WC2A 2LL
Tel: 020 7947 6159/6000
Email: customerservice.rcj@courtservice.gsi.gov.uk

The High Court is divided into three divisions – Chancery, Family, Queen's Bench – and hears both civil and criminal cases. Within the Queen's Bench there are several other courts such as the Commercial Court and Admiralty Court where you'll find cases about ship collisions or damages to cargo.

Court of Appeal

This court normally sits at the Royal Courts of Justice in the Strand, London. It hears both criminal and civil appeals.

House of Lords – see Chapter 3 for contact details

The Lords is the final UK court of appeal and is therefore known as the Supreme Court. There are twelve law lords but normally only five to seven hear an appeal. You can find more information about the judicial work of the lords from the parliamentary website: www.parliament.uk/judicial_work/judicial_work.cfm

Judgments are freely available from the parliamentary website by following the links to 'Judicial work' > 'Judgments': www.publications.parliament.uk/pa/ld199697/ldjudgmt/ldjudgmt.htm. Paper copies of the judgments (£5 each) are available by contacting: Judicial Office, House of Lords, London SW1A OPW. Tel: 020 7219 3111. Fax: 020 7219 2476.

OTHER COURT INFORMATION

Crown Prosecution Service

www.cps.gov.uk
50 Ludgate Hill, London EC4M 7EX
Tel: 020 7796 8000
Email: enquiries@cps.gsi.gov.uk
FOI Officer: Richard Pierce, Head of Information Management

Email: Richard.pierce@cps.gsi.gov.uk, but send requests to: FOIUnit@cps.
gsi.gov.uk
Publication scheme: www.cps.gov.uk/publications/foiapubeng.html

The CPS is an independent government department responsible for examining the evidence in police cases to determine whether a case can go to court. It is covered by the FOIA. The CPS proved surprisingly receptive to FOI and provided one of the most significant disclosures of 2005. In response to my request for conviction data by crime type and area, the CPS responded promptly with detailed databases that showed varying conviction levels across the country. This is the sort of data that should be released regularly to the public so we can have an informed debate about criminal justice based on fact, rather than politicised rhetoric. In Scotland, the *Sunday Herald* (8 January 2006) used FOI and found that out of 1,672 rape cases reported only 83 get to court with a third never making it past the police station. The damning figures were never before available to the public, and showed a litany of instances where rapes likely took place but were dropped either for 'insufficient evidence', the victim withdrew their allegations, or detectives decided 'no crime' occurred. The CPS standard for prosecution is heavily weighted against the victims of sexual crime because it demands empirical evidence. Further investigations using the FOIA into the failure to prosecute sexual crimes including rape are ongoing.

HMCPS Inspectorate

www.hmcpsi.gov.uk
26–28 Old Queen Street, London SW1H 9HP
Tel: 020 7210 1197 (enquiries)
Email: office@hmcpsi.gov.uk

If you want more information about the efficiency and effectiveness of the Crown Prosecution Service you could try this public body. Its reports and recommendations are not legally binding, but could prove interesting.

County court judgments

County court judgments are one way of getting an idea of someone's credit history. If they have failed to pay someone, that person will get a judgment against them for the money owed. The register of county court judgments is a statutory public register, which means it is open to all, though that doesn't mean it is easily accessible. In

2006, a new Register of Judgments, Orders and Fines was created that comprises all fines handed down in magistrates' courts, the High Court and county court along with county court administration orders, judgments and Child Support Agency liability orders. You can either access a county court judgment in person at the court where the judgment was held or by contacting the Registry Trust Limited, which holds the new register.

Registry Trust Limited
www.registry-trust.org.uk
173–175 Cleveland Street, London WIT 6QR
Tel: 020 7380 0133
Email: info@registry-trust.org.uk

This former government service was privatised in 1985 and now sells public information back to the public, and also to the main credit reference agencies. The Trust comes under the scope of the FOIA because the records it holds are public records held on behalf of a public authority (HM Court Service and by default the Department for Constitutional Affairs). This is the place to go if you want to check your own or others' creditworthiness. You'll find the records of any county court judgment against you that may be affecting your credit rating.

You can search either in person or by writing in, but not by telephone. The website can generate a form for you to post. A name and address you provide is used to search through all the records for the past six years. The cost for each search is now a whopping £8 whether you apply online, by post or in person for every search term (so that's £8 per time even if you're trying to find one person and have to go through variations of names such as Brook, Brooks, or Brooke). The Registry Trust also has registers for small claims information from Scotland and some information for Northern Ireland and the Isle of Man. For each judgment, you'll get the name and address of the debtor or limited company, the original amount and date of the judgment and the court where it was made.

You will need the name of the court if you want details of the claimant, plaintiff or pursuer, as this information is only available from the court, and sometimes not even then. In some jurisdictions, the plaintiff's name may only be available to the defendant. The lack of accessibility and anonymity of plaintiffs allows 'bully boy' claimants to aggressively pursue people for unfounded claims. For example, gym clubs and mobile phone companies have been known to harass former customers for further membership fees even after a contract is satisfied. It would benefit the public to know who is abusing the system in this way.

Wills and probate records

Wills and other probate court records are publicly available, though not yet online. To access these records in person you can go to the London or York Registry offices which have full indexes of all wills and probate in England and Wales. You can also request records from your local registry office, but they may not have all the indexes you need so phone ahead. You can search the indexes for free and they are useful for finding out the date someone died, where they lived, their relatives and solicitor.

If you want the clerks to search for you or if you want to view the full will or administrative documents, the standard cost is £5 and covers a four-year search. Longer searches are charged an additional £3 for every four-year period. Once you've made your request and paid, a scanned copy of the will should be sent to the Registry within the hour. Among the more interesting documents you can access are wills of significant people such as Charles Darwin, Winston Churchill, Princess Diana, Florence Nightingale, Richard Burton and John Lennon.

London Registry
The Principal Registry of the Family Division, First Avenue House, 42–49 High Holborn, London WC1V 6NP
Tel: 020 7947 7022 (searches); 020 7947 6939 (general enquiries)

York Probate Registry (for all postal applications)
First Floor, Castle Chambers, Clifford Street, York YO1 9RG

Public Guardianship Office
www.guardianship.gov.uk
Customer Services Unit, Public Guardianship Office, Archway Tower, 2 Junction Road, London, N19 5SZ
Tel: 0845 330 2900
Email: custserv@guardianship.gsi.gov.uk
Publication scheme: available by calling or on the website under the 'Freedom of information' section.

This executive agency provides services that protect the wellbeing of people with mental incapacities, such as older people with dementia. It is the administrative arm of the Court of Protection. Information available includes annual reports, research reports, minutes from board meetings and answers to parliamentary questions.

The Criminal Cases Review Commission

www.ccrc.gov.uk
Alpha Tower, Suffolk Street Queensway, Birmingham B1 1TT
Tel: 0121 633 1800
Fax: 0121 633 1804/1823
FOI Officer: Boris Worrall, Head of Communication
Tel: 0121 633 1806
Email: info@ccrc.gov.uk

The Criminal Cases Review Commission is an independent body set up by Parliament in 1997 to investigate suspected miscarriages of justice in the criminal courts. It is a public authority under the FOIA and holds information on the results of their investigations.

LEGAL PROFESSIONALS: SOLICITORS AND BARRISTERS

Solicitors and barristers and their professional bodies are self-regulating private organisations, so they do not come under the Freedom of Information Act. However, in 2006 a wide-ranging review concluded that self-regulation was not effective and a new regulator – a kind of 'Oflaw' – was needed. Such an organisation would presumably be subject to the Act. These reforms were set to go through Parliament before 2007. The proposals would:

- set up an Office for Legal Complaints (OLC) to independently investigate complaints
- set up a Legal Services Board (LSB) to regulate legal services
- enable different kinds of lawyers and non-lawyers to work together on equal footing to provide legal and other services.

The regulatory system as it stands in 2006 involved three law organisations that are public authorities under the FOIA: the Legal Services Ombudsman, the Law Commission and the Legal Services Commission.

The legal professions certainly need to improve their record on public accountability and transparency. A review by the Legal Services Ombudsman criticised the profession's inability to police itself effectively and a *Which?* investigation published in November 2003 found that the Law Society helpline, set up to keep the public informed about solicitors cited for misconduct, failed to inform callers about restrictions on disciplined solicitors. In March 2004 the Office for the Supervision of Solicitors was scrapped only a few years after it replaced the previously failing Solicitors' Complaints Bureau.

Legal Services Ombudsman

www.olso.org
Office of the Legal Services Ombudsman, 3rd Floor, Sunlight House, Quay Street, Manchester M3 3JZ
Tel: 0161 839 7262 or 0845 601 0794
Fax: 0161 832 5446

The Legal Services Ombudsman is the final adjudicator for complaints made against solicitors and barristers. The current ombudsman is Zahida Manzoor and her annual reports present a candid view of the current self-regulatory system and how it could be improved. The reports and details of her investigations are available on the website or by contacting the office.

The Law Commission

www.lawcom.gov.uk
Conquest House, 37–38 John Street, Theobalds Road, London WC1N 2BQ
Tel: 020 7453 1220
Fax: 020 7453 1297
Email: chief.executive@lawcommission.gsi.gov.uk

The Law Commission reviews the law of England and Wales and promotes reform. A range of publicly available information can be found on the website such as annual reports, consultation papers, reports and outlines of current law reform projects.

Legal Services Commission

www.legalservices.gov.uk
Legal Services Commission, Secretariat Department, 85 Gray's Inn Road, London WC1X 8TX
FOI Officer: Jacquie Elliott, Information Compliance Manager
Tel: 020 7759 0428
Email: secretariat@legalservices.gov.uk
Publication scheme: www.legalservices.gov.uk/aboutus/ati/foi_publication.asp

The Legal Services Commission is the executive agency (quango) that replaced the Legal Aid Board in 2000 and is responsible for spending nearly £2 billion of public money. It funds legal services for those with low incomes or who meet certain criteria. The system suffers from the reputation that it is a gravy train for lawyers. The latest

LSC annual report is the best place to find information about how money is spent. You can find this on the website or by contacting the commission.

Solicitors

The Law Society
www.lawsociety.org.uk
113 Chancery Lane, London WC2A 1PL
Tel: 020 7242 1222
Complaints helpline: 0845 608 6565
Email: enquiries@lawsociety.org.uk
Publication scheme: www.lawsociety.org.uk/publicationscheme.law

The Law Society is a private organisation and not subject to the FOIA. It regulates solicitors and all solicitors are required to behave within professional standards that are set out in the *Guide to Professional Conduct*. You can get this online at www.guide-on-line.lawsociety. org.uk. This is a lengthy document but is divided into sections. The most relevant section involves conflicts of interest and charging. The *Client's Charter* sets out clients' rights and the service they can expect. You can get these on the website, or for printed copies email at customerguides@lawsociety.org.uk or telephone the Law Society.

Complaints and negligence

There were 17,074 complaints about solicitors in 2004. You might like to know who the complaints are against, particularly when looking for a solicitor. The first way is to look up a name on the *Solicitors Directory* www.solicitors-online.com to see if they can still practise, then contact the Law Society to see if there are any conditions imposed on their practising certificate.

Barristers

The Bar Council
www.barcouncil.org.uk
3 Bedford Row, London WC1R 4DB
Tel: 020 7242 0082
Complaints Commissioner: Michael Scott
Complaints Department: Northumberland House, 3rd Floor,
303–306 High Holborn, London WC1V 7JZ
Tel: 020 7440 4000

The Bar Council regulates barristers who must adhere to the council's code of conduct. You can find this on the Bar Council's website under the section 'Rules and guidance'. The Bar Council is more organised and transparent than the Law Society.

Disciplinary tribunal results – Here you'll find details, findings and sentences passed by the disciplinary tribunals and summary procedure panel. The page is updated regularly, but you should call the Bar Council's records department on 020 7242 0934 for the exact practising status of a barrister. Available online under 'Complaints'.

Minutes – these are available online.

All barristers must be members of one of the Inns of Court. These gothic piles rather symbolise the elitist and out-of-touch nature of the law. With a social calendar of balls, banquets and garden parties, the Inns are more like country houses than the headquarters for a working profession. Few people seem to know that the grounds are usually open to the public, and the private buildings can often be toured by appointment. Because the Inns are private clubs, they are not subject to the FOI, but they are slowly pulling themselves out of antiquity. They all have websites now with histories and general information and most have virtual tours of the buildings, so even if you can't get in, you can at least know what you're missing!

- *Lincoln's Inn Fields* www.lincolnsinn.org.uk
- *Grays Inn* www.graysinn.org.uk
- *Inner Temple* www.innertemple.org.uk
- *Middle Temple* www.middletemple.org.uk

FOR MORE INFORMATION

Understanding the Law, Geoffrey Rivlin (Oxford University Press, Oxford, 2004) – an accessible and interesting look at all aspects of the justice system and legal professions.

Understanding and Using the British Legal System, Jeremy Farley (Straightforward Publishing, London, 2002) – brief outline of the court system, going to small claims, suing for damages and gaining compensation, noisy neighbours, bankruptcy, making a will.

The English Legal System, John Wheeler (Longman, London, 2002) – a 'law student' type of book that outlines the various courts, legal process and how to conduct legal research.

Eddey & Darbyshire on the English Legal System by Penny Darbyshire (Sweet & Maxwell, London, 2001) – a fairly detailed yet easy-to-understand guide to the law and legal system.

McNae's Essential Law for Journalists by Tom Welsh, Walter Greenwood, David Banks (Oxford University Press) – written for journalists, but members of the public will find it enlightening as is lays out all the restrictions on freedom of expression in the UK and provides a clear outline of the courts: what they do and public access to them.

The Solicitors and Barristers Directory (Waterlow Publishers) – this is your best source for getting addresses and contact information about individual solicitors and barristers, chambers and firms, magistrates, coroners and high sheriffs. It also includes a section on 'courts and offices' with contact information including phone numbers, addresses and relevant names for all courts and tribunals in England and Wales and some other territories.

Shaw's Directory of Courts in the United Kingdom (Shaw & Sons, London, annual), www.shaws.co.uk, tel: 01322 621100 – a comprehensive directory of the High Courts, Crown Courts, County Courts and courts of summary jurisdiction (such as Magistrates' Courts) in England, Wales, Northern Ireland and Scotland, as well as a list of coroners, contact details for the Crown Prosecution Service and prisons.

The Law Society also publishes the annual *Directory of Solicitors and Barristers* (Law Society, London).

8
Law Enforcement and Civil Defence

'Seeking to achieve trust and confidence through the demonstration of fairness will not in itself be sufficient. It must be accompanied by a vigorous pursuit of openness and accountability across Police Services ... [W]e consider it an important matter of principle that the Police Services should be open to the full provisions of a Freedom of Information Act. We see no logical grounds for a class exemption.'

Stephen Lawrence Inquiry – Report of an Inquiry
by Sir William Macpherson of Cluny, 1998

Who watches the watchers? The window into the world of law enforcement and civil defence certainly needs a good clean! Of course, a level of secrecy is necessary to deter, outwit or capture those who seek to harm society. But how can we ensure that those charged with protecting us don't abuse their powers and end up becoming a threat to our civil liberties themselves? Equally importantly, how can the police and other agents of the state gain the trust and assistance of the public if they cloak themselves in secrecy?

The police in the UK suffer from this lack of trust most noticeably and dramatic changes are necessary to restore public confidence. The police are only just learning that secrecy is not the way to build public trust; what is needed is more transparency and public oversight. We need to know that complaints against the police are taken seriously and investigators are not abusing their powers. Greater transparency and accountability would also benefit other parts of the system. In prisons, information is increasingly hard to get as private companies take over. Coroners wield tremendous power and yet they are virtually unaccountable to the public and they are not obliged to release the results of their investigations even to relatives of the deceased. The public are forbidden to see fire safety inspection reports, and we cannot judge the robustness and effectiveness of our civil defences because they are top secret.

Fortunately, the Freedom of Information Act covers these authorities. There are still many exemptions that will protect sensitive information but, apart from information supplied by, or relating to, the security services (section 23 of the Act), most of these exemptions are subject to a public interest test. The kneejerk reaction to any inquiry can no longer be blanket secrecy.

POLICE

Imagine being able to enter your address onto a police website and download detailed crime statistics for your street, or look up the name of your babysitter to see if s/he has a previous conviction. Want to know which officer has received the most complaints from the public? How about spending the evening with a police officer on duty?

Police departments in the United States provide these services to the public. They learned several decades ago that if they wanted to earn the trust and goodwill of the public, they would have to become more open, transparent and directly accountable to the people they served. Even in the supposed backwater states of the Deep South, I found police and sheriff's deputies committed to community policing, diversity, public involvement and transparency. They knew that to keep secrets raised suspicion, and they developed a stronger relationship with the public through openness. Police departments in the US are primarily funded through local taxes and answer directly to local councils with sheriffs answering directly to the electorate. Tax bills show exactly how much of the public's taxes go to the police and police budgets are detailed and widely publicised. I worked as a crime reporter in the US, and though I wouldn't say that the police always enjoyed having their budgets and methods scrutinised, they at least accepted the value of openness and understood why it was important to account to the public.

This is the opposite to the situation in the UK, and the comparative levels of openness in the two countries' law enforcement directly reflects the public's subsequent trust in them. Until very recently, the police in the UK were totally unaccountable to the local community in which they worked. They answered only to the Home Secretary and complaints made against them were investigated by... guess who? Other police officers! The government set out to change this, but couldn't quite face giving local communities such power, so what we have now is a compromise that makes a muddle of something simple. A triumvirate of the Home Office, the police forces (the actual police) and the police authorities oversee policing. Police authorities are a kind of genetically modified local government that sits between the public and police forces. They have very little power to affect police operations; instead, they oversee provision of buildings and equipment and monitor performance.

FOI in practice

The FOIA has provided a real opportunity for citizens to find out directly about their local force. In the first year of FOI, the police received about 21,000 requests across all forces, according to DCC Ian Readhead who works in the FOI unit at the Association of Chief Police Officers (ACPO). He says the police have managed to respond within the time frame in 94 per cent of cases and have disclosed in full or in part in 65 per cent of cases. Most requesters report a good service from the police. ACPO, while not a public body, decided to take the lead on FOI across all police forces and act as a central advisory service. ACPO can also provide advice to the public wanting to make requests. On one occasion, I made a 'national' FOI request to all police forces in England and Wales and I did this by sending my request to ACPO who then forwarded it to all 43 police forces. If you seek information from one or just a handful of forces, then it's probably best to contact those forces directly. I have posted the FOI contacts for all UK police forces on the www.yrtk.org website.

Prior to the Act, police feared the main users would be disenfranchised members of staff unhappy about their treatment within the force (what does that say about the force?). As it turns out, most requests have been from the public about operational policing matters and high-profile cases such as the Soham murders, the shooting of Jean Charles de Menzes on the London Underground or the policing of Islamic protests. Some notable police disclosures include:

- All the Greenham Common files during the period when it was a nuclear airbase
- The investigating officer's report into Soham and other high-profile cases
- Documents related to the policing of the anti-apartheid movement in the 1960s and 1970s
- Most chief officers' expenses are now routinely published online
- ACPO policies, such as how police deal with fox-hunting since the ban
- The numbers of police officers with convictions for drunk driving and violent offences, caught speeding and let off, or working second jobs.

The police have definitely made great strides in tackling a very entrenched culture of secrecy, but there remains an underlying inequality in the way information is shared. The police expect and often demand information from the public, but all too often they are unwilling to share anything in return. We cannot as a society have an informed discussion about policing without meaningful information from the police.

Local crime statistics

Crime statistics ought to be widely available to the public. After all, we have a pressing and direct need to know how safe we are. As it is, our knowledge of what crimes have occurred is based solely on inconsistent factors: a personal relationship between a reporter and a police officer, a call to the media from an enthusiastic witness or the subjective decisions of individual police officers about what they think the public ought to know. This is fine if you have complete trust that the police know best, but there is always scope for mistakes and political motivation. Maybe the police fail to spot that a string of sexual assaults are connected or that one street is particularly prone to burglaries and therefore they don't caution residents. Or perhaps a case puts the police in a negative light so they would prefer that the public did not know about it.

Accurate and consistent crime information allows us to make our own informed decisions about our safety. I would like to know on a weekly basis, for example, what sort of crimes have occurred in my neighbourhood. The more people who have access to this type of detailed crime data, the better we can monitor the safety of our neighbourhoods and the effectiveness of police. In the US, campaign groups and the media often help the police, by analysing this publicly supplied crime data in new ways to uncover connections. Domestic violence campaigners in the US have access to all police reports so they can see the scope of the problem. The British public, by contrast, are dependent upon taxpayer-funded studies directed by politicians for their knowledge. In such a centrally controlled system, it is politicians not the public who set priorities. The injustices suffered by victims of rape, domestic violence or so-called 'honour' killings, remain hidden until central government authorises a study, revealing the extent of the problem. Under FOI, this is now starting to change as anyone can ask for statistics from the police and Crown Prosecution Service.

Some police forces are making crime incident information available to the public. Hampshire Constabulary will give out crime figures by street. If you're considering moving, this is invaluable information. The goal would be to have the information available online. Check out this page in the *St Petersburg Times* (Florida): www.sptimes.com/crime. It allows you to see crime reports by neighbourhood block. In the US, you can even get crime figures for universities – www.securityoncampus.org/crimestats – something that many parents would like to know before sending their children away for the first time.

Publishing local incident reports can be done in an informative yet anonymous way such as by street or block. Making these reports public also shows us what police officers have to tackle on a daily basis, and this would go a long way to winning public trust for the police. Encourage your local force to release detailed crime incident reports.

Criminal records

Technically, all criminal convictions are public records – they are handed down in open court. However, the reality is inconsistency, confusion and overriding paternalism. True, the records are public, but only if you happen to go to every court hearing in every court in the entire country. If a newspaper reporter happens to cover a trial then that person's conviction will be in the paper's archives and therefore publicly accessible. Yet all these supposedly public records are available in one central location – the Criminal Records Bureau (CRB). The problem is that in their collected form, the public have no right to access these public records!

The private company Capita was given £400 million of public money to build a criminal records database and received another £68 million in 2004, despite being late and overbudget.

Access to this publicly funded database is granted only to the police and companies or voluntary organisations that apply for registration. Some professions require mandatory criminal records vetting, but who decides which ones? Recently, various categories of workers have been added, such as care-home workers and child minders; even church bell ringers were being considered. But this allows the state rather than the public to determine who should be vetted. What about people who run holiday camps or university professors? We should be able to decide for ourselves who should be vetted. Another problem is the cost: originally free for volunteers, and £12 otherwise, charges have risen to £31 for a standard disclosure and £36 for an advanced report, making it difficult for small organisations to afford vetting all their staff, and some may choose to forgo the £300 cost of registration altogether.

There is an argument that publishing criminal records will prevent ex-offenders from gaining employment and hinder their rehabilitation. But the reality is that ex-offenders already face these difficulties under the current system. Many professions require all new or prospective employees to waive their rights to privacy and allow the employer to vet them through the CRB. So the big employers and others who can afford to pay the fees already have access to full criminal history checks. And the standard disclosure details *all* convictions including 'spent' convictions – that is, those that happened some time ago and normally no longer need to be revealed, along with cautions, reprimands or warnings.

Contrast this to the system in the US. Any convictions handed down in open court are put on a central database accessible to the public. You can search most local and state courts on the internet or pay a small fee (about $29 or £20) to an agency to search all records nationwide. Such openness has not led to lynchmobs roving the country or whole sections of society left unemployable. A rehabilitation system allows convictions to be struck from the public record after a certain number of years, in much the same way that points are removed from your driving record. Everyone can access the same information regardless of wealth and the public are protected from career criminals. In the UK, these are the very people who benefit the most from the current inconsistencies.

Sex offenders

The situation becomes even more muddled when it involves sex offenders. Individual police forces maintain and feed information into the main sex offenders' registry, but there is no consistency or public debate about the sort of behaviour that warrants inclusion on the list. It is not restricted to those found guilty in court of sex offences. People with a police caution, those involved in a consensual relationship with a teenager, or just someone the police think suspicious – all can be included on the list. Even more dubious is politicians' involvement in deciding who should be classed as a menace to society. In 2006, then Education Minister Ruth Kelly revealed there were seven governmental blacklists barring people from working with children and vulnerable adults. Surely these lists would be more effective (both in terms of cost and operational effectiveness) if they were unified. And if the lists were public then such needless duplication and cost-wasting would have been exposed years ago. Secrecy has created a system that has no consistency and is open to abuse by those who control the lists, namely the police and politicians.

The other question is one of fairness. Why should only police and politicians have access to these records? It is unreasonable to expect the police to monitor and keep tabs on all suspicious persons. We, the people, are much better placed to protect our own children. The public's right to know about potential dangers in the community must be taken into consideration. Currently the system is skewed in favour of the privacy rights of criminals.

Claims that an open system would lead to vigilantism are misplaced. The United States makes public not only all criminal records, but also keeps a publicly accessible list of sexual offenders and they do not suffer from vigilantism. Vigilantism is the product not of open records but rather a breakdown in trust between the public and the criminal justice system. That is why we see vigilantism in countries where the rule of law has broken down and people feel the need to take matters into their own hands. Cases of such vigilantism in Britain are rare, that's why the same story is always trotted out – that of the paediatrician attacked after the *News of the World* named and shamed convicted paedophiles. The fact is people are attacked every day for a number of reasons. Is it sensible to put innocent people in danger's way just because of the irrational, and criminal behaviour, of a miniscule minority? Because let's not forget that assault and harassment are already crimes, and the police would do well to concentrate on prosecuting such crimes, rather than censoring information to the vast bulk of law-abiding people.

Rather than closing the system even more, the way to solve this problem is to make the courts and court records more transparent so the people can see with their own eyes and hear with their own ears exactly how justice is being done. Only then will we feel confident that the system is working properly and justly.

Criminal Records Bureau

www.crb.gov.uk
CRB, PO Box 110, Liverpool L3 6ZZ
Tel: 0151 676 1421
FOI Officer: Julie Pemberton. Freedom of Information Section, CRB, Shannon Court, 10 Princes Parade, Princes Dock, Liverpool L3 1QY
Email: freedomofinformation@crb.gsi.gov.uk
Publication scheme: www.crb.gov.uk/rights_freedom_publication.asp

If you are the average citizen then you have no rights to access criminal records, despite the fact that they are handed down in so-called open court and they are collected on a central data system that you paid for. About the only thing you can get from the publicly funded Criminal Records Bureau is a list of administrative reports on their website under 'Resource Library'. You can find their latest annual report and complaints summary. You can access records if you can prove you have a valid reason (such as vetting employees) and pay the £300 registration fee.

Offenders index database

This is a Home Office database that holds criminal history data for offenders convicted of standard list offences from 1963 to the present, although it runs about six to nine months behind. The information comes from the Court Appearances system and is updated quarterly. Enquiries, tel: 020 7273 4122; 020 7217 8790. However, you'll only get the information if you can convince a bureaucrat that you are a 'bona fide researcher'.

How to get information about the police

All police forces and police authorities must have a publication scheme (like all other public authorities under the Act) and in addition, police authorities, as a spin-off of local government, must also adhere to

---

The process for finding police information

1. Determine who holds the information you want: the Home Office, police force, or police authority. The Home Office holds a wide range of national statistics and makes national policies about policing and crime reduction, so if your query concerns the police generally or you want national figures, address your request to the Home Office. If you want information specific to a local area then contact the police force. They hold local information about all operations: incident reports, investigations, local crime statistics and budget information. The police authority has information about the local police force's performance (how well they are meeting set targets on diversity, successful prosecution of cases, adherence to the budget). They also hold general information about the authority such as the members' allowances and expenses.
2. If it is held by a force or authority, find the one you are interested in. A guide to all UK police forces is available at www.police.uk. A list of all police force FOI officers is available on the www.yrtk.org website.
3. Check the publication scheme to see if the information you want is already publicly available.
4. If not, telephone or email the general enquiries contact.
5. If they can't help you, or deny you the information, make an FOIA request to the FOI officer or relevant department.

all the local government openness laws such as allowing the public access to their books and accounts for a period of two weeks a year.

Home Office Police Information

www.homeoffice.gov.uk/crimpol/police

For initial enquiries contact the Direct Communications Unit, 2 Marsham Street, London SW1P 4DF

Tel: 0870 000 1585

Email: public.enquiries@homeoffice.gsi.gov.uk

FOI Officer: Jane Sigley, Information Access Manager

Tel: 020 7035 1306

Emails: info.access@homeoffice.gsi.gov.uk (state 'FOI request')

Publication scheme: www.homeoffice.gov.uk/about-us/freedom-of-information/publications-scheme/

Disclosure log: www.homeoffice.gov.uk/about-us/freedom-of-information/released-information/

The Home Office sets national targets and outlines government policies on policing and reducing crime and provides the bulk of police funding. *The National Policing Plan* 2005–08 sets out the main objectives: http://police.homeoffice.gov.uk/national-policing-plan/policing-plan-2008.html. The Home Office also has responsibility for Prisons and Probation and oversees the Forensic Science Service, the Criminal Records Bureau, the UK Passport Service and the Immigration and Nationality Directorate (see Chapter 4 for obtaining information from the last two agencies).

Intrusive surveillance code of practice – www.homeoffice.gov.uk/security/surveillance. Find out the police policy for wiretapping your house. The police are also supposed to make a record of all authorisations to carry out intrusive surveillance, so you could request these about yourself under the Data Protection Act.

Complaints – there are several documents available (from the website or by contacting the Home Office) that shed light on problems within the police force. One to note is 'Police Corruption in England and Wales: An assessment of current evidence'.

Police pay – all the latest pay scales are publicly available. On the website follow the links to 'Inside the police' > 'Pay and conditions'.

Police reform http://police.homeoffice.gov.uk/police-reform/Force-restructuring and www.policereform.gov.uk. The results of ongoing force restructuring updated here.

Women and minorities in the force – each force has its own breakdown of this information, but national figures are with the Home Office.

National Crime Statistics www.homeoffice.gov.uk/rds/a-zsubjects. html. This link leads to the Research and Development part of the Home Office where you can find an A–Z listing of statistics on everything from arrests to violence against women. General neighbourhood crime statistics are available from the Office of National Statistics by entering your postcode at the website: http://neighbourhood. statistics.gov.uk. In March 2003, the Home Office launched a similar service at www.crimestatistics.org.uk where you can compare local figures to the national average. These are compiled annually and you can only drill down to local authority level.

Research on CCTV www.homeoffice.gov.uk/rds/cctv2.html

Forensic evidence – each force must pay for its own forensic analysis, although some have their own labs. Those that don't, use the national lab, which is run as a quango answering to the Home Secretary.

Forensic Science Service

www.forensic.gov.uk
London Laboratory, 109 Lambeth Road, London SE1 7LP
Operational HQ: Trident Court, 2920 Solihull Parkway,
Birmingham Business Park, Birmingham B37 7YN
Tel: 020 7230 6700
Publication scheme: www.forensic.gov.uk/forensic_t/inside/FOI/class/index.htm

The nation's crime lab provides scientific support for criminal investigations and expert court evidence for both prosecution and defence with clients including the Crown Prosecution Service, the police and the Ministry of Defence, along with foreign and private organisations. The Service also maintains the National DNA Database on behalf of the Association of Chief Police Officers (ACPO). The database, launched in April 1995, holds DNA profiles from anyone suspected, cautioned or convicted of an offence, as well as from the scenes of unsolved crimes. The police have the power to take a non-intimate sample such as a mouth swab and the cells are then analysed to create a DNA profile that is put on the database.

Police forces

There are 44 police forces in England and Wales, eight in Scotland and one in Northern Ireland. Each is under the direction of a Chief

Constable (in London, the Metropolitan Commissioner) who has considerable autonomy over the budget, priorities and activities of the force they command.

The Metropolitan Police is the largest force with a colossal budget of £2.5 billion. Any public authority which spends this kind of public money deserves some close scrutiny.

Metropolitan Police
www.met.police.uk
Public Access Office, 20th Floor, Empress State Building, Empress Approach, Lillie Road, London SW6 1TR
Tel: 020 7161 3500
FOI Officer: Denise Brown, head of Public Access Office
Email: denise.brown@met-police.uk, but send requests to: publicaccessoffice@met.police.uk
Tel: 020 7161 3554/3559

The Metropolitan Police publication scheme follows the model set up by the Association of Chief Police Officers, which most police forces have adopted, so I'll use it to illustrate the kind of information that all police forces should be making public.

Chief Constable's Annual Report – this document gives an overall picture of how your local police force is run, how much money it spends and on what. This should be available online or through the publication scheme.

Policies – these are useful because they state how the police force is supposed to conduct itself: for example, how a force deals with cannabis smokers, Islamic protestors, fox hunters along with guidelines for stop and search or rules for high-speed pursuit. A list of other Met policies can be found at www.met.police.uk/foi/our_policies.htm, though they have refused to release the controversial 'Shoot to kill' policy. The policies of other forces can be found in their publication scheme, online or by contacting the main headquarters.

Minutes from executive decision meetings – these contain discussion about the main issues under consideration and how decisions are made for spending money. An open force will provide an accurate account of these meetings. If the minutes are a page of meaningless jargon, then chances are that the force is not committed to openness.

Recording of stops and stop/searches – stops and searches are controversial as they often imply racial profiling. The Macpherson

Report into the death of Stephen Lawrence recommended that a record should be kept every time a police officer stops a member of the public. Recording and publishing this information is intended to avoid charges of institutional racism and shows a force's commitment to transparency. The Home Secretary has set 1 April 2005 as the date by which all forces should be recording stops. If you are stopped, you should also be given a copy of this record.

Performance figures – number of complaints, gender/ethnicity breakdown – comparison with previous quarter and previous year. These are sometimes also held with local police authorities.

Special Branch. This is a section of the Metropolitan Police Force and is responsible for combating terrorism, extremist activity and other threats to the UK government. Special Branch is also responsible for providing armed personal protection for ministers, foreign VIPs and others at risk from terrorist or extremist attack. They release information on how much this costs, but good luck getting much more from them!

Police authorities

Police authorities make up the third part of the police system. As a form of local government, they must adhere not only to the FOIA but also to the local government access laws. Therefore they must provide a register of members' interests and allow the public an opportunity to inspect all 'orders for the payment of money', which will include any purchases they have authorised, such as guns, cars or other equipment.

Local policing plan – before each financial year, every police authority must issue a plan of how it will police the local area. It includes a statement of the authority's priorities for the year, expected financial resources and how they will be allocated. It also assesses the force's meeting of performance targets and comparisons to previous years.

Other organisations for police information

HM Inspectorate of Constabulary
http://inspectorates.homeoffice.gov.uk/hmic/
Main Office: Ground Floor, Ashley House, 2 Monck Street, London SW1P 2BQ
There are offices in Bromsgrove, London, Wakefield and Woking
Tel: 020 7035 2177
Fax: 020 7035 2176

HMIC publishes a range of detailed inspection reports on police base command units, forces and joint areas, as well as best value and themes such as domestic violence and child safety. It also inspects the National Crime Squad and National Criminal Intelligence Service.

Independent Police Complaints Commission

www.ipcc.gov.uk
90 High Holborn, London WCIV 6BH
Tel: 0845 300 2002 (local rate)
Fax: 020 7404 0430
Email: foi@ipcc.gsi.gov.uk
Publication scheme: www.ipcc.gov.uk/index/resources/foi.htm

Complaints against a police force have traditionally been investigated by another force. This self-regulation has done little to inspire confidence in the quality or independence of investigations. On 1 April 2004, the Police Complaints Commission was replaced by the IPCC. Now all complaints must be recorded by the local police force, and there is a power of appeal by individuals to the IPCC if the police do not do this. The IPCC will have its own team to investigate complaints independently of the police, though many are ex-police officers. The IPCC can require Chief Police Officers to produce or allow access to any documents or material that it calls for. Complaints against police staff and contractors are also covered for the first time. So can you find out which officers have been disciplined? John Tate, the director of IPCC Legal Services, says the organisation will disclose as much as possible to the complainant and other interested parties (such as relatives of a victim), but if outside parties want information they will need to apply using either the Freedom of Information or Data Protection Acts. Complainants are also free to publicise information they receive, although this could mean investigators' reports are edited to avoid jeopardising ongoing investigations. In exceptional cases the IPCC will be able to decide if a disciplinary hearing can be in public.

Other police groups subject to the FOIA:

British Transport Police

www.btp.police.uk
Freedom of Information Manager, 25 Camden Road, London, NWI 9LN
FOI Officer: Paul Crowther, Chief Superintendent Area Commander
Tel: 020 7918 3554

Email: paul.crowther@btp.pnn.police.uk, but requests via: www.btp.police.uk/foi.htm

British Transport Police cover the national railways, London Underground, Docklands Light Railway, the Midland Metro Tram System and Croydon Tramlink.

The Ministry of Defence (MoD) Police
www.mod.uk/mdp
(contact details – Chapter 5)

Offences that occur on MoD property.

Royal Parks Police
www.royalparks.gov.uk/about/police.cfm
The Old Police House, Hyde Park, London W2 2UH
Tel: 020 7298 2000 (general enquiries)
Email: hq@royalparks.gsi.gov.uk
FOI Officer: George Hipwell, Head of Policy
Tel: 020 7298 2008
Fax: 020 7298 2005
Email: ghipwell@royalparks.gsi.gov.uk

The Police Information Technology Organisation (PITO)
www.pito.org.uk
Corporate Communication Team, PITO, New Kings Beam House,
22 Upper Ground, London SE1 9QY
Tel: 020 8358 5555

This is the organisation to contact if you're seeking information about the Police National Computer, the Police National Network and other police IT projects.

Serious Fraud Office
www.sfo.gov.uk
10–16 Elm Street, London WC1X 0BJ
Tel: 020 7239 7493 (switchboard); 020 7239 7000/7190 (general enquiries)
Email: information.officer@sfo.gsi.gov.uk
Publication scheme: www.sfo.gov.uk/publications/publication_scheme.asp

The SFO is an independent government department that investigates and prosecutes serious or complex fraud.

Association of Chief Police Officers (ACPO)
www.acpo.police.uk
25 Victoria Street, London SW1H 0EX

Tel: 020 7227 3434
Fax: 020 7227 3400
Email: info@acpo.police.uk

ACPO Freedom of Information Central Referral Team
Police Headquarters, West Hill, Romsey Road, Winchester,
Hampshire So22 5DB
Tel: 01962 814 730
For national requests or advice: FOI.referral@hampshire.pnn.police.uk
FOI Officer: James Fulton, Chief Inspector, ACPO FOI Central Referral Team
Email: James.fulton@hampshire.pnn

ACPO is a private members' organisation and so does *not* come under
the FOIA, but it is worth mentioning, as ACPO is the coordinating
organisation that links forces across England, Wales and Northern
Ireland and develops common policies, strategies, methods and
operations for all the forces. Its funding comes from a Home
Office grant, contributions from police authorities, membership
subscriptions and profits from an annual exhibition.

In 2004, the first ever *ACPO UK Police Directory* (published by
PMH Publications: www.pmh.uk.com) was released. It is the most
comprehensive sourcebook of police contacts and information
and includes direct telephone numbers to senior officers, maps of
jurisdictions, force organisation structures, and data from non-police
organisations with law enforcement responsibilities such as HM
Revenue and Customs, local government and Trading Standards.

HM Revenue and Customs

Revenue and Customs has two main purposes: to collect certain taxes,
such as duty or VAT, and to protect society from the illegal import and
export of prohibited and restricted goods such as drugs, pornography
and firearms. As part of its law enforcement duties it also works to stop
excise frauds such as alcohol and tobacco smuggling and other tax
fraud such as VAT evasion. The department used to have its own in-
house Solicitor's Office, but it came under criticism for not providing
a thorough and objective review of investigators' evidence. A number
of botched trials involving drug traffickers, smugglers and fraudsters
prompted the creation of the Serious Organised Crime Agency, more
akin to the Federal Bureau of Investigation in the US.

There was a little public accountability in the investigative arm of
the former Customs and Excise. A report by the Office of Surveillance
Commissioners listed 34 instances of 'bad practices' by police and

customs investigators, including spying on suspects and using informants without proper authorisation. Even the report, which was dated August 2003, was secret and only came to light in March 2004 when it was leaked to the media.

In 2004, a string of more than 200 smuggling cases were undermined when an internal Customs document showed that officers had withheld from judges and defence the fact that a crucial prosecution witness was a registered Customs informant.

It is essential that with the increased surveillance powers now available to investigators that there is some level of public oversight to ensure these powers are not being abused. HM Revenue and Customs has refused in the past to make public even its policy on using informants and surveillance.

Getting information about HM Revenue and Customs

Knowledge and Resources Team, Room 2/66, 100 Parliament Street, London SW1A 2BQ
Tel: 020 7147 2412
Fax: 020 7147 2197
Email: ccp.disclosure@hmrc.gsi.gov.uk
FOI Officer: John Sharpe
Tel: 020 7438 7812
Fax: 020 7438 7752
Email: john.sharpe@ir.gsi.gov.uk, but send requests to the email above
Publication scheme: www.ir.gov.uk/enq/index.htm

A good source for information about Revenue and Customs is the Spring Departmental Report that outlines the department's goals, activities and planned spending. How they met these goals and actual spending is outlined in the Annual Report. The Annual Report is a treasure trove of information, especially the appendices which show you how much Customs and Excise raked in from cigarette and alcohol taxes, how many vehicles were seized from tobacco smugglers (8,616), and how many aircraft passengers had to pay duty to Customs officers.

Standards and codes of practice – this charter sets out how the department will conduct itself and standards for dealing with the public. National service standards give an idea of how HMRC performs against certain targets, such as their response to telephone calls, and repaying duty refunds. You can also get a code of practice for when things go wrong, which includes how to make a complaint to HMRC and also to the Adjudicator's Office.

Revenue and Customs Prosecutions Office
www.rcpo.gov.uk
New King's Beam House, 22 Upper Ground, London SE1 9PJ
Tel: 0870 785 8073 (enquiries)
Director: David Green
Email: david.green1@rcpo.gsoi.gov.uk

This is the independent prosecuting authority for cases brought by HM Revenue and Customs.

The Adjudicator's Office
www.adjudicatorsoffice.gov.uk
Haymarket House, 28 Haymarket, London SW1Y 4SP
Tel: 020 7930 2292
Fax: 020 7930 2298
Email: adjudicators@gtnet.gov.uk
Publication scheme: www.adjudicatorsoffice.gov.uk/pdf/publication.pdf

The Adjudicator's Office is covered by the FOIA. It looks at complaints related to delays, mistakes and rudeness, but cannot deal with tax or duty decisions, which are considered by the VAT and Duties Tribunals.

PRISONS AND PROBATION

Prisons are becoming a big issue as the number of people locked up continues to expand beyond prison capacity. The average yearly prison population was 61,900 in 1997 and 74,300 in 2003, with projections that it would rise to 92,400 by 2009. Overcrowding means prisoners must be held in other locations, often at great expense, or released early and monitored. Several high-profile murders in 2005 and 2006 by prisoners on probation led to calls for an overhaul of the probation service. The revelation in April 2006 that 1,023 foreign prisoners were allowed to walk free when they were meant to be considered for deportation cast another shadow on the competence of the Home Office and its ability to manage prisons and probation.

Increasingly, many prisons are privately run and thereby less accountable to the public. The same is true for much of the probation service's electronic monitoring programme. Until these companies are added to the FOIA, the only way to find out about their work is to make an FOI request to the relevant public authority that has contracted out its services.

Cost of police cells

Did you know that it cost about £363 per person per night to hold someone in a police cell in 2002? Booking a room at the Dorchester would be cheaper! The total cost of holding prisoners in police cells in 2002 was £10.4 million.[1]

Getting information about prisons and probation

Want to know how many minorities are in prison or the number of inmates released on home detention? For general statistical information about the prison population contact the **Home Office**.

- *Prisons* www.homeoffice.gov.uk/rds/prisons1.html
- *Probation* www.homeoffice.gov.uk/rds/probation1.html

The Home Office publishes a huge amount of information about inmates (age, sex, ethnicity, religion and offence); sentence length, remands, and non-criminal prisoners; prison population projections; punishments in prison, and figures on the release of prisoners on temporary licence, home detention curfew and parole. A range of research studies are conducted each year, and the Home Office claims most of the results are made public either in reports or shorter four-page 'Research Findings'. You may also be able to get more detailed information if you can prove you are a 'genuine' researcher.

For further information on prison statistics, email to prisonstatistics@homeoffice.gsi.gov.uk, or Tel: 020 7217 5078/5204. For further information on prison research, Tel: 020 7217 8587/8614. If you want to contact someone you think is in prison but aren't sure of their location contact:

The Prisoner Location Service, PO Box 2152, Birmingham B15 1SD.

You must supply the prisoner's full name, details of any known aliases, date of birth, sentencing details (if known) and reason for getting in touch. The service takes about three weeks. If the person is found, your details will be passed on and they will be asked if they want their location details sent to you.

HM Prison Service
www.hmprisonservice.gov.uk
Cleland House, Page St, London SW1P 4LN
Tel: 020 7217 2661/6000
Fax: 020 7217 6403

1. *The Times*, 27 January 2004.

Email: opengovernment@homeoffice.gsi.gov.uk
Publication scheme: www.hmprisonservice.gov.uk/resourcecentre/
freedomofinformation

HM Prison Service is responsible for prison services in England and Wales directly or through private contractors. It answers to the Home Office and employs more than 45,000 people. There are 137 prisons in England and Wales comprising high security prisons, local prisons, closed and open training prisons, young offender institutions (for sentenced prisoners under the age of 21) and remand centres.

For a full list of all prisons go to www.hmprisonservice.gov.uk/prisons or telephone the number above for a hard copy.

HM Inspectorate of Prisons

http://inspectorates.homeoffice.gov.uk/hmiprisons
First Floor, Ashley House, 2 Monck Street, London SW1P 2BQ
To request inspection reports, Tel: 020 7035 2103

The Inspectorate of Prisons is not attached to HM Prison Service but works independently and reports directly to the Home Office. It was established in 1980 to inspect prisons and make recommendations to the Home Secretary, and all these reports are publicly available. The website lists all full announced and unannounced inspections as well as follow-up inspections. The newest reports are mentioned on the 'Press releases' page. The inspectorate also publishes thematic reviews about topics such as women in prison, the inspectorate's aims and functions, structure and responsibility and an annual report. The inspectorate also examines and publishes reports on immigration service custodial buildings which you can find on their website or by contacting the office.

The inspectorate has a staff of about 32 people plus a varying number of outside consultants; some have worked in prisons while others are specialists in areas such as health, education, buildings and farms. The reports do not shy away from criticism and contain many interesting facts. A report in February 2004 of HMP Wealstun in West Yorkshire provides a typical example with the revelation that although all prisoners had signed up to be drug-free, 95 per cent of them told the inspectorate that drugs were freely available in the prison, and some dormitory doors had notices saying 'no salesmen' in order to discourage dealers!

The Prisons and Probation Ombudsman

www.ppo.gov.uk

Ashley House, 2 Monck Street, London SW1P 2BQ
Tel: 020 7035 2876 or 0845 010 7938 (lo-call)
Fax: 020 7035 2860
Email: mail@ppo.gsi.gov.uk

The Prisons Ombudsman publishes an annual report that is a useful source for revealing any injustices occurring within the prison system. The Ombudsman gets about 2,000 complaints annually, of which a quarter result in a full investigation. The Prisons Ombudsman is independent of the Prison Service and investigates complaints from all prisoners in England and Wales about their treatment in prison.

The Prisons Handbook, by Mark Leech and Jason Shepherd (MLA Press, 2003), is an excellent source of information on prisons edited by the founder of UNLOCK, the national ex-offenders charity. It provides a huge trove of interesting facts about all the prisons in the UK including each institution's key officials, the daily regime for prisoners (e.g. '0730 unlock, continental breakfast in cell'), learning and work facilities, religions represented at the chaplaincy, governor's comments, complaints by prisoners and a particularly good section entitled 'Did you know?' highlighting major events or scandals at each prison.

National Probation Service
www.probation.homeoffice.gov.uk
National Probation Directorate, Home Office, Horseferry House,
Dean Ryle Street, London SW1P 2AW
Tel: 020 7217 0659
Fax: 020 7217 0660
Email: npd.publicenquiry@homeoffice.gsi.gov.uk

This division of the Home Office rehabilitates offenders released from prison and those with community sentences and enforces court orders. Overall it supervises about 175,000 new offenders each year with a caseload on any given day of more than 200,000. As of 2006, the Home Office had contracted out the management and enforcement of people on home detention curfew, curfew orders, and electronic monitoring to the following private companies: Serco Home Affairs (Monitoring), Austin House, Stannard Place, St Crispins Road, Norwich NR3 1YF, Tel: 01603 428 300; and G4S Justice Services Ltd, PO Box 170, Manchester M41 7XZ, Tel: 0161 862 1000.

HM Inspectorate of Probation
http://inspectorates.homeoffice.gov.uk/hmiprobation

Second Floor, Ashley House, 2 Monck Street, London SW1P 2BQ
Tel: 020 7035 2203
Fax: 020 7035 2237
Email: HMIP.enquiries@homeoffice.gsi.gov.uk

Has a similar role to the Prisons Inspectorate, but dealing with the Probation Service. It publishes a variety of inspection findings and reports.

The NAPO Probation Directory, edited by Owen Wells (Shaw & Sons, 2006) is compiled by a probation officer and provides names, direct numbers and useful contact information for the probation and prison services.

CORONERS AND INQUESTS

A baby dies in its cot – was it murder or an accident? A suspect dies while struggling with police – an accident or are the police guilty? These are the types of crucial decisions made by coroners every day, and yet families are not given access to essential documents and there has been almost no oversight of coroners themselves. Coroner records are hidden from the public for an amazing 75 years!

Coroners must hold an inquest into all deaths that are violent, unnatural or in prison. In 2005, coroners in England and Wales investigated some 230,000 deaths – nearly 45 per cent of total deaths. Inquests are open to the public, but if you can't attend then the only way to find out what happened is if a newspaper reporter happened to cover the inquest (increasingly unlikely) or if you can prove to the coroner that you have a recognised interest in the case. These interests are laid out in the 1984 Coroners' Rules (rule 20 subrule 2) and in the new Coroner Reform Bill (see below). Families are often badly treated by inquests. They have few rights to information and battle for years to access witness statements, investigation reports, and other written evidence. During a review of the coroner system in 2006, Julie Morgan MP cited as an example a constituent who was still waiting 15 months after the death of her son to know whether or not there would be an inquest.

In 2006, there were 128 coroners' districts in England and Wales, and for no good reason the boundaries were completely different from local or even police authorities. Using FOI, the contact details for coroners were made public for the first time in 2005, and I published the list on the Your Right to Know website. In due course the Coroners' Society followed suit.

Surprisingly, coroners are *not* considered public bodies under the FOIA because they fall under the same exemption as courts, and disclosure of the documents used in coroners' investigations is governed not by the FOIA but by Coroners' Rules. These allow the coroner to restrict disclosure only to those people who have paid the relevant fees and who are defined as 'interested persons', such as relatives, insurance companies, doctors or the police. The coroner also makes the decision as to whether relatives can see the postmortem (autopsy) report. These reports can make uncomfortable reading, but surely the decision to read them ought to rest with the relatives. I read my mother's autopsy report after she died in America and was oddly reassured by the clinical detail in it. I cannot imagine being forbidden the report by someone I'd never met and who never knew my mother, yet this can happen in Britain even with the new reforms.

Another problem can be the difficulty of obtaining medical records of a deceased relative or partner. While the Data Protection Act only covers living people, there are enough exemptions in the FOI Act to prevent disclosure of this material. The way to appeal is to request the records under the Access to Health Records Act 1990, which gives the patient's personal representative or any person who may have a claim resulting from the patient's death, the right to health records relating to the cause of death. That is, unless the record includes a note made at the patient's request that s/he did not want access to be given or the information was provided by the patient in the expectation that it would be kept confidential.

The coroner is an independent judicial officer, qualified as a doctor or lawyer, appointed by a local council and answerable only to the Crown. The Department for Constitutional Affairs is now the sponsoring department for coroners (previously it was the Home Office). The DCA lays down Coroners' Rules, and only the Lord Chancellor can remove a sitting coroner (something which is very hard to do). Local authorities appoint coroners and provide most of the money. The police may also provide money and often an office. Coroners are assisted by coroners' officers who are usually police officers, so you can see the danger that may occur in cases where the death was in police custody. As of 2006, there was no system of inspection or monitoring of coroners and coroners received little professional training unlike other judges, something that they themselves complained about. Instead they learn on the job, without even so much as an induction to guide them. The frightening reality is that a coroner can be appointed by a council one day and be running a major district tomorrow without any training in between! Even the training on offer is extremely limited – a three-day course hosted by the DCA only has room for 150 coroners a year yet Michael Burgess, head of the Coroners' Society, says there are easily 350 coroners and assistant coroners who need training.

Many families, and even coroners, are lobbying for a more open, fair and transparent inquest system. Michael Burgess told MPs in 2006 that 'broadly speaking we have no difficulty at all in putting our hands up and saying reform is needed and the sooner the better'.

Coronial reform

On 12 June 2006, a draft bill to reform the coroner system was introduced. The bill proposed to reform the system in six main ways:

- Bereaved people would have a clear legal standing in investigations and a right to appeal decisions and determinations made by local coroners.
- A Chief Coroner would be appointed by the Lord Chancellor to provide national leadership through unified standards, guidance and support. The Chief Coroner would be accountable to Parliament through the Lord Chancellor.
- Coroners would work full-time and current districts would be streamlined to match other law enforcement boundaries.
- Coroners would have new powers to conduct investigations.
- Coroners would be given better medical support and advice at both local and national level.
- A national Coronial Advisory Council would be created to devise national standards. The DCA says that the Council will include members of the public who have dealt with coroners.

This is all good news and the reforms are long overdue. However, the bill does have some points of concern. It would give coroners new powers to impose reporting restrictions and it would reduce the number of jurors required for a coroner's jury and the circumstances in which a jury is required. The bill was set to move through Parliament by 2007.

Although coroners themselves are exempt from FOI, you can target any public authority they come into contact with. For example, you could send an FOI request to the local council that appointed the coroner for information about the appointment. Some coroners are appointed purely out of nepotism because they are from the same law firm that has held the coronership for generations.

How to get information about coroners

Coroners' Society of England and Wales
www.coroner.org.uk
Coroner locator: from the homepage follow the links 'Public information' >
'Local coroners' offices'

This is a voluntary body and not covered under FOIA.

Department for Constitutional Affairs: Coroner, Burials and Cremations
www.dca.gov.uk/corbur/index.htm
Coroners Division, Ground Floor, 4 Abbey Orchard Street,
London SW1P 2HT
Email: Coroners@dca.gsi.gov.uk
Barrie Thurlow, Coroners, Burials and Cremations Team
Email: Barrie.Thurlow@dca.gsi.gov.uk
Tel: 020 7340 6672; 020 7340 6660 (section switchboard)

The DCA provides policy, practice, training and information about
the reform of the coroners system. There is also a *Model Coroner's
Service Charter* and the Coroners' Rules.

Inquest
www.inquest.org.uk
89–93 Fonthill Road, London N4 3JH
Tel: 020 7263 1111
Fax: 020 7561 0799

This group campaigns for more rights for the bereaved and reform of
the coroners system. Inquest keeps detailed statistics on all deaths in
custody or in prison where information is available. They also keep
information on police shootings and unlawful killing verdicts and/
or prosecutions. You can get these from their website or by calling
the office.

FIRE

In 1987, 31 people died in a fire at the Tube station for King's Cross
St Pancras. The Fennell Report into the fire found that many of the
dangers had been identified earlier in reports by the fire brigade, police,
and Railway Fire Prevention and Fire Safety Standards Committee,
yet they were hidden from the public on the grounds they were
'confidential'. This was one of the cases cited by the Campaign for
Freedom of Information when they began lobbying for a Right to
Know bill.

Amazingly there is still no public right to fire safety inspection reports, and it is unclear whether this will change under the FOIA because of a 1971 law that makes it illegal to disclose these reports to the public. This law is exactly the kind that must be reviewed under the terms of the FOIA, but through an oversight it was not discovered until 2004. The law needs to be repealed or amended to take into account the public interest in knowing the fire safety of buildings because, as it stands, even if you were buying a property, you couldn't find out if it had been cited for fire safety violations without the written permission of the current owner. 'It does actually make one of my officers guilty of an offence that could lead to a fine or jail,' Divisional Officer David Wilkinson of the West Yorkshire Fire Brigade told me.

However, this information could also be classed as environmental as fires directly relate to buildings, land and pollution. As requests made under the Environmental Information Regulations supersede domestic prohibitions on disclosure (see Chapter 10 for more on this), these reports could be released under the EIRs. As of May 2006, I was still awaiting a decision on this very question from the Information Commissioner.

All fire brigades keep records of inspections for hotels, restaurants, theatres, businesses, and so on. Fire services operate on a similar system to police forces, with a fire brigade and a locally accountable fire authority. The central government department with overall responsibility for fire services is the Department for Communities and Local Government. There are big changes coming to the fire services, so it is best to check with your local fire service or the DCLG to see if the changes affect who holds the information you seek. The Fire and Rescue Services Bill controversially called for the greater centralisation of fire services.

Where to get fire information

Department for Communities and Local Government (formerly Office of the Deputy Prime Minister)

www.communities.gov.uk/fireandrescue
Tel: 020 7944 4400 (general enquiries)
FOI Officer: Richard Smith, Information Management Division,
Ashdown House, Victoria Street, London SW1E 6DE
Tel: 020 7944 3146
Email: richard.smith@communities.gsi.gov.uk
Publication scheme: found in the 'Freedom of Information' section online

The DCLG's fire division is likely to increase in size if the fire services are centralised. The link above takes you to the fire page where you can get the latest information about fire reform and fire services. *Fire statistics* are published quarterly in the form of a Statistical Monitor via the DCLG website.

London Fire and Emergency Planning Authority

www.london-fire.gov.uk/about_us/foi/ps.asp
Information Access Team, 8 Albert Embankment, London SE1 7SD
Tel: 020 7587 2000 (switchboard)
Email: info@london-fire.gov.uk

I've used London as an example here to show how the fire brigade and authority fit together, but all other areas are similar. Fire authorities, like police authorities, come under the Local Government (Access to Information) Act 1985 and so must already make a wide range of information public such as minutes, budgets, accounts, and so on. One of the primary sources of fire authority information is the *Corporate Plan*. This is the main planning document and it outlines the authority's goals and objectives for the coming years and how it plans to implement them. It also includes the amount of days lost due to sickness and injury. Buying equipment usually requires fire authority approval and you will find this in the authority's minutes and agendas from meetings. If you are denied this information based on the overused 'commercial confidence' excuse, you should challenge it as the public interest in knowing these costs is likely to override this exemption.

London Fire Brigade

www.london-fire.gov.uk

The London Fire Brigade is run by the London Fire and Emergency Planning Authority (LFEPA) and FOI requests are handled centrally by the authority. The fire brigade is the actual firefighting operation that runs the various fire stations. It holds information specific to local fire stations. It also holds *Prohibition Notices*, which are the record of any buildings or business shut down by the fire brigade for endangering safety. All fire brigades keep lists of prohibition notices but only make public the name on the notice and when it was served. The details of the violation are kept secret. An excellent FOIA request would be to ask your local fire brigade for all prohibition notices in the past year and details of the violations. This is the kind of information that should be readily available on a publication scheme.

Chief Fire Officers' Association (CFOA)
www.cfoa.org.uk
9–11 Pebble Close, Tamworth, Staffordshire B77 4RD
Tel: 01827 302 300
Email: enquiries@cfoa.org.uk

This is the official organisation for principal fire officers in the UK and has a membership of almost all the chiefs in the United Kingdom. Although it is not covered by the FOIA, it is a source of information about the fire services. Importantly, it provides a clickable map on its website to help you find UK fire services in your area.

EMERGENCY PREPAREDNESS (CIVIL DEFENCE)

When the Chief of the Metropolitan Police described a terrorist attack on London as 'inevitable' it suddenly brought the issue of civil defence to the fore. It is in the area of emergency readiness that the culture of obsessive secrecy could directly lead to substantial loss of life because those in charge have the mistaken belief that greater secrecy means greater security. When the London Resilience Forum meets it is in complete secrecy at a top-secret location. 'I'm not able to say whether the response for a catastrophic [attack] is good or not,' the chair of all London's local authority emergency planners, David Kerry, told the *Guardian* (24 March 2004).

On the day of the London bombings on 7 July 2005, Sir Ian Blair told the public almost nothing about what had occurred. Instead, people informed themselves by posting accounts online and through the media. Documents obtained using FOI revealed that there was a breakdown in communications between ambulance staff on the morning of 7 July. Ambulance crews were not contactable once outside their vehicles. There were also delays to ambulances reaching bomb sites and disorganisation about what to do with the walking wounded and where to send patients, with some hospitals being inundated while others were left empty.

Information sharing is crucial to ensure a prepared and coordinated response to any emergency. So it comes as no surprise that the response to the July 7th bombings was chaotic in ways that were preventable, according to the London Assembly's report into the disaster issued in June 2006. Greater transparency in emergency planning ensures that a coherent plan is in place and everyone knows his or her part in it. As it was, police, medics and firefighters couldn't communicate underground, and crews had to rely on runners to send information. This is particularly unacceptable when exactly this problem was highlighted in the 1988 report into the emergency services' response to the King's Cross fire. Even a year after the London bombings, many of these failings had yet to be remedied. And without the pressure of transparency, those in charge can settle back into complacency. Already, the new digital radio network for London's Underground is running behind schedule.

Secrecy means that even those with an important role to play in responding to an emergency are kept in the dark. Doctors from London told *Which? Health* (June 2003) that they were unaware of any detailed procedures to follow for a major bioterrorist attack even though they were essential for containing an outbreak. They also didn't know who to contact in an emergency. 'The Government response should be slickly produced and rehearsed – instead there are haphazard details about who to contact, and what the protocols are. For example, if we come across a case of smallpox we should contact the communicable disease consultant – but we aren't quite sure who that is,' said North London GP Dr Naomi Craft.

The United States takes the opposite approach. The Department of Health and Human Services emphasised in its report on the country's emergency preparedness that information sharing is a key factor in producing effective and efficient emergency responses. The American Centers for Disease Control has a system in place that can connect more than 1,800 public health officials across the country for immediate sharing of emergent public health data, and the Department of Homeland Security conducts live, fully interactive webcast forums with members of the public to share information and discuss emergency plans. The belief is that public scrutiny ensures that any weaknesses in the system are found and fixed and this reassures the public that preparation is the best it can be. Where the American system failed – with Hurricane Katrina – secrecy and information hoarding were to blame.

Until we can find out what systems are in place in the UK, it is difficult to have any confidence that the level of preparedness is as good as it should be. If money is anything to go by, we are not in good shape. Over the past ten years, funding for emergency planning has been cut and the total civil defence grant given to local authorities in 2002/03 was just £19 million. Even after 11 September 2001, local authorities were given no extra funding to meet increased demands for emergency planning. London councils only receive

£80,000, enough for just two staff. The public have a right to know what preparations are in place, the better to judge whether they are effective. This is one area where the Freedom of Information Act may make a difference as the public have a vital interest in the release of this information.

How to find out about civil defence

UK Resilience
www.ukresilience.info

Overall control of UK civil defence is the responsibility of the Prime Minister and Cabinet Office. They have recently made a concession to the public's demand for information and now have a website – 'UK Resilience' – which provides links and information about a range of possible emergencies and crises. The site also provides basic emergency planning guidance and government information.

Who's in charge? – a listing of which department is in charge of various types of emergencies can be found at www.ukresilience. info/handling.htm

Terrorism – the Home Office Terrorism website includes a FAQ section with public advice and information: www.homeoffice.gov. uk/security. The current list of proscribed terrorist groups is at www. homeoffice.gov.uk/terrorism/threat/groups

London – information specific to an emergency in London can be found on the central government site 'London Prepared': www. londonprepared.gov.uk. More information is available from the London Emergency Services Liaison Panel: www.leslp.gov.uk. The website provides an overview of London's emergency services' joint response to major incidents within the capital. You can also download a copy of the LESLP Major Incident Procedure Manual.

9
Health

A culture of secrecy results in most cases in bad policies and distrust of government. In the health services, the consequences are far more serious. Secrecy in healthcare can literally mean life or death. When mistakes go unreported or are covered up, the same bad practices and bad doctors are allowed to continue. Around 5 per cent of the 8.5 million patients admitted to hospitals in England and Wales each year suffer some kind of adverse event that could have been prevented by following proper standards of care.[1] It is estimated that as many as 25,000 people a year may die unnecessarily due to preventable errors in the health services. One inquiry after another has said that greater public access to information and clearer lines of accountability are the main qualities needed for a safer and more effective health service. The Freedom of Information Act and Data Protection Act 1998 are your tools to ensuring the health services deliver on these points.

A culture of 'closed ranks' and a fear of blowing the whistle and naming names has made the National Health Service particularly vulnerable to scandals and malpractice. This was shown in two cases that have had a significant impact in changing the NHS structure. The unusually high death rates of children undergoing heart surgery at the Bristol Royal Infirmary were not investigated for more than a decade even though many people were aware of what was happening. There was no national audit in place to flag suspicious trends and each person involved thought it was someone else's responsibility to deal with the problem. In the meantime, between 1991 and 1995, 30–35 more children under one year old died after open heart surgery than in other comparable units. It wasn't until an anaesthetist at the hospital, Dr Stephen Bolsin, blew the whistle on the whole scandal that the matter was properly investigated. A public inquiry followed, and in the final report Prof. Ian Kennedy wrote in July 2001: 'It is still not possible to say, categorically, that events similar to those which happened in Bristol could not happen again in the UK; indeed, are not happening at this moment.'

1. Bristol Royal Infirmary Inquiry.

It would be nice to think everything has changed. Yet the inquiry into the serial murderer Dr Harold Shipman showed again the deadly effects of failing to collect and share information. The inquiry concluded that Dr Shipman had possibly killed as many as 200 patients while he was a doctor, and despite warnings to police, he was not properly investigated and the unusually high death rate of his practice wasn't picked up until too late.

Even if the system was perfect, the nature of healthcare is fraught with risk. The best physicians and hospitals can make mistakes, but if mistakes and accidents are preventable then every check should be in place to make certain they are prevented. Openness and public accountability are the main safeguards to ensure the system is working properly for the benefit of everyone concerned. Openness means everyone has access to the information they need to monitor the system and make informed decisions, and accountability ensures that when things go wrong, everyone knows whose job it is to fix the problem.

FOI IN PRACTICE

To some extent the NHS has learned its lesson from these tragedies. It has invested a lot of time and money in adopting a more open and transparent system and has actively prepared for the Freedom of Information Act.

Some of the major disclosures resulting from FOI requests in the health sector:

- Scottish surgeons were forced by the Scottish Information Commissioner to publish their mortality rates including each surgeon's name, location and number of operations. The pressure is now on English surgeons to follow suit.
- In February 2006, a report was published detailing life-threatening NHS blunders in 19 health authorities. It revealed how one patient died after air was allowed to enter a vein through a drip, one had forceps left inside, another received the wrong set of lungs during a transplant, a man had the wrong testicle removed and a woman underwent an unnecessary hysterectomy.
- The BBC found that hospitals in England were charging patients up to £1.5 million a year for car parking. The Department of Health figures showed that twelve hospital trusts each raised

more than £1 million in car parking charges. The University Hospital Birmingham raised the most – £1.5 million from fees in 2004–05.

- Incidents of MRSA were made public for the first time. Data from 63 of the 174 acute NHS trusts showed there were 34,432 hospital cases in 2004.
- *Nursing Standard* magazine obtained figures that showed a quarter of student nurses in the UK quit their training courses before they qualified, costing the taxpayer at least £57 million a year.

The new access rights are also highlighting problems where records are not kept or have been lost or destroyed. Haydn Lewis, a haemophiliac who contracted AIDS and Hepatitis C from contaminated blood was waiting for the FOIA to come into force so he could get answers about why the NHS used infected blood to treat his condition. 'There were 49 co-infected people in Wales in 1985. There are 18 left and the widows of those who have died want some kind of explanation,' he told the *South Wales Echo* (23 April 2006). But the Department of Health told him vital documents that could shed light on how 1,200 people came to be infected with HIV through blood were destroyed in a civil service blunder.

The health services make up the bulk of the public authorities to whom the Act applies. The NHS is the largest employer in the world, with 1.3 million staff. Individual doctors, dentists, optometrists, opticians and pharmacists come under the FOI Act, along with hospitals, Acute Trusts, Ambulance Trusts, Mental Health Trusts, Primary Care Trusts, Special Health Authorities, Strategic Health Authorities and the Department of Health. They must all have publication schemes and meet the obligations laid down in the law. In addition, private companies being paid with public funds and performing a public service such as running a hospital, also fall under the Act's purview – making this the first time that citizens have had a statutory right to information from these companies.

One of the main benefits of the FOIA is what's called 'migration of disclosure', which means that once one organisation makes information available, other organisations are pressured to follow. This is most likely to occur where several organisations provide the same services, such as in local government or the NHS. So if Trust 'A' discloses their rate of MRSA infection, the residents served by Trust 'B' will want to know why their Trust doesn't do the same.

The NHS is embarking on a major overhaul of its records systems with contracts now signed to convert all paper records to electronic format. The Secretary of State for Health has promised that every patient in England will have an electronic medical record by 2010 and the records from more than 30,000 GPs and 270 trusts will be unified onto a single secure database. The NHS IT programme will be the world's largest civil computer programme – costing the taxpayer between £6.2 billion and £30 billion (potentially more than twice the cost of the Channel Tunnel). Yet the project was approved in secret at a seminar chaired by the Prime Minister, and Downing Street has consistently refused to release information under FOIA. In the United States, this kind of money would need Congressional approval, but here Parliament was not even told until the programme had been approved. The Department of Health has also been defensive and reluctant to hold an honest conversation with the public about the risks. The FOIA has provided one of the only means of scrutinising the management, scope and cost implications of these massive public projects. *Computer Weekly* was in the process of appealing for the release of the government's Gateway Reviews and Downing Street documents.

ACCESSING PATIENT INFORMATION

Putting all patient information into electronic form could make accessing your own medical records a lot easier as files are less likely to go astray or be spread out amongst various practices. The Data Protection Act 1998 gives every living person the right to access their health records. The DPA replaced the Access to Health Records Act 1990, though that act still governs access to the health records of dead people.

However, two things hinder this powerful right of access: cost and exemptions. It used to cost just £10 to access medical records under the old law, but despite promises by the government that the new law would benefit, not disadvantage, patients, health authorities can now charge up to £50 to give you your records. More disturbingly, the exemptions allow a medical practitioner to withhold information from you and not even tell you they've withheld it. So you may request your file, think you've seen everything and never know that large sections have been censored. The precise terms are that access may be denied, or limited, where the data controller judges that information in the records would cause serious harm to the physical or mental health or condition of the patient, or any other person, or where giving access would disclose information relating to or provided by a third person who had not consented to the disclosure. There is no independent adjudicator to ensure that records are not being withheld merely to protect the practitioner, and many patient groups are lobbying for these obstructions to be removed.

The group Patient Concern is campaigning for free and uncensored patient access. They believe you should not have to wait up to 40 days, pay up to £50, only to find that doctors have removed anything they consider 'harmful'.

Patients can also be barraged with questions about why they want their records from staff who believe the only reason people want their records is so they can sue the NHS, says Peter Walsh, the chief executive of Action Against Medical Accidents. 'You shouldn't ever be made to feel awkward for asking for your medical records. You may want the records so you can get independent advice or perhaps you're just curious.'

You may find your records useful for any number of reasons, but the point is that these are *your* medical records and you do not have to justify why you want them. The unchecked power of practitioners to withhold information goes completely against the government's stated aims of patients' rights and openness. The latest information about accessing your medical records is available online at the Information Commissioner's website www.ico.gov.uk or you can request a leaflet on subject access to health records, by contacting their office.

Not all the information you need will be in your medical record. If you were the victim of some kind of medical malpractice, chances are

---

What is a health record?

- It can be in electronic and/or manual form.
- It is retrospective – you can get records prior to the law's implementation in 2000.
- It includes handwritten clinical notes, correspondence between other health professionals about you, laboratory reports, radiographs and other imaging records such as monitoring equipment, photographs, videos and tape recordings of telephone conversations.
- It applies equally to the private health sector and to health professionals' private practice records.
- It applies to employers' records relating to the physical or mental health of their employees, if the record has been made by or on behalf of a health professional in connection with the care of the employee.

the hospital will have conducted an internal investigation into what happened. Previously, the public had no right to this information, but had to rely on the goodwill of the doctor or hospital concerned and there are powerful motivations for them not to tell you the results of an internal investigation if it proves the doctor or hospital was negligent. A patient's only option prior to FOIA, was to go to court and use the legal process of discovery to access the information. Although there is an exemption for investigations in the FOIA, information should be released if it is in the public interest.

However, new 'reforms' proposed by the government's Chief Medical Officer may eliminate this new right. The reforms 'Making Amends' would make internal investigations privileged information and therefore exempt from all public disclosure laws. Patients would then find it near impossible to prove medical negligence (an already Herculean task). The excuse given for such secrecy is that more people will come forward to report wrongdoing or errors if confidentiality can be guaranteed. If this is really the goal, though, the government could beef up the puny laws that protect whistleblowers. A survey of 704 nurses by the Royal College of Nursing in Scotland showed that 59 per cent felt unable to report concerns publicly, and of these, 42 per cent feared 'damaging repercussions' if they did.[2] Of those surveyed, 10 per cent believed management would do nothing to investigate their concerns. Lack of protection for whistleblowers is the real problem, and yet even now not all NHS Trusts have policies in place to protect those who speak out.

The belief that greater secrecy will somehow improve things should have been buried along with all the victims who have died as a direct result. Total anonymity and secrecy is what we had before, and the result was not a candid flow of reporting and whistleblowers but instead a tragic string of scandals.

NAMING NAMES

Clear lines of accountability and transparency do lead to good practice, yet there is still a reluctance to name names even though anonymity protects bad practitioners at the expense of the public.

The National Patient Safety Agency (NPSA) is perhaps the best example of the belief that secrecy improves safety. It was set up in 2001 at the recommendation of the Bristol Royal Infirmary inquiry

2. *Nursing Times*, 15 March 2004.

to tackle the estimated 850,000 errors occurring every year in NHS hospitals. One of its early aims was to produce a 'blame-free culture' for the NHS. But is this really the answer? The Patient Safety Agency might consider 'blame' a bad thing, but if a surgeon has removed your only functioning kidney, you might think someone ought to take the blame for such actions!

'We all want to make sure that there are no scapegoats in the NHS, that one person at the end of the line is not blamed for the failures of a whole system,' stated Patient Concern, a campaigning group that represents patients, on its website. 'But when professionals are careless or negligent, patients want them to be answerable for their actions. We believe that a "blame-free culture" would remove personal responsibility and accountability.'

Due to the lobbying of Patient Concern, the NPSA changed its goals, but this focus on a 'blame-free' culture is predominant and infects most NHS reforms. The stated goals of the NPSA are to promote a more open and fair culture across the NHS and encourage staff to act as anonymous whistleblowers to report malpractice. Granting anonymity to whistleblowers is one thing, but those reported against are also granted anonymity, thus destroying any chance of holding individuals to account.

The NPSA says it's not its job to investigate; it only monitors performance and 'patient safety incidents' – that's what it calls mistakes and errors. The hope is that its monitoring efforts will prevent another Harold Shipman tragedy, but its effectiveness has yet to be tested, and if it refuses to identify badly performing doctors or Trusts, it is difficult to see how that improves patient safety. The public interest in knowing where the next Harold Shipman is practising is likely to win out over issues of confidentiality.

The new investigation arm of the NHS is the Commission for Health Audit and Inspection (CHAI) and came into effect in April 2004.

The public should be able to easily find out the names of people and institutions that CHAI finds guilty of maladministration or malpractice. But CHAI will not release even this minimal amount of information. Instead, only parties in the case will get a detailed report; the public are left with a meaningless anonymised report bereft of any useful information. This refusal to 'name and shame' is disappointing as naming and shaming is virtually the only power CHAI has to hold individuals and institutions publicly to account. It makes two sets of recommendations: one concerned with redress for the individual and the other for improvement of the services. Neither of these are enforceable by law. A more patient-focused watchdog would also publish warnings and complaints, allowing the patient to decide whether or not the information is relevant. Using the FOIA, you could ask for the detailed reports, warnings and complaints. You may not always get them, but at least the organisation will have to consider whether the public interest is best served by secrecy or openness.

PROTECTING BAD DOCTORS

In the past it has been difficult to get detailed information about individual doctors – exactly the type of information most of us would find most useful. The public had no right to information about complaints or investigations into doctors even when they have been upheld. 'Choosing a doctor can be one of the most important decisions you make, so it's a good idea to know if he or she has been convicted of unsafe practice in the past,' says Peter Walsh.

The General Medical Council (GMC) is responsible for regulating doctors and investigating complaints of malpractice. The main problem in accessing information about doctors' fitness to practise is the total lack of consistency and reasoning regarding the definition of 'public information', a problem endemic in all areas of British public life.

Under the GMC's disciplinary procedures, complaints against doctors or surgeons are not published until they reach a public hearing or a private conclusion, so patients cannot find out if their doctor is under investigation until a lengthy screening process is complete, which the GMC admits can take 15–18 months. Yet some of these complaints are already in the public domain in the form of minutes from GMC meetings. The GMC has admirably decided to conduct its meetings in public (except where privacy or confidence requires an issue to be discussed in closed session) and makes minutes from those meetings publicly available. So you can find information about the investigation by trawling through the minutes, but if you call up and ask if the doctor is under investigation, it may not tell you! A doctor's employer has the right to be informed of all complaints as soon as they are made, yet his or her patients have no right to it until many months later, if at all.

The GMC had to apologise to patients in April 2004 when it came to light that the organisation had not informed the public about a gynaecologist's previous record of serious misconduct in Canada that had led to two deaths. Richard Neale was allowed to operate on patients in the UK from 1988 to 2000 and a string of patients suffered botched operations and lifelong complications. In 2000 Mr Neale was found guilty of 34 acts of professional misconduct and struck off.

The problem of anonymity crops up in the Health Services Ombudsman's investigations where conclusions of serious wrongdoing against doctors or dentists are hidden behind such identifiers as 'Dr Z' or 'Dr P'. In the 2003–04 report, the Ombudsman upheld two serious complaints against a dentist only identified as 'Mr F'. In both cases, the Ombudsman found that the dentist failed to conduct a proper clinical examination of his patients, charged them private rates for services they could have received on the NHS and then charged the NHS for compensation on work he hadn't done.

PERFORMANCE FIGURES

The health system has little need for secrecy. It cannot lay claim to withholding information based on national security, so the only reason to withhold information should be for reasons of patient confidentiality. Yet although the NHS now publishes a range of performance figures and waiting times, these figures are often so anonymised and vague that they are not much use to the people who need them, namely patients. An article in the *British Medical Journal* (17 January 2004) said that patients could not be expected to make informed decisions about the quality of surgeons or operating outcomes because there was such a shortfall of useful data.

Useful, patient-friendly data should be:

1. detailed so you can identify your trust, practice, surgeon, consultant or GP
2. consistent across all trusts so you can make accurate comparisons
3. monitored so you have confidence that the results are an accurate representation of reality.

In all cases, if the information you seek is not provided or is unintelligible, the public authority is under an obligation to assist and help you to understand and locate the information you need under the terms of the FOIA.

Sometimes performance figures are simply wrong. This is the case with Ambulance Trusts where there is a severe lack of accurate and detailed information. Response time figures are often fiddled. The former government health watchdog (the Commission for Health Improvement) found that one-third of Trusts it inspected altered response times to make them look better. Trusts have also inflated their response times by altering the classification of patients from life-threatening to less serious, so some patients may get a slower response than they need. A *Which? Health* special investigation in April 2003 found that 'UK ambulance services are still providing an unacceptably poor service for patients' and estimated that 2,000–3,000 lives could be saved each year if better systems of monitoring were in place. Using FOI, the BBC replicated these findings for other trusts.[3] You probably want to know how well your Ambulance Trust performs. As yet, there is still a dearth of meaningful information. An ideal place to direct a hard-hitting FOIA request.

DRUG SAFETY

The FOIA provides a golden opportunity to finally uncover the shadowy world of drug trials and drug safety in the UK, and this is especially true with the decision in April 2004 to repeal section 118 of the Medicines Act 1968. This draconian law enforced a blanket ban on the release of clinical trial information without regard to the public's need to know. There has always been an overpowering public interest in drugs information being released, but in the past government paid more mind to the interests of drugs companies. Now the balance is shifting in favour of the public.

Pharmaceutical companies may put pressure on the Medicines and Healthcare Regulatory Agency (MHRA), which licenses drugs, to refuse requests about clinical drug trials. However, unless the information is a trade secret or an actionable breach of confidence, it should be released.

The extent of the collusion between the pharmaceutical industry and government drug regulators was laid bare in March 2004 when Richard Brook, the chief executive of the mental health charity Mind, resigned from an expert drug advisory group to protest at what he saw as a cover up of the dangers of anti-depressant drugs. He claimed that the MHRA had known for more than ten years that doctors had been handing out overly high doses of the anti-depressant Seroxat, increasing the risk of suicide especially among young people. As the

3. http://news.bbc.co.uk/1/hi/health/4113624.stm

only 'lay' member of the panel that advises the drug regulator (the rest all had connections with the pharmaceutical industry), he felt the public's interests were being ignored and they deserved to know the facts. In response, he was sent a letter from MHRA warning him that he could be prosecuted under the Medicines Act 1968 for such a disclosure. A number of MPs and health experts called on the government to launch an inquiry and overhaul the drugs regulatory and licensing system but it remains to be seen whether this will happen. 'These revelations [of the Seroxat trials] provide compelling evidence of the need for transparency in drug regulation. Had the evidence from these dose-ranging studies been made publicly available the regulators' errors would have been apparent years ago,' Charles Medawar of the consumer group Social Audit told the *Guardian* (13 March 2004) on the day Mr Brook resigned.

Medawar fiercely criticised the government's drug regulatory system in his book *Medicines Out of Control* (Askant, Netherlands, 2004) as dangerously secretive, riddled with conflicts of interest, and indelibly flawed by chaotic and incompetent procedures for evaluating drug benefits and risks.

Whether or not you agree, the fact is the public have until now had no right to accurate and detailed drug trial data. The drug companies' claim that such secrecy is necessary to protect 'commercial confidentiality' is proved false by the fact that this information is released to the United States Federal Drug Administration when pharmaceutical companies are seeking to sell drugs in the US. Prior to FOIA, this was the only way people in the UK (by filing an American FOI request) could find out information about drugs being taken by British patients.

ACCESS TO MEDICAL INFORMATION

If British patients want access to detailed and thorough medical information, they again have to rely on the openness of the United States. Medline is the world's largest open access database of medical information and is run by the US National Library of Medicine and National Institutes for Health. It is open simply because the US government believes that any information compiled by public servants in the course of their duties or paid for by the public should be freely available to the public. It's a simple principle, but one which British institutions have yet to embrace. So despite the fact that we have the largest healthcare system in the world funded entirely by taxpayers' money, if you want detailed information about diseases, cancer or surgery, the US government provides the most comprehensive resource.

Medline
http://medlineplus.gov

US National Library of Medicine
www.nlm.nih.gov

The British equivalent of Medline is the National Electronic Library for Health www.nelh.nhs.uk. It only has a fraction of the content of Medline and access to most of the information available is restricted to NHS staff. Patient UK, a private company, is also becoming a popular resource. Its website (www.patient.co.uk) provides free, up-to-date health information as provided by GPs to patients during consultations.

There are promising signs that more British institutions are embracing the idea of open access. The Public Library of Science (www.plos.org) was launched in 2004 as a non-profit organisation of scientists and physicians committed to making the world's scientific and medical literature a public resource. The founding ideal is that as most research is already funded by the public via governments or public universities, the public have a right to see the results of the research they have paid for. In June 2004, The Wellcome Trust announced plans for a £1.25 million open access archive of influential medical journals that it will place on the US National Library of Medicine website. Hopefully, these may mark the start of many such projects and perhaps push the UK government toward its own open access projects. Taxpayers' money funds a great deal of research, and it is only right that this be made easily, cheaply and widely available to the public.

WHERE TO GET INFORMATION ABOUT THE HEALTH SERVICES

The following is a breakdown of the major NHS organisations, their purpose and the information they hold.

Department of Health
www.dh.gov.uk
Freedom of Information Unit, Room 363C Skipton House, London SE1 6LH
FOI Officer: Jill Moorcroft
Tel: 020 7972 5872

Email: Jill.Moorcroft@gsi.gov.uk

Publication scheme: www.dh.gov.uk/PublicationsAndStatistics/
FreedomOfInformation/fs/en

Disclosure log: www.dh.gov.uk/PublicationsAndStatistics/
FreedomOfInformation/EreadingRoom/fs/en

The Department of Health is the central government department responsible for the NHS and it makes and implements health policies. It also develops public health campaigns such as those to combat obesity, drunkenness and smoking, and to improve the nation's sexual health. The NHS Plan (available online by searching the Department's website) provides the national strategy for improving health and health services and outlines various targets for specific services. The publication scheme directs you to minutes of meetings, annual reports, policies, public consultations, and internal guidance (such as the Data Protection Subject Access Request Handling Guide). Advertisements for current tenders for government projects are also available online. The Freedom of Information Unit is responsible for overall compliance and guidance on difficult FOI requests within the department. A correspondence management system allows staff to log and track FOI requests.

There is a searchable library of existing tenders and recently awarded contracts available online, which is useful if you want to know where the big money is being spent.

The operation of the NHS in Wales is the responsibility of the Welsh Assembly. In Northern Ireland, the Department of Health, Social Services and Public Safety is responsible for implementing health and community care policy.

There are a number of statistical publications available that can give a general picture of the NHS. You can find these online or by contacting the relevant agency.

Checklist – useful information and where to find it

- Waiting lists – DoH, Trusts
- Hospital episode statistics including individual doctors' success rates – Trusts
- A&E waiting times – DoH, Trusts
- Ambulance response times and clinical outcome statistics – Ambulance Trusts
- Complaints – General Medical Council for medical practitioners, Nursing and Midwifery Council, CHAI for all others
- Inspection reports – CHAI
- Financial information – available in the annual report of the relevant organisation
- Drug safety and clinical trial data – MHRA

- *Health Statistics Quarterly* – the Office for National Statistics
- *Health and Personal Social Services Statistics* – Department of Health
- *Annual Report of the Chief Medical Officer of the Department of Health* – Stationery Office
- *Scottish Health Statistics* – Information and Statistics Division, NHSScotland: www.show.scot.nhs.uk/isd
- *Health Statistics Wales* – National Assembly for Wales.

Health directories

Health directories are useful for finding the name and contact details for all Trusts and healthcare services. The most useful health directory is *Binley's Directory of NHS Management*, which is published three times yearly by Beechwood House Publishing, Essex, www.binleys.com. You can find a copy in most public libraries. It lists all NHS organisations, Community Health Councils/Patient Forums, healthcare interest groups such as charities, and professional associations. Binley's also has a fair amount of financial information, including a useful category on the amount paid out for clinical negligence, so you can see that while Chelsea and Westminster Healthcare NHS Trust spent nothing on clinical negligence, Barts & London NHS Trust racked up £4.755 million. Binley's has an online version but, with a £4,000 subscription fee, few libraries can afford it. If you can't find Binley's, look for the *NHS Directory* (Medical Information Systems), which has basic contact information for all NHS organisations.

The *Institute of Healthcare Management Yearbook* (published annually by The Stationery Office) is another worthwhile directory, particularly for information about independent healthcare providers and hospitals. It also lists NHS organisations with key management contacts, but the independent hospital section is most intriguing as it lists the facilities of each hospital along with single room rates. If you're shopping around for the best deal on a private hospital stay, then this is useful as you'll find that a night at the Priory Roehampton is a bargain at £254, compared to the one in North London which is £477. All are small beans compared to the whopping £625 per night at London's Princess Grace Hospital (prices correct at time of writing).

Strategic Health Authorities

The NHS Reform and Health Care Professions Act 2002 created 28 Strategic Health Authorities, each covering an average population of between 1.5 million and 2.4 million. These manage all the Trusts in their areas and ensure that performance targets are met. The Local Delivery Plan sets out their performance targets and priorities (such as maximum waiting times for planned treatment and A&E admission).

Primary Care Trusts

The 304 Primary Care Trusts (PCTs) make up 75 per cent of the NHS budget and are the main source for patient information. They must publish an annual prospectus that includes local patient surveys carried out by the patient forums, and, from 2003, PCTs and some Care Trusts must create local plans (similar to police authorities' local plans) that incorporate national healthcare priorities with the needs of the local community. These plans are also incorporated into the Strategic Health Authority's local delivery plan. Trusts usually manage between 50 and 100 General Practitioners and healthcare professionals. They decide what health services are needed and are responsible for providing adequate care. This includes making sure there are enough hospitals, surgeons, consultants, doctors, dentists, mental health services, walk-in centres, A&E centres, patient transport, pharmacies, opticians and NHS Direct centres. As such, if you want to know how many surgeons are on call at any one time or any other detailed information about your area or hospital, the local primary care trust is the first place to contact. An Audit Commission's review in 2004 recommended that all Trusts should be publishing more information on quality and outcomes to help enable patient choice and provide greater public accountability.

NHS Trusts

The 273 NHS Trusts are your point of contact for information about most NHS hospitals. They are accountable to Strategic Health Authorities.

Care Trusts

Care Trusts are a collaboration between the NHS and a local authority when the close integration of health and social care is required.

NHS Foundation Trusts

The first Foundation Trusts began operation in April 2004 after their set-up was approved by a slim margin in Parliament. The stated aim is that they will give local communities more power over their health services as they assume direct control of local hospitals, but as patient forums are excluded from Foundation Trusts, this promise rings hollow. A reasonable FOIA request would be to ask for the details of the contracts between your Foundation Trust and the PCT. These should include information about the forecast level of activity and expected cost of health services.

The Healthcare Commission (formal name is the Commission for Health Audit and Inspection)
www.chai.org.uk
Information Access Team, Healthcare Commission, Finsbury Tower,
103–105 Bunhill Row, London EC1Y 8TG
Tel: 020 7448 9200 (switchboard)
Fax: 020 7449 9311
FOI Officer: Natasha Dunkley, Information Access Manager
Tel: 020 7448 4536
Email: natasha.dunkley@healthcarecommission.org.uk, but send requests to:
information.access@healthcarecommission.org.uk
Publication scheme: www.healthcarecommission.org.uk/assetRoot/04/02/26/23/04022623.pdf

The Healthcare Commission is a goldmine of information and is not just useful as a storehouse of facts about the NHS but, importantly, it is one of the few places you can find accurate information about private healthcare. Before the Commission was created, private healthcare was almost unregulated and there is still a dearth of information available about private hospitals, doctors and consultancies. The Healthcare Commission became fully operational in April 2004 after passage of the Health and Social Care (Community Health and Standards) Act. It incorporates the former National Care Standards Commission, the Commission for Health Improvement (CHI) and the Mental Health Act Commission. It also takes over the Audit Commission's work in relation to health services and is charged with inspecting 2,000 hospitals and clinics each year along with private hospitals, psychiatric and maternity hospitals, hospices, doctors' consulting rooms and many clinics that offer laser and pulsed lights cosmetic treatments. These inspections are not currently made public, but because there is a strong public interest, it is worth making an FOIA request for them.

The Healthcare Commission also receives and investigates complaints about the health system, and as such, it maintains records of complaints, action taken and outcomes. Reports of all investigations and panel hearings are available on the website – but these are anonymised. While it's true that some complaints may be unwarranted, why is the balance of protection always weighted in favour of those in authority at the expense of the public? A system that truly believes in patients' rights would seek a more even balance.

The Commission's other role is to look for problems in the NHS and it says it will do this by feeding in anonymised 'baseline reports' into a system and then using 'mechanisms to identify recurring issues or clusters of complaints against a particular individual or department'. These will be integrated with other 'surveillance mechanisms' to flag up problems that warrant further investigation. But it is questionable how effective this will be if data is anonymised.

Health Service Ombudsman
www.ombudsman.org.uk
Ombudsman's Office, Millbank Tower, Millbank, London SWIP 4QP
Tel: 0845 015 4033
FOI Officer: Jane Kennedy
Fax: 020 7217 4000
Email: foi.officer@ombudsman.gsi.gov.uk
Publication scheme: www.ombudsman.org.uk/about_us/FOI/whats_available/index.html

The Ombudsman investigates serious cases of complaints against the NHS where the complainant is unsatisfied with previous action. The Ombudsman makes an annual report to Parliament and this is an excellent source of information. Individual Trusts are named, but individuals are not, except in rare instances where a practitioner has chosen to ignore the Ombudsman's ruling. You can get a copy of the report online or by contacting the office.

Commission for Patient and Public Involvement in Health
www.cppih.org
7th Floor, 120 Edmund Street, Birmingham B3 2ES
Tel: 0121 222 4500
Fax: 0121 222 4511
Email: enquiries@cppih.org
Publication scheme: www.cppih.org/FreedomofInformation.htm

The new Patient and Public Involvement Forums have many of the same legal rights as the old Community Health Councils, such as the right to inspect premises where NHS Trusts and Primary Care Trusts provide services or where primary care is provided, and the right to information from all Trusts and Strategic Health Authorities. They prepare a report on their findings and this is available to the public. The abolition of health councils was rushed through without any public consultation and patients were left without any representation for several months before the new forums took over. 'What does that say about the government's promises about empowering and listening to patients?' says Peter Walsh of Action Against Medical Accidents. 'The way it was handled will continue to dent confidence for years to come.'

Forums must hold open meetings when discussing matters of importance and provide agendas, minutes and background documents. A register should also be kept of members' interests – an important piece of information to ensure that members are representing patients and not the healthcare industry. There is major concern that forums are underfunded, and unlike the old health councils, forums do not have a statutory right to be consulted on major service changes such as proposed hospital closures or to appeal to the Secretary of State if they believe their Primary Care Trust has ignored their views. Community Health councils are still operating, in a revised way, in Wales.

Medicines and Healthcare products Regulatory Agency
www.mhra.gov.uk
Freedom of Information Unit, 9 Elms Lane, London SW8 5NQ
Tel: 020 7084 2729
FOI Officers: Martin Bagwell
Tel: 020 7084 2729
Email: martin.bagwell@mhra.gsi.gov.uk
and, Stephen Wilson
Tel: 020 7084 2852
Email: stephen.wilson@mhra.gsi.gov.uk
Publication scheme and disclosure log available as links from 'Freedom of Information' section of website.

This agency, set up in 2003, is the place to direct queries about the safety of drugs, equipment and medical devices. This includes the safety of hip replacements, breast implants, pacemakers, prostheses, and so on. The agency gathers facts from a variety of sources and can prosecute manufacturers if they fail to meet standards, although typically enforcement is not rigorous. In 2001, DePuy International had to recall hip joints after they were found to be faulty, despite being approved by the MHRA. Patients in the UK cannot directly report problems they've experienced with drugs or equipment to the regulators, but have to do so via their doctor.

National Institute for Clinical Excellence (NICE)
www.nice.org.uk
MidCity Place, 71 High Holborn, London WC1V 6NA
Tel: 020 7067 5800
Fax: 020 7067 5801
FOI Officer: Julian Lewis, FOI compliance manager
Email: julian.lewis@nice.org.uk
Publication scheme: available online under 'Publications'

This public body is responsible for appraising the latest technologies, techniques and treatments for the NHS and it is their advice that determines what the NHS buys and uses. As such it is the authority that will decide whether local health trusts should provide Herceptin to patients with early stage breast cancer in England and Wales. It is also worth keeping an eye on the interests of board members to ensure business is not funnelled to particular companies where they have something to gain. NICE produces guidance for the NHS in England and Wales. NHS Quality Improvement Scotland and the Scottish Intercollegiate Guidelines Network produce guidance for the NHS in Scotland.

REGULATION OF HEALTHCARE PROFESSIONALS

If you want to know if your individual doctor, dentist or other healthcare practitioner has been censured or warned for misconduct, contact their regulatory body. If they won't tell you, then file an FOIA request. All UK healthcare regulatory bodies come under the FOIA. You can also make a request to the Trust that employs that person. Historically, healthcare regulators have been unnecessarily secretive, but they are beginning to open up their disciplinary proceedings.

General Medical Council (GMC)
www.gmc-uk.org
Regent's Place, 350 Euston Road, London NW1 3JN
Tel: 0845 357 8001
Fax: 020 7915 3641

FOI Officer: Andrew Ledgard
Tel: 020 7189 5418
Email: foi@gmc-uk.org
Doctor's registration: www.gmc-uk.org/register
Publication scheme: www.gmc-uk.org/publications/right_to_know/
publications_scheme.asp

The GMC is the regulating body for the medical profession in the UK. As discussed earlier, it already publishes the minutes of its meetings and final results of investigations. 'The mood is toward greater transparency,' Michael Cotton, the GMC's planning development manager in the Fitness to Practise Directorate, said in 2004. The GMC has changed its rules for disclosure and there is now a greater emphasis on publishing more information. New changes to the law were planned for 2006/07 that would give the GMC a 'duty to publish' various types of information.

You can check a doctor's registration online, though this information is provided for guidance only and is not the legal register. The GMC states that the absence of a record does not necessarily mean that the doctor is unregistered. For further information about a doctor's registration you can call 020 7915 3630 or email to registrationhelp@gmc-uk.org

General Dental Council
www.gdc-uk.org
37 Wimpole Street, London W1G 8DQ
Tel: 020 7887 3800
Email: information@gdc-uk.org
Publication scheme: www.gdc-uk.org/News+publications+and+events/
Publications/

All dentists, dental hygienists and dental therapists must be registered with the General Dental Council to work in the UK, but this self-regulating body falls short of the standard set by the General Medical Council. The Health Ombudsman's 2003–04 report highlighted three complaints made against dentists who unscrupulously charged NHS patients private rates without telling them. The Office of Fair Trading conducted a survey and found that just 21 per cent of the 749 practices it visited published their charges. The Consumers' Association filed a 'super-complaint' against dentists and the OFT's resulting report in March 2003 concluded that the GDC's standards are neither routinely monitored nor enforced and that NHS patients do not get the information they need about prices or how to find an NHS dentist. As the private dentist business expands, there is an increasing need for patients to have access to detailed information about dentists. You can search the GDC register online and telephone the office for further information.

There is a definite need for more detailed public information about dentists, and as the General Dental Council is classed as a public body under the terms of the FOIA, this should provide the opportunity to get it.

The Nursing and Midwifery Council
www.nmc-uk.org
23 Portland Place, London W1B 1PZ
Tel: 020 7637 7181 (switchboard)
Fax: 020 7436 2924
Registration enquiries: Tel: 020 7333 9333
Publication scheme: follow links on website

All nurses, midwives and health visitors must be registered with the Nursing and Midwifery Council to practise in the UK. The Council sets standards for education, practice and conduct, and investigates allegations of misconduct or unfitness to practise due to ill health. You can find detailed information about the recruitment of foreign nurses, and the popular destinations of British nurses in the Statistical Analysis of the Register. Performance figures available online also show staff turnover and how quickly complaints are investigated.

Royal Pharmaceutical Society of Great Britain
Pharmaceutical Society of Northern Ireland
www.rpsgb.org.uk
Information Access Team, 1 Lambeth High Street, London SE1 7JN
Tel: 020 7735 9141
Fax: 020 7572 2499
FOI Officer: Susan Em, Records Manager
Tel: 020 7572 2212
Email: Susan_Em@rpsgb.org.uk, but send requests to: infoaccessteam@rpsgb.org
Publication scheme: www.rpsgb.org/members/society/index.html

Only those on the register of pharmaceutical chemists can practise. You can search the register online by the name of the pharmacist or premises. The Society also publishes online the names of members investigated for complaints by the disciplinary committee: www.rpsgb.org.uk/members/statutorycommittee

The General Optical Council
www.optical.org
41 Harley Street, London WIG 8D3
Tel: 020 7580 3898 (switchboard)
Fax: 020 7436 3525
Email: goc@optical.org
FOI Officer: Philip Ireland, Director of Corporate Resources
Email: pireland@optical.org
Publication scheme: www.optical.org/index_files/news_room/news_3.asp

The professional body that regulates optometrists (ophthalmic opticians) and dispensing opticians in the UK. You can search the register online by practice number or surname. A summary and full transcript of 'fitness to practise' hearings is also available online and it identifies those investigated.

The Health Professions Council
www.hpc-uk.org
Park House, 184 Kennington Park Road, London SEI I 4BU
Tel: 020 7582 0866
Fax: 020 7820 9684
Email: info@hpc-uk.org
Registration: Tel: 0845 300 4472
Fax: 020 7840 9801
Email: registration@hpc-uk.org

The Health Professions Council is covered by the FOIA. It sets and monitors standards for other health professionals such as arts therapists, biomedical scientists, chiropodists/podiatrists, clinical scientists, dietitians, occupational therapists, orthoptists, paramedics, physiotherapists, prosthetists and orthotists, radiographers, and speech and language therapists. The Register can be searched online or in person by going to Park House. The Register is stored electronically and there is not a hard copy, so you will be given access to a computer or a member of staff can search for you.

The Council for the Regulation of Health Care Professionals
www.crhp.org.uk
1st Floor, Kierran Cross, 11 Strand, London WC2N 5HR
Tel: 020 7389 8030
Fax: 020 7389 8040
FOI Officer: Julie Stone, Head of Policy and Fitness to Practise
Email: julie.stone@crhp.org.uk
Publication scheme: follow links online to 'Publications'

The regulator of the regulators! The Council was set up in April 2003 to address concerns that self-regulating organisations such as the General Medical Council favour their fellow professionals over patients and don't enforce their standards rigorously enough. However, the Council has little power. Instead, its main purpose appears to be to ensure consistency among all the regulatory organisations and to report on their activities to Parliament so it can hold them to account. Patient groups have expressed concern that it also fails to cover unregulated practitioners such as complementary therapists. The Council is a public body as defined by the FOIA.

In addition to these regulatory bodies there are other professional organisations such as the British Medical Council (for doctors) and the British Dental Association, but these are voluntary organisations that lobby for their members and as such do not fall under the remit of the FOIA.

10
The Environment

In the past few decades, people have become increasingly concerned about the air they breathe, the water they drink and the overall quality of their environment. Tougher laws introduced in 2005 make it harder for governments and private companies to suppress environmental information, but excessive fees, restrictive government copyright and secrecy are hindering the public's new right to know.

The BSE crisis clearly showed how secrecy extended and escalated the seriousness of the epidemic, yet there are enough exemptions in the current access laws to allow the government to cover up any future crisis in exactly the same way. The ownership of land is still far from transparent with fees restricting access to a full account of 'who owns Britain'. Inspections of restaurants and food businesses are now being published, but in piecemeal fashion. There is still no clear statutory right for the public to see all food hygiene inspections, so we remain in the dark about the quality of those places in which we eat and shop.

All environmental information is exempt from the Freedom of Information Act and access is governed instead by the Environmental Information Regulations 2004. Why two systems? Because the government had to concede that the FOI law did not provide enough freedom of information to meet European Union requirements for openness. Instead of beefing up the FOIA, politicians decided to create another law, and another layer of bureaucracy.

The Environmental Information Regulations (EIR) are the implementation in UK Law of an EC directive on accessing environmental information, in much the same way that the Human Rights Act was the UK's version of the European Convention on Human Rights. Initially, the plan was to integrate the requirements of the European law with the new Freedom of Information Act, but it soon became clear that the FOIA not only failed to protect the access rights required by the new EC directive, it didn't even guarantee the same access rights granted by the previous EC directive passed a decade earlier! The Department for the Environment, Transport and the Regions (which later became the Department for Environment, Food and Rural Affairs) insisted that environmental information be removed from the Freedom of Information Act and then took charge of drafting its own access regime for environmental information to meet the demands laid out in the directive.

The upshot is that you should avoid the FOIA where you can and request information using the Environmental Information Regulations. It is a much better law and places more value on the public's right to know. The definitions of 'environmental information' and 'public authorities' are sufficiently broad, so you can use the EIR for a wide range of topics, including transport and energy policies.

EIR IN PRACTICE

Not a lot of people know about the Environmental Information Regulations. They're the shy sister of flashy freedom of information, which gets all the publicity. Even the UK Information Commissioner seems unfamiliar with the law, as he mistakenly issued a judgement on an environmental complaint citing the Freedom of Information Act. The EIR does give the public more rights to information than the FOIA, so it's worth having some knowledge of the law to increase your chance of successfully getting the facts you need. It may not be clear which law is best, in that case I recommend you use both and see how the public authority responds.

Some of the major environmental disclosures using the access laws:

- Detailed accounts of EU farm subsidies.
- A previously secret list drawn up by Nirex, the radioactive waste management agency, of sites that were considered for Britain's long-term nuclear waste dump in the 1980s. The shortlist of twelve sites were abandoned in 1997 but could re-emerge as potential candidates.
- Food hygiene inspection reports.
- In Birmingham, residents won compensation from the council after their MP used the access laws and discovered that houses were built on a former metal tip and the gardens poisoned with chemicals including arsenic and cadmium.[1]

Campaign group Friends of the Earth has been the primary organisation using the EIR to date. They are mainly pleased with the law and their solicitor Phil Michaels says they are seeing information

---

1. *Birmingham Mail*, 9 February 2006, 'Relief over plans for toxic land'.

that they would never previously have seen. 'It's certainly better than the old system,' he said, illustrating the point with a letter dated April 2004 that read simply: *The information relating to the closure of Drumshambo Landfill site is not available for release to the general public. Yours sincerely...* 'That should not happen now. It sometimes does, but we would pull them up on it. A public authority must give a reason under the law if they want to withhold information.' Some information that was once only supplied by Friends of the Earth such as 'Factory Watch' is now available online through the Environment Agency.

Obstacles to the law's effectiveness mirror those with the FOIA: delay and weak enforcement by the UK Commissioner. Of 108 requests made by Friends of the Earth in 2005, 81 involved public authorities who failed to respond within 20 working days. Of those, 27 gave no explanation for the delay. Also, exorbitant charges plagued early requesters. However, this should start to change as a result of the Tribunal ruling in *David Markinson* v. *Information Commissioner* that set strict limits on the amounts public authorities can charge for environmental information (see Chapter 1). Another obstacle is restrictive copyright, particularly for address and mapping details. The main way to display and use environmental information is by linking it to geospatial data such as maps. Yet Crown Copyright restricts the free use and reuse of this information even though it was created at public expense (see Chapter 3 for more on restrictive copyright).

There are many areas to investigate using the EIR – it's virgin territory just waiting to be discovered! The public knows very little about pesticide testing, agriculture run-off, land-use planning, GM crop trials, and the impacts from industry – particularly fishing, off-shore mining and quarries.

While environmental information is exempt from the FOIA, the process for appeal and enforcement is the same as for the FOI law.

Why Environmental Information Regulations are better than the FOIA

1. Requests cannot be denied on the basis of cost as with the FOIA.
2. There are no absolute, or 'blanket', exemptions.
3. There are fewer exemptions, and these are narrowly prescribed and must meet a public interest test.
4. Requests can be made verbally, not just in writing.
5. The exemption for commercial confidentiality must meet a stronger harm test.

The Regulations have been constructed to encompass the strengths of the FOIA so requests must be answered in the same time – 20 days (though there is an allowance to extend this to 40 days if the authority satisfies itself that the request is overly complicated). If your request is denied you have the right to appeal to the Information Commissioner. All the exemptions must meet a well-defined public interest test.

You can technically request environmental information using the FOIA even though it is exempt under section 39 because public authorities have the power to disclose whatever they want – all exemptions are discretionary. But in most cases it will be to your advantage to use the EIR instead.

Lewis Baker, the Freedom of Information Officer at DEFRA, advises that if in doubt, it is best to err on the side of the Regulations. 'We want to make it easy for people. In most cases it won't matter what law they use because if the information can be released then the procedure for staff is the same for either law. The differences will arise when someone does *not* want to release the information. Then they'll find that the EIR requirements for openness are more stringent than the FOIA. So in that sense, the EIR is better.'

A brief history of accessing environmental information

- 7 June 1990 – Council Directive 90/313/EEC on the freedom of access to information on the environment passed. The Environmental Information Regulations 1992 are the UK version of the law.
- Aarhus Convention, 1998 – all member states and the EU signed an agreement on the Convention on Access to Information, Public Participation in Decision-making and Access to Justice in Environmental Matters, more simply known as the Aarhus Convention. The three main objectives of the convention were to make environmental information more widely and easily available to the public, to give the public greater access to justice in environmental matters, and to provide the public with specific rights of access to environmental data held by authorities. It provides more liberal definitions of what is a public authority and environmental information, includes a harm test, narrows the exemption for commercial confidence and gives a right to have refusals reviewed.
- Environmental Information (Amendment) Regulations 1998.
- 28 January 2003 – the EC integrated and expanded on the Aarhus requirements to sign into law Directive 2003/4/EC.
- 22 July 2004 – the new draft Environmental Regulations introduced for public consultation.
- 21 December 2004 – EC directive transposed into UK law with passage of the Environmental Information Regulations (EIR).
- 1 January 2005 – EIR comes into force.

Is access to environmental information a human right?

The Aarhus Convention (see box on previous page) is remarkable because it places great value on the public's ability to easily access information. It doesn't raise the issue to quite the level of a fundamental human right, but it is a step in that direction.

One particular case has paved the way for this new rights-based way of looking at public access to information. In *Guerra* v. *Italy*[2] the applicants lived next to a highly toxic factory that had previously exploded causing widespread poisoning to locals. Residents tried for years to get information about the factory's emissions and safety procedures from the local authority but were constantly denied access. The applicants then took the case to the European Court of Human Rights. The court ruled that their right to a private and family life under Article 8 of the European Convention on Human Rights had been breached because they were denied vital information for so long. However, the case does imply that the right to information is not guaranteed – it only applies where information is so vitally important that to refuse it would infringe on some other fundamental human right such as the right to stay alive!

It would be better if you didn't have to prove your life was in danger to get information, but the ruling does imply that an authority has an obligation to disclose information that could affect public health or interfere with any of the fundamental rights laid out in the Human Rights Act.

What's new about the Environmental Information Regulations?

- A reduction in response time from two months to 20 days (though it can be extended to 40 for complex requests).
- The requirement of a public interest test for all exemptions (there are no absolute exemptions).
- A wider definition of what is 'environmental information' includes radioactive waste, biodiversity and genetically modified (GM) organisms.
- Expanded legal definition of organisations subject to EIR – includes organisations that provide public services in relation to the environment, such as private waste contractors.
- You can appeal to the Information Commissioner if your request is denied.

WHO IS SUBJECT TO EIR?

The EIR is a tougher law, but who is subject to it? One of the easiest ways for an authority or company to wriggle out of their duties is to

2. (1998) 26 EHRR 357.

claim the law does not cover them. That is what happened under the previous regime. The Campaign for Freedom of Information reported that requests made using the 1992 Regulations were often not complied with because 'certain bodies advanced the most distorted accounts of their functions in order to circumvent the... definitions'.

If the spirit of the EC law is adopted then private companies that perform public functions would be included. However, public utility suppliers are inclined to believe that they aren't covered by the new regulations. For example, do water companies provide a public service in relation to the environment? Most of us would say 'yes', but the water companies do not always agree, though Friends of the Earth report that water companies are increasingly accepting that they are covered by EIR.

The definition of a public authority is laid out in Article 2(2) of the EC directive. It includes government, public administration and public advisory groups at national, regional and local level, including those that do not have specific responsibilities for the environment. It also includes individuals and other groups performing public administrative functions or providing public services in relation to the environment. Some in the legal profession[3] believe that 'public administrative functions' clearly includes private companies that have some public administrative functions imposed on them, and the explanatory notes to the EC law also give a further indication that privatised utility companies should be included.

The Campaign for Freedom of Information lobbied for private companies to be specifically included to avoid utility companies using the ambiguity as a means of exempting themselves from their responsibilities to disclose information. On the other hand, the vagueness could also be used to *extend* the definition so that possibly even airlines, rail operators or other public transport companies could be covered.

Industry and purely private companies will likely argue that they have no public administrative functions and it will be harder to prove they are subject to the law even though industry has an enormous impact on the environment. In these cases, you can also make requests to the various oversight agencies that regulate emissions into the environment. All discharges into water courses, for example, must be registered and approved by the Environment Agency.

3. 'Freedom of Environmental Information: Recent Developments and Future Prospects' by Daniel Wilsher in *European Public Law*, Volume 7, Issue 4, December 2001.

Any ambiguity in the law will have to be clarified by case decisions made by the Information Commissioner, Information Tribunal and courts. In the meantime, you have nothing to lose by making EIR requests to any agency you think remotely applicable.

AVAILABILITY OF INFORMATION

The law requires those who hold environmental information to proactively make it public; this would ideally be done by putting in on the internet. Many companies and bureaucrats complained that this would cost too much, even though they could give no figures estimating the amount. The government let them off the hook by saying only that a public authority 'should' take reasonable steps to organise environmental information with a view to making it public. They don't have to. And they could meet these obligations through existing public registers.

WHAT IS ENVIRONMENTAL INFORMATION?

Environmental information includes anything to do with the atmosphere, water, soil, land, landscape and natural sites, biological diversity and its components, including genetically modified organisms, and the interaction among these elements. It also includes factors affecting the environment such as energy, noise and radiation. An important addition includes activities or measures, including administrative measures, environmental agreements, policies, legislation, plans and programmes, affecting or likely to affect the environment, along with cost-benefit and other economic analyses and assumptions used in environmental decision-making.

The inclusion of 'cost-benefit and other economic analyses' is very broad and could include any government policy that affects the environment where economic calculations are made, such as transport and energy policies. These definitions are explained in Article 2 of EC Directive 2003/4/EC. The full text of the new Environmental Information Regulations can be found on the DEFRA website listed below.

EXCEPTIONS

As stated earlier, the directive, and therefore the EIR, has no blanket, or absolute, exemptions, giving it a major advantage over the Freedom of Information Act. There are 13 main categories of exemption that are called 'exceptions', but they can only be used to withhold information if it is in the public interest. The law states the exceptions must be interpreted restrictively. The exemptions are laid out in Article 4 of the EC Directive and Part 3 of the Environmental Information Regulations.

1. *Personal information in accordance with the Data Protection Act* – see Chapter 14 for more about what constitutes personal information. The definition is currently defined very narrowly to include only that individually identifiable information which adversely affects a person's privacy.
2. *Information not held* – information is exempt if it is not held by or for the authority. But if the authority knows where it is, then it should either transfer your request to that authority and inform you of this or tell you where to send your request.
3. *Manifestly unreasonable* – this could include requests that place a substantial and unreasonable burden on resources.
4. *The request is too general* – but the authority should tell you of this as soon as possible and help you to narrow your request.
5. *For future publication* – if an authority uses this exemption they must tell you the name of the authority preparing the material and the estimated time of completion.
6. *Internal communications* – this is an overly broad exemption widely open to abuse. It is being used with gusto by secretive public authorities.

For the following exceptions to be used, an authority must also show that the disclosure would produce some harm or 'adverse affect':

7. *Confidentiality of proceedings* – only where confidentiality is required by law.
8. *International relations, public security or national defence* – public authorities have been known to abuse this exemption. Friends of the Earth report a council using this exception to refuse the release of a tree-felling contract!
9. *Investigation and justice* – information can be exempt if it would stop someone getting a fair trial or hinder an authority's ability to conduct an inquiry. Once the investigation or trial and appeals are over, the exemption no longer applies.
10. *Breach of confidence* – similarly to the FOIA, this only applies to information that is a *legal* breach of confidence. Emission

information can override commercial interests and confidentiality if it is 'relevant for the protection of the environment'.
11. *Intellectual property rights.*
12. *Information supplied voluntarily* – but what this also means is that information that was *not* supplied voluntarily (i.e. it was legally required by the public authority such as safety trial data) is not subject to an exception.
13. *To protect the environment* – such as the location of rare species.

AGRICULTURE AND LAND

Land subsidies

Up until passage of the EIR and FOIA, government agencies had refused to reveal the amount of public subsidies paid out to large farmers. In Britain, the European Common Agricultural Policy subsidies are worth £3.5 billion. Oxfam conducted a large-scale research project to investigate subsidy transfers based on land ownership and found the richest landowners were receiving the biggest handouts of taxpayers' money in the form of subsidies.

'In no other sector do taxpayers spend so much and have so few rights to information about the use of their money,' an Oxfam spokesman said (press release, 22 January 2004). 'This raises fundamental questions about transparency and accountability in the use of taxpayers' resources.'

The Duke of Westminster, who is Britain's richest man with assets totalling £5 billion, receives £1,000 a day in subsidies. It is doubtful the public approve of their money being distributed in such a way. But to change policy, people needed facts. They finally got some in 2005 when the Rural Payments Agency released details that showed Oxfam was right. The biggest subsidies went to royalty, wealthy aristocrats, and huge agribusinesses such as Nestlé, Unilever and Tate & Lyle. Small farms get next to nothing. We can now have an informed debate about the allocation of these subsidies.

Across Europe, citizens are trying to get their own governments to release this information. The cost of the subsidies are close to €43.5 billion a year, more than 40 per cent of the EU's entire annual budget. This works out at about €100 a year for each EU citizen! So the figures published in England (Scotland and Wales were refusing to release the names of recipients at the time of going to press) are just the tip of the iceberg. A collective of interested journalists and citizens have created a farm subsidy project intent on gathering all this data across the EU. See: www.farmsubsidy.org

Land registration

The Land Registration Act 1988 allowed the public to access the land register for the first time, ending centuries of secrecy about land ownership. Although the majority of landowners are registered on the Land Registry, there are a few who are not, and these people happen to own quite a lot of land. These are the aristocratic landowners, like the Duke of Westminster and the royal family, who conduct their business in relative secrecy. You can conduct a search of the land register online at www.landreg.gov.uk

DISEASE

The BSE crisis is an example of the enormous costs and tragedy that can result from withholding information from the public. The public inquiry found that the government's failure to release accurate and timely data to the public was directly responsible for extending the crisis. Vets and farmers weren't given vital information about what symptoms to look out for in their cattle or told about the seriousness of the problem until it became such a huge catastrophe that the government could no longer hide the truth. The FOIA was spurred into existence in part by this inquiry, so it's ironic that almost all of the data so vitally needed during the BSE crisis could still be withheld under the many exemptions of the FOIA – a clear indictment of the weaknesses of the Act. However, the government would find it much more difficult to withhold the data under the Environmental Information Regulations.

AIR

The public have been able to access pollution registers since the passage of the Environmental Protection Act 1990. That's not to say that the authorities that hold these registers have publicised them, and often the only way to inspect them was to make an appointment and visit the register in person. That is starting to change and more registers are being put online, but this should be followed through with educating the public about how to use them and making them more user-friendly. Your local authority is responsible for local air quality and will hold a public register of air-quality readings. Other registers are available from the Environment Agency (see below).

The UK National Air Quality Information Archive
www.airquality.co.uk

This is an excellent website that provides access to the archive of Air Quality Bulletins. These hourly updates of air pollution figures are derived from the UK's automatic air quality monitoring network. There are over 1,500 sites across the UK that monitor air quality. The website allows you to choose your location by clicking on a map. It shows where the data is collected (including a photograph) and provides air-quality data by the hour and week for that area. You can retrieve statistics back to 1960.

National Atmospheric Emissions Inventory (NAEI)
www.naei.org.uk

You can find emissions data about greenhouse gases and pollution from airports on this website. It is not as user-friendly as the air-quality information archive, but it does provide a lot of advice about how to find emissions data.

WATER

Water companies spend vast amounts of public money, have powers of taxation (water rates), and build reservoirs and sewage works. They also control trade effluent into public sewers in England, Wales and Scotland. Despite all this they are not considered a public authority under the FOIA and it is unclear whether they are covered by the EIR. Many water services were privatised in 1989. At first, regional boards included members of the local community, but over the years that requirement has vanished, leaving water company boards much like any other corporate board of directors, with no public representation.

Water companies and agriculture are responsible for the majority of serious water pollution incidents, according to the Office for National Statistics. In 2002, the Environment Agency investigated 866 pollution incidents that had led to a serious impact on water.

Seawater

Accurate and detailed information about pollution in the sea has always been difficult to ascertain due to the difficulties of monitoring and enforcing dumping restrictions. It is easier to control and monitor the amount of waste being discharged from a landmass. Around the UK coast, certain areas have been designated as bathing areas and the EC Bathing Waters Directive sets pollution limits. For the latest pollution data from these areas visit www.seasideawards.org.uk or www.blueflag.org

Where to get water information

Ofwat
www.ofwat.gov.uk
Library and Information Services, Office of Water Services,
Centre City Tower, 7 Hill Street, Birmingham B5 4UA
Tel: 0121 625 1373/1361
Fax: 0121 625 1400
Email: enquiries@ofwat.gsi.gov.uk
Publication scheme: www.ofwat.gov.uk/aptrix/ofwat/publish.nsf/Content/pubshome

Ofwat is the economic regulator for the water and sewerage industry in England and Wales and it is your main source for information about private water companies as it is covered by the FOIA. The most useful information it holds is:

- *Directors' Register* – this includes every water company's licence, information about terminations, transfers or conditions of a licence, any changes to the service area, and enforcement orders.
- *Leakage performance* – Ofwat collects data and publishes details of companies' leakage performance in a press notice each July. A report titled 'Security of Supply, Leakage and the Efficient Use of Water Report' follows later in the year.
- *Price setting* – Ofwat publishes the results of customer research that it uses to make pricing decisions.

Consumer Council for Water (formerly Water Voice)
www.watervoice.org.uk
Victoria Square House, Birmingham B2 4AJ
Tel: 0121 345 1017
Fax: 0121 345 1010
Email: central@watervoice.org.uk

The Consumer Council for Water represents the customers of water and sewerage companies in England and Wales. Of most interest is the database it holds about complaints made about water and sewerage companies. Minutes of their meetings are available online.

FOOD

The food safety and labelling regimes in the UK suffer from the usual bureaucratic problems of poor leadership and lack of transparency. Although we are the ones who eat in restaurants, we cannot easily see restaurant inspections! It is also difficult to get detailed information about the ingredients and processes used in the manufacture of that food. A good example of a consumer-centred regime is found in any state government in the US. San Francisco, California offers a comprehensive yet simple website for searching hygiene reports: www.dph.sf.ca.us/eh/Violations/Loc_Search.asp

Food hygiene reports are obviously in the public interest, so councils look foolish refusing such requests. But that doesn't stop some of them: Norwich City Council refused a request from the *Eastern Daily Press*, but when the paper ran an article slamming their secrecy, the council backed down and disclosed all the records.

Councils conduct thousands of inspections a year, and each one can be a multi-page form, so it's wise to narrow your request. Councils keep a listing of all food premises by risk category. It is now fairly common to get the electronic database of a council's food premises categorised by risk that lists the business address, inspection date and food risk category for all food premises inspected. Risk is categorised from A to F with 'A' being the highest risk. With such data, it then becomes possible to target all high-risk food premises for further investigation.

There are two types of inspections – food standards and food hygiene. Food standards cover the labelling and composition of food. Food hygiene deals with the cleanliness of venues, storage of food and hygiene of staff. In a city like Birmingham there are about 5,000 food hygiene inspections a year. So unless the council proactively makes these public (and few do), you need to specify which of these reports you want.

There is no central agency in charge of overall monitoring and regulatory enforcement of food safety. The Food Standards Agency is the most likely candidate but it lacks any real power to act for the public. And what little power it has, it doesn't always use. For example, the FSA refused to issue any guidance to councils about publishing their food hygiene inspection reports even though its guiding principles are: 'putting consumers first, being open and accessible, and being independent'. The reality is that the FSA U-turned on its proposal to introduce a national register of food business convictions and it has failed to push for public access to food safety inspections.

Local authorities are charged with monitoring food safety in their areas, yet they are loathe to make it fully transparent to the public. This means we don't have a list of all the manufacturers who are guilty of labelling food incorrectly. And local councils have few inspectors for the number of businesses they are meant to regulate, so inspections can be infrequent. Until the UK has a transparent and publicly accessible system, the public's health is not being adequately protected.

WHERE TO GET INFORMATION ABOUT THE ENVIRONMENT

Department for Environment, Food and Rural Affairs (DEFRA)
www.defra.gov.uk
3–8 Whitehall Place, London SW1A 2HH
Tel: 020 7238 6000
FOI officer: Lewis Baker
Tel: 020 7238 6591
Email: lewis.baker@defra.gsi.gov.uk, but send requests to: accesstoinfo@defra.gsi.gov.uk
Publication scheme: www.defra.gov.uk/corporate/opengov/pubscheme/index.htm
Disclosure log: www.defra.gov.uk/corporate/opengov/inforelease/index.htm

DEFRA collects a huge amount of information, and because it is one of the more open departments, a large proportion is already public. The publication scheme contains major publications as well as internal administrative policies, annual reports and business plans for the entire department. If you don't find what you need in the publication scheme, try the Information Asset Register, which is a comprehensive list of all published and unpublished data held by DEFRA. A roundup of the main environmental statistics can be found in the Digest of Environmental Statistics available on the website or by contacting DEFRA: www.defra.gov.uk/environment/statistics/

DEFRA and its associated quangos collect information about all manner of environmental issues: agriculture (for example, GM crops), disease control (the foot-and-mouth or BSE crises), farms, woodlands, forestry, organic farming, pesticides and plant health. It is also the UK department overseeing the EU Common Agricultural Policy and Common Fisheries Policy and holds data on dairy produce quotas, fisheries, the horse industry, flood and coastal defence, veterinary medicine, climate change, biodiversity, radioactive substances and environmental waste.

Waste information is divided between DEFRA and local authorities. The UK produces more than 400 million tonnes of waste each year according to the Office for National Statistics. Most is from agriculture, industry or construction, but household waste makes up a good portion. Contact your local authority for local figures, and DEFRA if you want national data or information about waste policies.

In Wales, the implementation of environmental policies and programmes is being devolved to the National Assembly for Wales. The Scottish Executive and Scottish Parliament oversee environmental policies in Scotland.

DEFRA sponsors a number of government groups. The main ones that hold information of interest are listed below and they are all subject to both the FOIA and the Environmental Information Regulations. A fuller listing of all the associated agencies and bodies can be found on the DEFRA website and publication scheme.

The Environment Agency

www.environment-agency.gov.uk
Tel: 08708 506 506 (general enquiry line)
Email: enquiries@environment-agency.gov.uk
FOI Officer: Chris Jarvis
Tel: 01454 28 44 26
Email: Chris.Jarvis@environment-agency.gov.uk
Publication scheme: follow the links to 'Freedom of information'

The Environment Agency is charged with protecting and improving the environment, which involves regulating and controlling pollution, managing water resources and improving flood defence. The Scottish Environment Protection Agency (SEPA) carries out these functions in Scotland. The agency is one of the best public authorities for the amount and user-friendliness of the information it provides, though none of its main registers were fully online in summer 2004. The most noteworthy examples of easily accessible information are the online environmental guidelines for small businesses ('NetRegs'), the flood-warning and advice service ('Floodline') and best of all:

- *What's in Your Backyard* – this popular database allows users to examine pollution sources and data by specific area. You'll find the database under the heading 'Your environment' from the homepage. The information is also available from your local Environment Agency office. For the location of your nearest office, call the number above or check the website.
- *Local Environment Agency plans* – these public documents highlight the main environmental issues in local areas and the Agency's plans for addressing these issues over a five-year period.
- *Water quality and pollution control register* – all effluents discharged into water must be approved by the Environment Agency (and regional equivalents). They issue a consent and then monitor the water quality. Information about water quality, performance and compliance, authorisations for discharge and monitoring is available for public inspection, though not yet online.
- *The Register of Radioactive Substances Information* – this gives details for all applications for registration or authorisation including supporting material such as maps and photographs. Again, this ought to be online but is currently only available for inspection in hard copy.

Centre for Environment, Fisheries and Aquaculture Science

www.cefas.co.uk

Lowestoft Laboratory: Pakefield Road, Lowestoft, Suffolk NR33 0HT

Tel: 01502 562 244

Email: lowlibrary@cefas.co.uk

Publication scheme: www.cefas.co.uk/publications/scheme

Conducts environmental research and monitoring for fisheries management and aquaculture health and hygiene. This is the place to go if you want detailed information about the health and safety of fisheries. There are three laboratories: Lowestoft, Suffolk; Weymouth, Dorset, and Burnham, Essex.

Pesticides Safety Directorate

www.pesticides.gov.uk

Mallard House, Kings Pool, 3 Peasholme Green, York YO1 7PX

Tel: 01904 640 500

Email: information@psd.defra.gsi.gov.uk

Publication scheme: online under 'PSD publications'

Responsible for ensuring the safe use of pesticides. The Directorate is under tremendous pressure from the pesticides lobby not to release environmental information. In 2002, Aventis Crop Science (now owned by Bayer), the maker of a controversial weedkiller, and the pesticides industry's trade body, the Crop Protection Association, took the Pesticides Safety Directorate to court over its decision to release information to Friends of the Earth. The environmental charity had made a request for company data on the environmental effects of the weedkiller using the 1992 Environmental Information Regulations. There was concern even among government scientific advisors about the potential for the weedkiller chemicals to wash away in heavy rain and pollute surface or ground water.

Pesticides manufacturers are required to submit a number of scientific studies to the Directorate during the approval process and DEFRA's position was that this information was not subject to a blanket commercial confidentiality as the public has an interest in knowing the safety of products. They argued that information is only exempt if a company can prove release would cause actual commercial harm. DEFRA and Aventis settled out of court in spring 2003 and Aventis agreed to let Friends of the Earth inspect the documents at its office. You may be able to get more of this type of information by making a request using the new EIR.

Rural Payments Agency
www.rpa.gov.uk
33 Kings House, Kings Road, Reading, Berkshire RG1 3BU
Tel: 0118 958 3626
Send FOI requests to: Customer Relations Unit, Rural Payments Agency, PO Box 69, Reading RG1 3YD
Tel: 0118 9531 282
Fax: 0118 9393 817
Email: customerrelations@rpa.gsi.gov.uk
Publication scheme: available online but only by searching the website

Responsible for all payments under the Common Agricultural Policy (CAP) in England and some throughout the UK. The site has information about the various allowance and quota schemes.

Veterinary Laboratories Agency
www.defra.gov.uk/corporate/vla
New Haw, Addlestone, Surrey KT15 3NB
Tel: 01932 341 111
Fax: 01932 347 046

The VLA is the agency charged with protecting the public from another foot-and-mouth epidemic. Its stated aims are to protect public health, prevent farm animal disease and promote animal health and welfare by delivering high-quality veterinary surveillance, research and laboratory services.

Veterinary Medicines Directorate
www.vmd.gov.uk
Woodham Lane, New Haw, Addlestone, Surrey KT15 3LS
Tel: 01932 336 618

Responsible for licensing and regulating all animal medicines including those in feedstuff. As part of this remit, it is also charged with protecting consumers from any potentially hazardous residues in food.

Food Standards Agency
www.food.gov.uk
Corporate Secretariat, Consumers and International Division,
Aviation House (Room 615c), 125 Kingsway, London WC2B 6NH
Tel: 020 7276 8000 (switchboard)
FOI Officer: Steven Johnson
Tel: 020 7276 8664
Email: Steven.Johnson@foodstandards.gsi.gov.uk
Publication scheme: www.food.gov.uk/aboutus/how_we_work/foia/100025
Disclosure log: www.food.gov.uk/aboutus/how_we_work/foia/foirelease/

The FSA was set up in 2000 by an Act of Parliament to protect public health and consumer interests in relation to food. As such it is responsible for national food safety and standards. It sets targets for reducing food poisoning, promotes healthy eating campaigns, food labelling, promotes best practice within the food industry and is charged with improving the enforcement of food law. Local authorities enforce food safety laws in two areas: trading standards (labelling of food, its composition and chemical contamination); and environmental health (food hygiene, microbiological contamination, and food unfit for human consumption).

The FSA does require each local authority to send in reports of their total inspections and other visits to food premises, the total food samples taken, and the numbers of formal enforcement actions taken (ranging from written warnings to prosecutions). However, these are generic statistics and do not give the most vital information the public needs to know – the names of the businesses! In the case of food poisoning, complaints are usually dealt with by the local authority in which the food business operates.

The Food Standards Agency is the main organisation collecting data on BSE: www.food.gov.uk/bse/facts. Other publicly available information includes a list of incidents worldwide, breaches in BSE controls in imported meat, results of testing, and an annual report on the findings of specified risk material in imported beef and sheep meat. There is also a section devoted to GM crops, though it is not particularly detailed.

The Food Standards Agency oversees a number of advisory boards that provide more detailed information about particular foods or food processes. The FSA publication scheme lists the latest contact details for all these boards. Agendas, minutes and background information from the boards are publicly available on the FSA website for the following advisory committees:

- Advisory Committee on Animal Feeding Stuffs
- Advisory Committee on Microbiological Safety of Food
- Advisory Committee on Research
- Consumer Committee
- Committee on Toxicity of Chemicals in Food, Consumer Products and the Environment
- Meat Hygiene Advisory Committee (MHAC)
- Meat Hygiene Policy Forum (MHPF)

Natural England (amalgam of The Countryside Agency and English Nature)

www.countryside.gov.uk
John Dower House, Crescent Place, Cheltenham GL50 3RA
FOI Officer: James Paterson, Records and Information Rights Manager
Countryside Agency
Tel: 01242 521 381
Email: foi@countryside.gov.uk or info@countryside.gov.uk

English Nature

www.english-nature.org.uk
Northminster House, Peterborough PE1 1UA
Tel: 01733 455 100/101/102
Email: enquiries@english-nature.org.uk
FOI Officer: Darren Green, Corporate Data Manager,
Information Delivery Group
Tel: 01531 638 513

Fax: 01531 638 501
Email: darren.green@english-nature.org.uk

The Countryside Council for Wales
www.ccw.gov.uk

Scottish Natural Heritage
www.snh.gov.uk

The Countryside Agency and English Nature were set to merge by 2007. The contacts for both are above as it was unclear which section would be handling freedom of information. Natural England will take over the duties that were formerly split between the two groups. The organisation is responsible for implementing the Countryside and Rights of Way Act 2000 that gives the public greater access to open country and registered common land – the right to roam. There is a website portal devoted to land access in England: www.openaccess. gov.uk/wps/portal. Campaigners were lobbying for similar access to rivers – a right to paddle. The British Canoe Union states that canoeists only have an automatic right of access to just 2 per cent of waterways.

English Nature's share of responsibilities included promoting wildlife conservation and the preservation of natural features in England, Wales and Scotland. Council papers and minutes are freely available and council meetings are open to the public.

Forestry Commission
www.forestry.gov.uk
Silvan House, 231 Corstorphine Road, Edinburgh EH12 7AT
Tel: 0131 334 0303
Email: enquiries@forestry.gsi.gov.uk

Manages nearly 1 million hectares of public forests throughout Britain. The service is devolved so responsibility for English, Scottish and Welsh forests rests with each government.

11
Local Government

'It is but a small portion of the public business of a country which can be well done, or even safely attempted, by the central authorities.'
John Stuart Mill

Local governments conduct more types of business than most multinational corporations. From housing and planning to council tax and rubbish collection, we are all affected in some way by local authorities. Councils in England spend over £91.9 billion of taxpayers' money and employ more than 2 million people. Add another £5.7 billion for Wales. With such a large budget of public funds, it's worth keeping an eye on how your local council is spending its share. Are you getting value for money? If not, you'll need access to information to find out what's going on and how to improve matters.

Although local authorities have been subject to their own FOI law for two decades, vital information is consistently not made public. Trading Standards Officers investigate businesses for trade violations, yet the public are refused access to the results. Hearings to consider pub licences or planning applications are frequently held behind closed doors. Environmental Health Officers inspect restaurants and takeaways for food hygiene violations, yet their reports are not easily available. Major decisions on redevelopment are made in secret cabinet meetings where the public and even other councillors are excluded.

The Local Government Act 2000 handed councils secrecy on a plate under the guise of 'reform'. Instead of becoming more open, the law brought in new cabinet-style councils. Decision-making power was taken away from open committees and given to mostly single-party cabinets.

No surprise then that by 2005, regional daily and weekly newspaper editors ranked secrecy among public bodies of high or very high significance.[1] Why should this affect you if you're not a journalist? Firstly, when a reporter can't get into a council meeting, he can't

---

1. The Newspaper Society survey 'The Challenge for Freedom of Information, Press Freedom Survey', released 17 February 2005.

report to the public what happened. Secondly, when someone employed to find out information has trouble getting it, the rest of us will likely find it even more difficult.

The astounding level of paranoid secrecy and obstruction operating in some local authorities constantly surprises me. Councils have had decades to get used to openness and yet it seems to have made no difference to their attitude toward the public. A radical shift is needed if councils are to retain public trust.

FOI IN PRACTICE

Local councils are receiving more FOI requests than any other type of public body. As a result there are literally dozens of stories a week in the local press resulting from FOI requests. Some of the more noteworthy disclosures include:

- Contractual details and financial information about a super casino at Birmingham City Stadium. In what was believed to be the first legal challenge of its kind, Las Vegas Sands tried to stop the council releasing the documents under FOIA, but failed after the High Court refused the appeal.
- Parking enforcement contracts, revealing incentive packages to boost ticketing
- Councillors' expenses and use of council mobile phones
- Cost of consultants
- Minutes and documents from closed council meetings
- Restaurant inspections

But even these cases where the public interest is obvious had to be fought. The *Birmingham Post* newspaper had two cases awaiting a decision from the Commissioner: Solihull Council's refusal to release documents relating to the £100-million redevelopment of Shirley town centre, and Birmingham City Council's demand for £9,000 to release details of taxi and first class train journeys made by staff and councillors. The paper argued in the latter case that it was wrong for the council to pass on the cost of making the council accountable to the taxpayer. Tony Lennox, acting editor of the *Birmingham Post*, said: 'Details of spending on travel by a local authority are of obvious public interest and ought to be freely available. The media cannot be held to blame because Birmingham City Council has no proper system of recording journeys by staff and councillors.'[2]

2. *Birmingham Post*, 2 February 2006, 'Ruling on council's Information Act bill'.

The Birmingham fees case highlights the way FOI saves the taxpayer money and as such is a cost worth bearing. A battalion of consultants or regulators would doubtless have charged the taxpayer even more to highlight this inefficiency! Instead, FOI gives every citizen the opportunity to scrutinise.

Lydia Pollard from the Improvement and Development Agency (IDeA) told MPs that FOI, 'has raised information management and records management much higher up the agenda for local authorities'. She said councils are now 'valuing their information and thinking much more carefully about how they can make best use of it. That in turn has a very positive knock-on effect for service improvement.'[3]

A brief history of accessing local government information

- **Public Bodies (Admission to Meetings) Act 1960** – Margaret Thatcher introduced the first 'freedom of information' law for local authorities in 1960. It gave the public a right to attend council meetings of local authorities, including parish and community councils, unless 'confidential' information was discussed – then they were automatically excluded. There does not have to be any consideration of the public interest to close the meeting.
- **Local Government Act 1972** – gave the public an additional right to attend council committee meetings, but the previous exclusion of the public and press applied if 'confidential' information was discussed.
- **Local Government (Access to Information) Act 1985** – this Act updated the 1972 law to include subcommittees to the list of council meetings open to the public and press, and gave a right of access to reports held by the authority where the report and related documents are to be discussed in a meeting, unless the information is exempt or confidential. It also replaced the blanket 'confidential' information with exempt information, and the exclusion of the press and public was no longer automatic but had to be formally proposed, seconded and voted upon. The council's word alone was no longer enough to prove an item was 'prejudicial to the public interest'; it had to give an actual reason usually referring to a section of the Act.
- **Local Government Act 2000** – this law changed the structure of local governments from committees and councils to an executive that mirrored the structure of central government with an all-powerful mayor and/or cabinet working with political advisors. Decision-making was transferred from council and committees to the executive (the mayor, and/or cabinet, cabinet leader, council manager or council officer). A few councils still operate under the old system, but the majority have adopted this 'modern' arrangement. The previous FOI laws only provide access to meetings of the council and its committees and subcommittees, not to the cabinet. Therefore, the public's ability to see and influence decision-making has decreased. Initially, New Labour provided no new public rights to information and held that local government executives should be

▶

---

3. 28 March 2006 – uncorrected transcript of oral evidence, published as HC 991-ii.

able to make their decisions in secret – just like the central government Cabinet. After sustained criticism, a new concept was invented – 'key decisions'. Where a decision is held to be 'key' it should be taken in public, though what constitutes a 'key decision' is open to interpretation. The decision can still be held in secret if it meets the exemptions.

Current rights

1. Local authorities must provide access to reports, agendas and background papers used in meetings five days in advance.
2. Local authorities operating under the new executive system must provide a forward plan to the public that sets out the key decisions to be taken in the next four months and list related background documents.
3. Cabinet meetings where a 'key decision' will be discussed or taken must be open to the public (however, the definition of what is a 'key decision' is left to individual authorities to determine, allowing ample scope for inconsistency and secrecy).
4. Councils must produce a record of all decisions taken, key or otherwise, and the reasoning behind them.
5. Your rights to parish and community council meetings are slightly different, governed by the 1960 and 1972 laws. You have a right to attend and get the agenda and minutes for all full council and committee meetings, but not subcommittee meetings (though it's unlikely a parish will have subcommittees). Background documents do not have to be given out by law, but often are in the interest of open government.
6. In all local authority structures, the budget and policy framework must be set by the full council meeting in public.

In addition to the FOIA, there are a handful of separate, older laws that deal specifically with the public's right to attend council meetings and access relevant information. Some of these laws give the public greater rights than the FOIA, such as the right to background information about major decisions or to inspect the council's accounts prior to an audit. But in other ways, the laws are more restrictive; for example, when councillors decide to close a meeting to discuss exempt or confidential information, they do not have to consider the public interest.

In some situations, local authorities can close a meeting based on a 'confidential' document that would have to be disclosed under the FOIA. What cannot happen is that information available under one law will be denied because of another. Instead, you can use whichever law offers the best access.

It's important not to get too concerned with which piece of legislation you use to gain access to local authority information. All you have to do is ask in writing for the information. You do not have to explain how the laws give you the legal right to make a request: the FOIA is in place automatically without mentioning it and the local authority is responsible for abiding by all the laws that affect it, so it cannot refuse to give you information to which you have a statutory right.

You might think that having been subject to FOI legislation for so long (the first Open Access law was in 1960), councils would be an example of openness and at the forefront of preparation for the new Act. This is not the case. The Local Government (Access to Information) Act 1985 sets out the main rights the public have to attend council meetings and access relevant information from those meetings. It updated an earlier Local Government Act from 1972. However, there is widespread concern, especially among regional newspapers, that councils do not always observe these laws and frequently close meetings for spurious reasons.

'We have reports that councils will often slip in a confidential piece of information just so they can have the meeting closed,' says Santha Rasaiah of the Newspaper Society. The most common reasons for denying information to the public are for reasons of 'commercial confidence' or an incorrect interpretation of the Data Protection Act where whole documents are suppressed just because they mention someone by name (see Chapter 14 for more about proper use of the Data Protection Act). Residents trying to find out why their local leisure centre is being closed or why the council has chosen one company over another to collect rubbish, previously had no way of challenging council decisions to go into closed session. The FOIA should help to provide greater access to this information, but the problem of being shut out of meetings will remain until the laws governing access to the decision-making process are amended.

Publicity is one way of shaming councils into openness. More than 70 local residents in Sheffield objected to the construction of a large statue of the Buddha in the town, but after sitting through two hours of a meeting in May 2004, the council told them the Buddha debate would happen in closed session and they were kicked out. After the ban was publicised in the media, the Sheffield council admitted it had been wrong to ban the press and public from the debate.

GOING BACKWARDS, NOT FORWARDS –
LOCAL GOVERNMENT 'REFORM'

As stated previously, the new executive arrangements laid out in the Local Government Act 2000 significantly changed the way local councils operate. The stated goal of the new system was to provide clarity as to who was responsible for making decisions. Many local authorities have upwards of 50 councillors and numerous committees, so there is validity in the point that the decision-making process was murky and cumbersome. It may be right to have a smaller group in charge, but there is no benefit to the public if these people are all from the same party and their decisions are made in secret. If only six people have any real power in a council then let's just have six councillors and save the money spent on the other 45 who sit around shuffling papers.

The Local Government Act also created scrutiny committees in an effort to provide some means of challenging the executive, but in reality these committees have little power and are often ignored by the mayor and/or cabinet. According to a study by the Economic and Social Research Council, many local scrutiny committees lack power to properly oversee and question cabinet proposals. Prior to the FOIA, members of scrutiny committees only had a right to documents containing exempt or confidential information if the information was defined as 'relevant' to their work as scrutinisers. And the people who decide this are the same people the scrutiny committee is meant to be scrutinising. Again, why are we paying for all this official oversight? Save the money and hold the meetings in public.

Political advice

The 2000 law created a new exemption for the advice of party political advisors or mayor's assistant. Even the scrutiny panel cannot access information prepared by these advisors, creating another level of unaccountability and secrecy. It is now possible for an executive to make a decision based entirely on the suggestion of an advisor and neither the scrutiny committee nor the public could access this information.

The good news is that the Freedom of Information Act makes it more difficult to justify this secrecy. Although there are exemptions for information used to formulate policy (section 35) and information that would prejudice the effective conduct of public affairs (section 36), both these exemptions must satisfy a public interest test for the information to be withheld.

Key decisions

Key decisions must be taken in public. A key decision is defined as an executive decision that is likely to:

1. result in the local authority incurring spending or savings that are significant in relation to the authority's budget for the service or function to which the decision relates, or
2. be significant in terms of its effects on communities within two or more wards in the area of the local authority or electoral divisions.

Although key decisions are central to the operation of local authorities, their definition is scrupulously ambiguous, leaving it up to individual councils to decide for themselves what constitutes a key decision. The danger is that an executive will simply not define a decision as 'key' if it wants to conduct a debate about it in secret. A better and far simpler system would be one that allows public scrutiny for all decisions.

Secret cabinet meetings

Even in those instances where the cabinet must meet in public, the chance of a full public debate is often stifled because the main players have already made their decisions at a secret meeting. In London's Tower Hamlets, a Leader's Advisory Board, consisting of all cabinet members and the corporate management team, meets prior to the public cabinet meeting. Even if this group is not technically breaking the law (that is, it is not formally a decision-making body), the Audit Commission said in a 2002 report that there is a danger the meeting 'could be seen as a "secret" cabinet meeting which inappropriately excludes the wider council' – not to mention the public! The minutes and papers from these meetings are considered confidential and information presented in them is not listed in the background material for items on the cabinet agenda.

Is your council doing this? One way to find out is to go along to a cabinet meeting. If it's over in less than an hour with no real discussion, then the chances are the real decisions were made beforehand in secret. In Tower Hamlets, some meetings are over in 15 minutes, even before all the opposition or the public have arrived!

Commercial confidentiality

While the government's favourite catch-all phrase for denying information is 'national security', local government can hardly claim to be handling state secrets. Though they do try! A request by Friends of the Earth for a road bypass contract with particular reference to the terms and conditions concerning bats was rejected by Buckinghamshire Council on the grounds that to release such information would be a danger to national security: 'there is a likely possibility of harm from demonstrations to all concerned'.

A more common blanket refusal used by councils is 'commercial confidentiality'. Under local authority legislation, a small piece of commercially sensitive information was enough to close an entire discussion and prevent the public from seeing whole documents. Under the FOIA, the commercial confidence exemption must include both a public interest and a harm test. Also, whole documents cannot be suppressed, but rather the sensitive information can be removed and the rest of the document must be released.

If a public service is contracted out by a local authority, then that authority is deemed to 'hold' the information, said Graham Smith, Deputy Information Commissioner. This is a contentious area, though, and may have to be settled by court cases. The local authority can consult the third party, but if the information is not exempt it must give you the information even if the third party would prefer to keep it secret.

WHAT YOU CAN GET

Accounts and audits

One of the most powerful rights of access comes under the Audit Commission Act 1998. It gives local council taxpayers a right to view all the accounts and accompanying documents for the annual audit for 20 full working days. This includes the right to inspect all books, deeds, contracts, bills, vouchers and receipts relating to the audit. You also have a right to make copies of any part of the accounts and these documents.

By the end of June each year, most larger councils finish preparing their accounts for the financial year ending on 31 March. Local councils have until 30 September to approve their accounts, so look out for an advertisement in your local paper around this time or call the Treasurer's department for the exact dates. This is one of the best ways to get information and certainly sheds light on dodgy dealings, though often too late to stop bad projects going through. For example, if citizens had been able to access Lancaster City Council's finances before the final audit, they may have been able to halt a £2 million council-funded theme park in Morecambe that closed its doors just 13 weeks after it first opened. The Audit Commission found the council behaved in an imprudent, irrational and unlawful manner for pushing through and publicly funding the Crinkley Bottom Theme Park. That's money that could have been much better spent elsewhere.

The Audit Commission Act allows for no exemptions for commercial confidentiality, and is therefore one of the only ways the press and public can find out about a council's full dealings with private companies.

For more information about your rights to see and question council accounts visit the Audit Commission's website: www.audit-commission.gov.uk/reports

Annual report

You can study a council's annual report either in person or electronically. An annual report should consist of a presentation of the council's budget and overall financial position – how much they spent, on what and where that money came from. If you've never investigated government financing before, this is a good place to start as you can see more directly the money you put in (through council and income tax, rent, service charges and other fees) and where it goes. Once you've done this exercise, you'll get an idea of how governments manage money and may want to find out the same figures for other authorities.

Councillors' interests

Every authority must establish and maintain a register of councillors' interests according to law. Ideally this should be online or at the very least in an authority's publication scheme, but councillors often vote against such openness, so you may need to call and find out where the register is kept – it is usually held by the Monitoring Officer. The Local Government Act 2000 also introduced a Code of Conduct for councillors and gave the Standards Board for England responsibility for enforcement (Wales has its own). Interests must be registered within 28 days of election and any changes made within the same period. The code requires that councillors must declare:

- employment and business interests
- election expenses
- financial interests where holdings are greater than £25,000 or 1 per cent of issued share capital
- land owned, leased or rented for more than 28 days in their authority's area

- membership of or offices held at companies, charities, trade unions and professional associations. In January 2004, the Standards Board for England added freemasonry to this list.

Councillors must also specify their interests during meetings where there may be a conflict with an item on the agenda. One problem with the current law is the high threshold – £25,000 per shareholding – so many interests go unrecorded. Councillors must also declare any personal interests, and this includes links not only where they personally could be seen to gain but also relationships with friends, family and partners.

Allowances and expenses

Councillors are not employees of the council and do not receive a salary. However they do get allowances and expenses, and these can often be significant amounts of money. All councils must publish details of their payment schemes and the amount each member receives annually. The latest legal regulations governing the allowance system and payment panels are available by searching the website of the Department for Communities and Local Government for 'Members' Allowances'.

All councillors are eligible for a basic allowance, so it might be worth requesting councillors' attendance records to see how many meetings they actually attend. A growing number of councils have stopped their attendance allowances in favour of a beefed-up basic allowance, decreasing the amount of administrative paperwork but also the incentive for some councillors to turn up to meetings. The amount of allowances claimed by each councillor must be sent to the local media each year. The online site IDeA Knowledge has also begun compiling a database of allowances across councils, so you can see how yours compares.

Gifts

Councillors must notify the Monitoring Officer of their council of any gifts or hospitality they receive worth more than £25, and there's no reason why this information should not be made public. MPs are now required to make public all gifts and services they've received above a certain value, so if your council is not doing the same then it is worth asking why.

Salaries

You may find these in the budget or you can request them directly from the relevant department. Provisions in the Data Protection

Act may prevent you from getting information about identifiable employees, but remember that information can be denied only if it affects someone's privacy and there is an argument that public employees cannot have an expectation of privacy for their publicly funded salary. At the very least you should certainly be able to get salary information for senior staff. Another good source for salary information is job advertisements – check out the 'Society' section of the *Guardian*, the 'Public Sector' section of *The Times*, and local government magazines such as *Public Finance, Local Government Chronicle* and *Municipal Journal*.

Council rules

The council's Standing Orders outline how the council conducts its business. These will tell you if the council provides any rights to information or to attend meetings other than those granted by law. You can find copies in your local library or from the council's main information office.

Performance reports

On 31 March every year, each authority has to publish its Best Value Performance Plan (BVPP). These indicators are often controversial and confusing to the public, but the report contains a summary of the council's plans for efficiency and improvement, a review of its progress, future performance targets and how it plans to meet them, along with an outline of the authority's finances.

WHERE TO GET INFORMATION ABOUT LOCAL GOVERNMENT

Of course, the first place to go for local government information is your local authority. The two main documents you'll find useful are the authority's publication scheme and forward plan. There are also a number of other organisations that hold useful information about local government.

The Audit Commission

www.audit-commission.gov.uk
1st Floor, Millbank Tower, Millbank, London SW1P 4HQ
Tel: 020 7828 1212
Fax: 020 7976 6187

The Audit Commission annually reviews local authorities and produces a very informative Comprehensive Performance Assessment

(CPA). Its intended audience is the local authority as a means of helping them improve, but as a stakeholder, it's a useful document that is easily accessible online or by contacting the Commission. The CPA looks at the council's delivery of services, its cost-efficiency, professionalism and openness. The reports include a brief description of the authority, its annual turnover and council composition. The Audit Commission also individually inspects various service departments. In November 2004, it published its first performance assessment of the Greater London Authority, including Transport for London, the London Development Agency and the Metropolitan Police. You can search alphabetically, by name, postcode or region, and compare your council with past years and other councils.

Department for Communities and Local Government (formerly Office of the Deputy Prime Minister)
www.communities.gov.uk
Tel: 020 7944 4400 (general enquiries)
FOI Officer: Richard Smith, Information Management Division,
Ashdown House, Victoria Street, London SW1E 6DE
Tel: 020 7944 3146
Email: richard.smith@communities.gsi.gov.uk
Publication scheme: found in the 'About us' section online

This is the central government department responsible for local authorities and regional government. If you are interested in overall policy relating to local governments then contact the DCLG. If your query is localised, then direct it to your local council.

Local Government Ombudsman
www.lgo.org.uk
Tel: 0845 602 1983 (advice line)
To order publications or copies of the Ombudsmen's reports, ring the London office on 020 7217 4683
FOI Officer: Hilary Pook, Commission for Local Administration
10th Floor, Millbank Tower, London SW1P 4QP
Fax: 020 7217 4755
Email: foi.officer@lgo.org.uk
Publication scheme: www.lgo.org.uk/publications.htm

The Local Government Ombudsman investigates complaints of maladministration by local authorities. There are three Local Government Ombudsmen: one in England, one for Wales (www. ombudsman-wales.org), and one for Scotland (www.ombudslgscot.

org.uk). Local government complaints in Northern Ireland are handled by the Northern Ireland Ombudsman (www.ni-ombudsman. org.uk). The main document of interest is the digest of cases, which includes a summary of completed investigations. Report summaries are available online and full reports are available on request. Some reports are not published where exemptions apply, but these could still be published with the exempt information redacted. Investigation reports are available free of charge for up to five reports, and for six or more reports they are £1.00 each.

Local records offices

www.a2a.org.uk
Access to Archives, National Archives, Kew, Richmond, Surrey TW9 4DU
Tel: 020 8876 3444
Fax: 020 8487 9211
Email: a2a@pro.gov.uk

If you are searching for older records, they may be held by your local record office rather than the council. Every English county and most Welsh counties have a record office, as well as some historic cities such as Hull, Coventry and London. These offices contain archived material from local government including rate books and council minutes. They also hold unofficial material donated by individuals, companies or clubs. You can find a listing of all the local records offices and links to their websites at the Access to Archives website. You can now also search a number of catalogues online.

Neighbourhood statistics

A wealth of general information is available from the Office of National Statistics 'Neighbourhood' section: www.statistics.gov.uk/ neighbourhood and also from www.upmystreet.co.uk

Improvement and Development Agency (IDeA)

www.idea-knowledge.gov.uk
Layden House, 76–86 Turnmill Street, London EC1M 5LG
Tel: 020 7296 6420
Email: ihelp@idea.gov.uk

This is a non-profit organisation created by local government for local government. It is not covered by the FOIA but it is a useful site that holds a good deal of information on local authorities, particularly relating to their performance. IDeA conducted a survey of FOI sections across local government and their findings make interesting reading.

The survey is available to download at: www.idea-knowledge.gov.
uk/idk/core/page.do?pageId=263274

The 'Local Authority Information' section provides contact details,
economic and demographic data, budgetary information and a
summary for each local authority in England and Wales, along with
a link to each authority's website.

Local Government Association
www.lga.gov.uk
Local Government House, Smith Square, London SW1P 3HZ
Tel: 020 7664 3131
Fax: 020 7664 3030
Email: info@lga.gov.uk

The LGA is the representative body for local authorities in England
and Wales. It is a voluntary lobbying organisation and is not subject
to the FOIA, but as the main coordinator across local authorities, it
played a major role preparing local authorities for the new law and
offers a dedicated FOI information section on its website. It also
holds some information centrally about all councils such as total
spending. A breakdown of the £91.9 billion spent by English councils
in 2004/05 is at: www.local.odpm.gov.uk/finance/stats/ro0405tab1.
xls. The same report for Wales is at: www.statswales.wales.gov.uk/
tableviewer/document.aspx?FileId=554

The National Association of Local Councils
www.nalc.gov.uk
109 Great Russell Street, London WC1B 3LD
Tel: 020 7637 1865
Fax: 020 7436 7451
Email: nalc@nalc.gov.uk

The NALC represents the 10,000 community, parish and town councils
in England and Wales, in partnership with 52 county associations. It
is a voluntary organisation and not covered by the FOIA.

LOCAL AUTHORITIES AND WHAT THEY DO

In order to request information about your local authority, you first
have to know who holds it. Unfortunately, local authorities today
are divided in such a confusing way that it's often difficult to know
which authority is responsible for what service. Say you live in a
two-tier system – some services may be the responsibility of your

Principal local authorities

Going from the larger to the smaller, the local government system looks like this:

1. **County councils (34)** – these are not the same as the historic shires, but are more recent structures. Some county councils contain unitary authorities, such as Plymouth in the county of Devon, and thus Devon no longer looks after services in Plymouth.

Services: usually responsible for strategic planning, highways, traffic and passenger transport, social services, education, fire, libraries, rubbish disposal, consumer protection.

2. **Metropolitan borough councils (36)** – also known as metropolitan district councils.

Services: responsible for education, housing, planning applications, strategic planning, highways and traffic, social services, libraries, leisure, waste collection and disposal, environmental health, council tax collection, electoral registration, and joint authorities to run some services in a wider area such as fire and civil defence.

London – London boroughs (33), Corporation of London, Greater London Authority. The GLA itself costs £36 million, most of which comes from a central government grant and about 11 per cent from Londoners. It has eight main functions: transport, policing, fire and emergency planning, economic development, planning, culture, environment and health. The main contact points are:

- *GLA main Office*: City Hall, The Queen's Walk, London SE1 2AA. Tel: 020 7983 4000 www.london.gov.uk
- **London Development Agency**: Devon House, 58–60 St Katharine's Way, London E1W 1JX. Tel: 020 7680 2000
- *Transport for London (TfL)*: Windsor House, 42–50 Victoria Street, London SW1H 0TL. Tel: 020 7941 4500 – most public transport in London including fare structures and future investment (see Chapter 6 for more details)
- *Metropolitan Police Authority (MPA)*: 10 Dean Farrar Street, London SW1H 0NY. Tel: 020 7202 0202
- *Fire and Emergency Planning Authority*: 8 Albert Embankment, London SE1 7SD. Tel: 020 7587 2000

London metropolitan boroughs – same responsibilities as other metropolitan boroughs with the exception of those services administered by the GLA.

Corporation of London: same as metropolitan boroughs, but with its own police department.

3. **District councils (England) – (238)**

Services: local planning, housing, environmental health, markets and fairs, rubbish collection, cemeteries, crematoria, leisure services, parks, tourism, electoral administration, council tax collection.

4. **Unitary councils (46)** – mostly cities in England. Wales is divided into 22 unitary councils and Scotland into 32.

Services: same responsibilities as metropolitan borough councils and also passenger transport. Wales and Scotland – councils responsible for all council services; Northern Ireland – leisure, rubbish collection and disposal, environmental health.

district authority and others provided by the county council. To add to the confusion – your parish may be responsible for upkeep of the village hall, a private company probably collects rubbish, and a regional transport board oversees bus routes. Fire and police are separate authorities again.

For the basic structure of local government think of a set of Russian dolls with the smaller one resting within the larger one. So district councils and unitary councils, for example, Chester or Bournemouth, sit inside Cheshire County Council and Dorset County Council respectively. But in the last major reorganisation, many artificial 'county' councils proved to be so unpopular, as in the case of Avon, that they were abandoned in favour of informal 'areas' with new metropolitan borough councils or unitary councils solely responsible for their area.

There are several directories that can quickly tell you how your area slots into the system and who is responsible for the major service departments. The books are detailed at the end of this chapter and are available at most libraries or at your town hall.

Parish (town) councils

In Wales and Scotland these are called community councils or local councils. Parish councils are mostly found in rural areas but are gaining popularity in urban communities. They must have at least one meeting a year, but most meet on a six-weekly cycle.

Services: allotments, footpaths, commons, tourism, crime prevention, recreation facilities, bus shelters, public clocks, community halls, drainage. Parishes can also influence planning applications and social housing projects. There are moves to give parish councils more funding and additional responsibilities, as historically it was in the parish council that people felt they had the greatest influence.

Cities

The title of City is an honorary title granted by the Queen or Royal Charter. Many large cities govern their own affairs either by being a metropolitan district (or borough) council, such as Birmingham City Council and Manchester City Council, or they are a unitary council like Bristol City.

National Parks

National Parks are independent special-purpose local authorities that operate as separate authorities. They are statutory unitary planning authorities for their areas.

Regions

Regional assemblies are not covered by the FOIA, lending weight to the accusation that they are secretive and anti-democratic. However, the minister in charge of freedom of information said they were being considered and stated 'it is the Government's expectation that regional assemblies will comply with the spirit of the Act'.[4]

There are nine Regional Development Agencies in England that were set up by the 1998 Regional Development Agencies Act. They are covered by the FOIA and members appointed by the government. These agencies are responsible for economic development in their area, and as such will have information about job creation, sustainable development, regeneration, skills training and business efficiency. The London Development Agency is a very good place to direct some FOIAs about its dealings with private companies in preparation for the 2012 Olympics.

COUNCIL FUNCTIONS

Councils will allocate service provision through various council departments or, increasingly, they will contract out services to another authority, agency or private company. There has been a quango explosion in recent years with 6,000 new bodies created to oversee services and functions once the sole domain of the local council. Most of these newly created positions have been at the expense of elected members, as the boards of quangos are appointed by politicians rather than elected by residents as before.

Various laws set out the responsibilities of a local authority. This means there is no 'one size fits all' for local authorities. Say you live in a small town and want to know how much is spent on CCTV cameras on a particular street. The authority responsible may be either your local parish council, district council or county council – or it could even be the responsibility of the police authority. You may have to telephone around to find out who is responsible. The main council departments and the type of information you could request are listed below. Councils differ in the way they organise their services, so check your council's A–Z for more information.

Administration

This department deals with the day-to-day running of the authority and includes such things as the treasury, personnel, standards and

4. Baroness Ashton of Upholland, written answer to Lord Goodhart on 19 April 2006.

expenses. Every authority must keep separate accounts of what they spend on publicity, but increasingly councils are blurring the line between information and propaganda. Find out how much your council spends on promoting itself and whether this cost is justified.

Economic development

This department is responsible for promoting and improving the economic development of the area. This includes regeneration projects such as skills training, adult education or childcare.

FOI requests:

- *Regeneration* – the huge amounts of money involved in regeneration projects have often led to corruption. In Tower Hamlets, councillor Kumar Murshid was censured for failing to declare his relationship with the chief executive of a training company that had received £2 million of public funds. You could also request minutes from regeneration committee meetings and operational budgets to find out who is benefiting from these big, publicly funded projects.

Education

Education accounts for the largest proportion of local authority spending (41 per cent). A council's education department is responsible for schools, education, student awards, special education, and youth services in its area. It also contributes toward adult education. More detailed information can be found in Chapter 12.

Environmental services

This department covers a wide range of topics: pest control, environmental nuisance (dog fouling, dumping, noise), rubbish collection, waste management, food safety, health and safety, recycling, skip hire, energy efficiency, air and water quality, contaminated land, biodiversity, drainage, abandoned vehicles and street cleaning. Some authorities have bizarre divisions in their waste sections with different offices responsible for rubbish collected on housing estates, pavements and streets. Waste *disposal* requires more resources, so it's usually the responsibility of a county council in two-tier systems. In other areas there are joint arrangements either mandated by law or voluntary, and in London, waste disposal is overseen by the London Waste Regulation Authority. Greater detail on environmental matters is provided in Chapter 10.

Details of traders prosecuted for food hygiene convictions should be made public, but very few local councils do this. Their secrecy protects unscrupulous businesses at the expense of the public. Birmingham City Council was the first to implement a more open system – www.birmingham.gov.uk – and more councils should follow their lead.

FOI requests:

- *Noise complaints* are the most common form of neighbour problem. Under section 8 of the Environmental Protection Act 1990 the council has a duty to stop noise nuisance. How many prosecutions for noise nuisance does your local council pursue?
- *Dog fouling* – 60 per cent of dog owners allow their dogs to foul public spaces, according to the *Local Government Chronicle* (20 January 2004). If the smell of dog mess on your shoes is getting right up your nose, find out how many wardens the council employs, how many cautions they issue and how many people they actually fine or take to court. Tower Hamlets is renowned for its 'tough' stance on negligent dog owners, but it still only has three wardens who issued a meagre 90 citations for 2002/03.
- *Waste* – if waste is contracted out to a private company in your area, request the contract and service terms. How many staff do they employ? How many sick days were taken last year? How much waste is collected each year and where does it go?
- *Recycling* – how many households recycle? How much of the total waste is your local authority recycling? What is their future plan for improving levels of recycling? What are the cost differences between recycling, landfills and incineration of waste?
- *Pollution and disease* – get air-quality readings to find out the most and least polluted part of your area.
- *Health and safety* – get safety inspection reports for local playgrounds, offices and shops.
- *Food safety* – inspection reports for local restaurants, takeaways and school or hospital kitchens.

Highways and transport

Local authorities are responsible for minor roads while major roads (trunk roads and motorways) are built and maintained by the Highways Agency under the direction of the Department for Transport. In some councils, environmental services may take care of some tasks such as street cleaning and picking up abandoned cars.

FOI requests:

- *Traffic lights* – if you think you spend half your life at a certain set of traffic lights, why not request the timing schedule of the light (ratio of time on red to green), the policy on traffic management, a listing of all traffic lights by type (timed or sensor), or expand the survey to all traffic lights and discover the lights most often on red in your area? The Mayor of London came under criticism for supposedly altering the timing schedule of lights to give the impression of less traffic when the Congestion Charge was first introduced – requesting the above information would provide conclusive evidence if your council tried to do the same.

- *Parking and clamping* – parking fines are a major source of revenue for councils, so they have an interest in maintaining a system that generates as much money as possible, often at the expense of the public. The chief parking adjudicator for London has said that local councils treat drivers who contest parking fines unfairly, and pointed out that appeals took too long, there was often insufficient evidence given for rejection and appeal forms were hidden from the public. A man in Bury, Greater Manchester, won an appeal against a £60 parking fine from NCP after an independent adjudicator concluded that the car parking company had faked a photograph to prove its case. So it's always worth requesting photographs and other evidence if you're ticketed. You can also ask for figures on how many cars are ticketed or clamped and where, to find out which streets are the most prevalent for tickets and clamping. Find out if parking officers are acting properly by requesting their enforcement policies. If the service is contracted out to a private company, ask for the contract to see what incentives are given to encourage maximum ticketing.

- *Roadworks and maintenance* – what is the most dug-up road in your area? You could ask for a list of all roadworks by street or get figures on the costs and time spent on each. How many penalties were issued for improper roadworks?

- *Humps and speed limits* – how many humps are in your area? Which streets have the most humps? How much do they cost? You could request all the facts and information used when the

decision was first made to install humps. How many humps
are on bus routes (many bus drivers complain that driving over
humps gives them back pain)?

- *Abandoned vehicles* – which street has the most abandoned
cars? How long does it take the council to pick them up?

Housing

Local authorities have a statutory duty to house the homeless. They
also provide central government rent subsidies to poor tenants.
Housing Associations are also considered public authorities under
the FOIA. These days, many councils are selling off their housing
stock to registered social landlords, often against the will of residents.
If you feel you're getting a biased picture from the council you can
use the FOIA to gather information.

FOI requests:

- How many empty or derelict properties does the council
own?
- How many repair calls does it receive? Average waiting time for
repairs? Total cost? This can show you if there's a backlog.
- Benefit fraud: how many reports of fraud does the council
receive and how many do they investigate? You may find your
council has a very poor record of tackling benefit fraud.
- How many tenants are evicted for bad behaviour, and where
are they moved?
- Get your council's 'allocation scheme'. Every council is required
to have a scheme detailing how they prioritise those waiting
for housing.

Leisure

This sector is least subject to central government mandates and
covers parks and open spaces; tree maintenance; sports facilities
such as tennis courts, swimming baths or football pitches; sports
development; museums; arts; allotments; civic halls; orchestras;
repertory theatres and nature centres.

FOI requests:

- *Rundown parks, amenities* – ask for the budget and schedule
of maintenance. How many hours per week are spent on
upkeep?
- *Pools* – chlorine content and results of water testing. How many
people use the pool a week? How often do they change the
water? How many accidents?

- *Parks* – how much does the council spend on plants, and who supplies them? The cost of vandalism? Safety of play equipment in parks? If you're concerned about your council selling off parks or leisure facilities, you could ask for a list of all the open spaces and leisure facilities the council has sold in the last ten years and request minutes from meetings where the sell-off was discussed.
- *Libraries* – what are the most popular lends? How many books are bought per year and at what cost? What's the policy on choosing which books to purchase (you could find out if books are being censored)? How many books are lost/stolen? Have opening hours changed over time (many libraries have cut back their opening hours to the point that they are quite inaccessible)? What subscriptions does the library pay for?

Planning

Planning is divided into strategic (or forward) planning and development control. Planning is quite an open system (at least in principle), and many councils have information online or you can look at plans or request copies for a fee. Planning consent is subject to appeal to central government. An electronic Planning Portal – www.planningportal.gov.uk – was launched in May 2002 to make planning more transparent and accessible. The site contains a guide to planning, an online application service and a system for national appeals.

FOI requests:

- Get plans of new buildings or proposed work in your area.
- How many planning applications has the council received?
- How many has it approved?
- How many has it rejected, and why?
- A list of committee members and their interests – this can reveal if those who make decisions on projects will directly benefit from them.

Procurement

This is the section that oversees all the council's commercial transactions. It will have information about purchases and also contract information for partnerships with private companies. The 'Best Value' officer has overall responsibility for ensuring that the council gets a good deal on goods or services. The contracts/direct services officer has overall responsibility for overseeing the tendering process and resulting contracts.

FOI requests:

- Service contracts and terms.
- Amount and details of unsuccessful bids.

Social services

Social services make up the second largest proportion of council spending (19 per cent) and include care services to adults and children (fostering, adoption, child abuse investigation) as well as registration of childminders, playgroups, nurseries and nursing homes. A great deal of social work is done by private sector and/or voluntary agencies such as daycare centres, private nursing homes, residential homes, drug action teams and charities like Age Concern, Home Start and MENCAP. Agencies responsible may vary between the local government, NHS Trusts and other authorities such as Ofsted in the case of childminders' inspection reports. As of April 2002, a new group – the National Care Standards Commission – www.carestandards.org.uk – regulates and inspects all fostering services, care homes and daycare centres for mentally ill people. Social workers are regulated and registered by another new quango, the General Social Care Council in England: www.gscc.org.uk

FOI requests:

- *Vetting* – those registered to work with children must be vetted. How many applicants for registration has the council received? How many has the council processed (this can show if there is a backlog)? What percentage of applicants were turned down, and why?
- *Abuse* – number of abuse cases investigated over time (wide variations in the number could signal an overzealous or lackadaisical approach by social workers who either unnecessarily prosecute innocent parents or fail to investigate suspected abuse cases).
- *Nursing homes/daycare* – inspection reports: how many accidents?

Trading standards

A goldmine of interesting information is held within this department. Many councils have their own websites outlining the many areas they regulate. A partial list includes: markets, estate agents, weights and measures, consumer credit, overloaded goods vehicles, animal health, hallmarking, safety of consumer goods, food composition and labelling, sale of poisons, trade descriptions, piracy and counterfeit goods, animal feed and pet foods, misleading advertisements, price marking, holidays and timeshare property.

FOI requests:

- *Markets* – have there been illegal or unsafe goods sold at the market? How often are inspections made?
- *Inspection reports* – for trades such as plumbers, businesses, shops, factories and farms. How often are they made? What are the results?
- *Complaints* – does your local Trading Standards department warn the public about businesses that have unduly high levels of customer complaints? How many complaints does the department receive and how many do they actually investigate? What are the results? You may find that a handful of staff are responsible for investigating thousands of businesses, and as a result proper standards are not enforced.

You might encounter some resistance getting this kind of information as traditionally, many Trading Standards departments keep their inspections and results secret (see Chapter 13 for more detail about getting information on private companies). Some counties like Surrey have taken a proactive approach and publish the names of unscrupulous traders, so if your local Trading Standards Office isn't revealing names, ask why.

Council contact information

The Municipal Yearbook – this 2,000-pages-plus 'bible' of local government comes in two volumes and contains a listing of all local governments in Britain and contact details for councillors, department heads and committee chairs. There are also sections detailing the structure of councils and statistics on the gender of chief executive officers.

Shaw's Local Government Directory – a condensed version of the Municipal Yearbook with contact details for the main departments in all UK local governments.

The Local Government Companion (The Stationery Office) – this directory lists all UK local governments along with a description of each authority, councillors, council functions and chief officers, contact details, an A–Z of chief executive biographies (including photos), and a listing of local education authorities and local government organisations.

OTHER USEFUL SOURCES

The *Guardian* has a local government website with all the latest news and issues: www.society.guardian.co.uk/localgovt

The 'Rotten Boroughs' column in *Private Eye* provides numerous examples of local government mismanagement and questions to ask about your own council.

Public Finance and *Local Government Chronicle* are the two major 'industry' magazines about local government.

Sign up for free email bulletins about your chosen areas of interest in local government: www.info4local.gov.uk

12
Education

Parents are the main beneficiaries of greater openness in schools. From the amount spent on school dinners to the way schools select pupils, the Freedom of Information Act is being used to delve into all areas of schools' performance and operation. The Act is also holding local education authorities to account and, for the first time, private finance deals are being made public. Yet awareness of the Act among parents is minimal and this is hindering the law's effectiveness.

All schools in the public sector, including government-maintained nursery schools and faith schools, are subject to the FOIA. Independent, private and Academy schools are not covered, though with enough public pressure they could be designated as public bodies under the law. As it is, the only way to get information about privately funded schools is to target public bodies with whom they have a relationship. Apart from the main educational public authorities such as Ofsted and the Department for Education and Skills, the Office of Fair Trading (contact information is given in Chapter 13) is an important source of data about private schools, particularly in relation to price fixing. In 2004, for example, the OFT ordered a large number of the country's leading independent schools, including Eton, Charterhouse and Winchester College, to hand over documents so it could investigate an alleged price-fixing cartel. This came at a time when private schools had adopted record fee increases averaging 9 per cent.

Schools are fairly open in many areas with school league tables and inspection reports made public. What they have been less forthcoming about are problems related to internal discipline problems. Bullying was for years not taken seriously, and parents can often feel ignorant about what happens inside the school gates. Hence, the FOIA is one of the best ways of obtaining hard facts on issues such as student discipline, funding, performance, professional conduct and educational policy.

Parents can use the Act to explore the admissions policy of schools and find out precisely why their child was rejected. Faith schools are coming under scrutiny as incubators of sectarianism in a predominantly secular society. The Act gives people the opportunity

> ### Educational organisations covered by the FOIA
>
> - **Schools and nurseries** – the governing body of every maintained school or nursery in England and Wales which includes individual community schools, foundation schools, voluntary schools and special schools. In Northern Ireland, the managers of controlled schools, voluntary schools, grant-maintained schools and pupil referral units.
> - **Colleges/further education** – this includes general, sixth form, specialist and designated colleges. Many colleges are run by Further Education Corporations, and in these cases, the corporation rather than the governing body is caught by the Act.
> - **Universities/higher education** – all universities in England, Wales and Northern Ireland are covered. The Information Commissioner has also stated that any college, school, hall or other institution of a university that receives its funding from the same source as a university in England and Wales is also included.
> - **Student unions** – if student unions are part of an institution's organisational framework then they come under the Act. If they are defined as independent, then they do not.
> - **Local Education Authorities.**
> - **Central government departments** – Department for Education and Skills and associated organisations such as Ofsted.

to examine the curriculum, teaching methods and funding of such schools for the first time. Educational policies are being probed. In Scotland, a man requested the names of officials involved in the development of the education department's guidance on teaching sex education in Scottish schools. The Scottish Executive appealed in May 2006 to overturn the Scottish Information Commissioner's decision that the names must be released.

The Act can certainly make a difference, so it is disappointing that so few parents are using their new rights. 'The Act hasn't been a big issue for schools,' says Collin Crooks, the FOI Officer for the Department for Education and Skills. He maintains this is because schools already have to publish large amounts of information. Most of the requests received at the DfES relate to issues in the news such as school meals or sex offenders in schools.

But there is also little awareness of the Act among parents in the absence of any official promotion. Schools are not doing a great deal to tell parents about their new rights to access official school data. Awareness generally comes through local media, and journalists have catered to parents' desire for more knowledge by conducting their own investigations into schools. *Kent Messenger* editor Bob Dimond told the *Press Gazette* (5 January 2005): 'Public confidence in councils and schools can often hinge on their willingness to be open. We felt parents and others in the wider community were entitled to know the full background to events at the school.'

Some important disclosures using the Act include:

- The *Cambridge Evening News* found that more than 1,000 pupils were banned from Cambridgeshire County Council schools in a single term. The bad behaviour included verbal abuse against staff and pupils, violence, sexual misconduct, theft, and drug taking and dealing (31 March 2006).
- The same paper asked for the number of school days lost because of teachers who called in sick and found that the sickness rate was decreasing, but still higher in Cambridgeshire than the national average.
- The *Surrey Mirror* (23 February 2006) discovered there were 52 incidents in 2005 of Surrey school pupils possessing drugs or an offensive weapon.
- The *Kent Messenger* newspaper used FOI to delve into the unexpected resignation of a head teacher.
- Documents released under FOI showed how De Montfort University had lowered pass grades so pharmacy students could continue to study even though they had failed their exams.
- Details of lists kept of individuals who may pose a risk to children. Essex newspaper the *Yellow Advertiser* used the Act to get details of workers on the secret list, sometimes known as list 98, of suspect people employed by Essex schools.[1]
- In line with the spirit of openness, local education authorities released the amounts spent per pupil per meal. The Soil Association came up with a league table that showed most schools spent less than 40p.[2]

Further and higher education

The Joint Information Systems Committee is the coordinating body for Freedom of Information requests to further education institutions. JISC is a subsection of the university funding councils and is itself a public body under the Act. The Committee stepped in to prepare universities and colleges for the Act in the absence of any central

1. 'County Council gives "threat" teacher details to YA', *Yellow Advertiser*, 27 April 2006.
2. 'Big divide on school meals revealed in spending survey', *Guardian*, 24 March 2005: http://education.guardian.co.uk/schoolmeals/story/0,,1444601,00.html

---

Where to find school information

* National curriculum and national education policy – Department for Education and Skills
* Administration of council's school buildings, PFI contracts and other county-wide school services – Local Education Authority
* Issues specifically about an individual school – chair of the School Governors.

---

guidance from the Department for Education and Skills, but 'it was a role DfES was happy for us to take,' says Steve Bailey, the records and information manager for JISC. The Committee continues to provide a central point for higher education institutions covered by the Act. It runs an online forum (www.jiscmail.ac.uk) and in May 2006 awarded a contract worth £200,000 to build a central repository for FOI disclosures, case law and guidance. It was unclear how much of the repository would be publicly accessible.

A recent survey showed that universities and colleges received 2,068 FOI requests in 2005[3] and answered 63 per cent of those in full. The biggest users of the Act in the first year were journalists (45 per cent) followed by members of the public. The most popular topics for requests were information on university management and administration, followed by human resource issues, and financial information. The prevalence of journalists making requests highlights the need for more promotion of the new law to citizens. On average, English universities received about three FOI requests a month, while their Scottish counterparts received an average of six. A bigger budget for FOI promotion in Scotland has obviously translated into more public activism.

Better records management was cited as the single biggest factor affecting the processing time of FOI requests according to the JISC survey. Another fact to emerge was how few higher education institutions have disclosure logs – only 4 out of 76 respondents published FOI requests and responses.

Primary and secondary schools are not covered by JISC. The Department for Education set up an FOI sector group in the summer of 2005 to coordinate FOI policy, but there is still no equivalent central coordinating body for FOI in primary and secondary schools. This means there are no statistics available on how many FOI requests

---

3. Survey by the Joint Information Systems Committee, Universities UK and the Standing Conference on Principles: www.jiscinfonet.ac.uk/foi-survey/foi-survey-results-2005

are sent to these schools and overall compliance with the law. The Information Commissioner's Office has guidance on accessing educational information that you can find on their website. There is also a model publication that tells schools what they ought to make public on demand. But you will still find wide variation in the way each school handles an FOIA request. There may be confusion as information released by one school is refused at another. Also, a lot of time and money can be wasted if schools do not pool their knowledge and experience. Many are doing this voluntarily, but others are not, and without a central coordinator, compliance with the law is likely to be piecemeal. Some schools may not open up until challenged by the public, the media or the Information Commissioner.

Without central guidance, some schools could adopt a mercenary approach to the public's right to know by charging the maximum amount for any information supplied to the public. Any attempt to do this, however, could legitimately be challenged as guidelines state that public bodies can only charge a reasonable amount for information. Other schools are refusing to put the minutes from public meetings online. Sometimes this may be justified due to clashes in IT systems, but usually it is for no other reason than to make it more difficult for the public to see what these groups are doing. Schools may cite confidentiality concerns, but if the information can be disclosed in hard copy, there is no reason it cannot also be provided online.

ACCESS TO SCHOOL RECORDS

Everyone has the right to access his or her personal information from any organisation under the Data Protection Act 1998. In addition, the data protection law gives school students additional rights to access educational records held within the state education system. Educational records are defined as the official records that are the responsibility of head teachers. They can be in electronic or paper form, or a mixture of both. The main difference is that these records should be supplied within 15 days instead of the usual 40 (though it is 40 days in Scotland and Northern Ireland). You cannot be charged to see your record, but you may be charged a fee for a paper copy.

Otherwise, your rights to school records are similar whether you went to a state or independent school. Regardless of age, everyone can request his or her school pupil record. If students are unable to exercise their right (for example, because they are too young), then parents can request the information on their behalf. The Data

Protection Act also gives you the right to receive a description of any personal data in the record including where the information came from, who else has seen it or received it, and the purpose for which it was collected.

Several exemptions might limit the amount of information given to you. These are similar to the exemptions used to withhold health records – information that might cause harm to you or another person, or hinder the prevention or detection of crime. The problem with these exemptions is that because only the school is involved in deciding whether or not an exemption applies, information might be withheld for improper reasons; for example, to protect a school or teacher from outside scrutiny. An external check is needed to ensure information is being withheld for legitimate and reasonable purposes.

Another problem in accessing school information occurs when schools wantonly destroy information just so they don't have to provide it under the Data Protection Act. Representatives from Oxford's student union were furious when they discovered that tutors had been instructed to tear up notes made when marking final exams just so tutors would not have to hand them over to students who requested them under the DPA. This drastic action was taken based only on anecdotal evidence that students were increasingly exercising their rights under the DPA. The university had no actual figures on how many students had used the Act to request the information or how many had used the DPA to challenge their grades.

How to request your school records

- Apply in writing to the head teacher of the school concerned (see sample letter in the appendix).
- If you are a former student of the school, some form of identification may be needed. Check with the school.
- Although not required, it is helpful to include attendance dates.
- If a fee is charged, include payment.
- Keep a copy of the letter you send and also keep a note of any further contact or correspondence.
- The school has 15 school days to respond to your request for school records, and 40 days for other records.

School performance

It's very easy to access school inspection reports for either state or independent schools. The reports are freely available on a searchable database on the Ofsted website or the Independent

Schools Inspectorate's website. What is harder to gauge is how accurately these inspection reports mirror what is actually going on in schools. Schools used to have ten weeks to prepare for an inspection, and during that time many embarked on radical refurbishment programmes to present their best image to the inspectors. A failing school in Hull hit the headlines in March 2004 when it borrowed eight experienced teachers from another school and sent away nine disruptive pupils to a vocational college course during its inspection. To counter this kind of makeover madness, Ofsted announced plans to change the inspection regime and give schools just 48 hours' notice of inspections. This would certainly present a more accurate picture. For those parents who are not satisfied with the final report, an FOIA request could provide the more detailed notes taken during the inspection process.

Teachers

You might think parents would have a right to information about the quality of those people teaching their children. Are teachers under disciplinary procedures? Where did they qualify and what subjects did they specialise in? Remarkably, the public did not have a right to any of this information prior to 2005. The General Teaching Councils of England, Wales and Scotland are the regulatory bodies of the teaching profession. The Councils have three main functions: maintaining the register of qualified teachers, advising the government on issues regarding teachers and teaching, and regulating the profession in the public interest. Quite how the councils are taking the public interest into account is debatable as they seem reluctant to tell the public any useful information about teachers. Employers, on the other hand, have rights to know where a teacher qualified, the subjects studied, whether they passed their induction and if there are any restrictions in force. There is no reason parents should not be given the same information. Many regulatory agencies such as the General Medical Council have learned from bitter experience that keeping the disciplinary problems of its members secret leads only to a breakdown in public trust. The results of the teaching council's disciplinary hearings are public but it can be difficult to get timely notice of the hearings and subsequent detailed minutes. If you face difficulties then call the teaching council and ask for the record from these hearings.

Attendance

The governing body of a school must keep an Admissions Register, which gives the details of every pupil currently enrolled at the school, and an Attendance Register, which shows whether each pupil was present or absent from school and if an absence was authorised or unauthorised. These registers could be used to find out how well a school is tackling the problem of truancy.

WHERE TO GET EDUCATION INFORMATION

Department for Education and Skills

www.dfes.gov.uk
Public Enquiry Unit, Castle View House, East Lane, Runcorn WA7 2GJ
Tel: 0870 000 2288 (Information Line)
Fax: 01928 794 248
Email: info@dfes.gsi.gov.uk
DfES publications: Tel: 0845 602 2260
FOI Officer: Collin Crooks, Level 2 Caxton House, Tothill Street,
London SW1H 9NA
Tel: 020 7273 5026
Email: collin.crooks@dfes.gsi.gov.uk
Publication scheme and disclosure log: www.dfes.gov.uk/foischeme

The DfES is the central government department that oversees education policy and the disbursement of educational funding. It also collects national statistics on education, though it is not the central coordinator for FOI. If you want national educational data, contact DfES; for detailed local information, contact your Local Education Authority or school directly.

Local Education Authorities – an A–Z list of all LEAs can be found on the DfES website: www.dfes.gov.uk/leagateway. It features a clickable map to help you locate your LEA and provides contact details.

School contacts – if you need basic information about schools such as an address, the name of the headteacher or LEA number then you can search the EduBase database for schools by area, name or postcode. EduBase is a register of all educational establishments in England and Wales and is maintained by the DfES – www.standards. dfes.gov.uk/locate/management/tar/edubase

School governors www.governornet.co.uk. This DfES gateway to information for and about school governors and school governing bodies contains a wealth of information about their responsibilities to parents, students, the DfES and Local Education Authorities.

Performance tables www.dfes.gov.uk/performancetables. This link gives performance tables for primary and secondary schools dating back to 1992.

National education statistics – the most up-to-date statistics including exam results for young people in England are available on the 'Statistics' section of the website: www.dfes.gov.uk/statistics/ DB/SFR

Parent centre www.parentcentre.gov.uk. A DfES gateway containing information for parents, including a school locator which gives details of school location, performance tables and the latest inspection reports.

Educational organisations – the DfES publication scheme maintains an updated list of all its partner educational organisations and contact details. Currently there are just over 20 such agencies, including the Adult Learning Inspectorate, Qualifications and Curriculum Authority and the Teacher Training Agency and Universities UK.

The Office for Standards in Education (Ofsted)

www.ofsted.gov.uk
Alexandra House, 33 Kingsway, London WC2B 6SE
Tel: 020 7421 6800 (switchboard)
Email: geninfo@ofsted.gov.uk
FOI Officer: Anna Greenbank
Email: enquiries@ofsted.gov.uk
Publication scheme: www.ofsted.gov.uk/foi

Ofsted is an independent non-ministerial government department created by the Education (Schools) Act 1992. Its purpose is to improve the quality of education, and it does this by inspecting schools, colleges, teacher training bodies and Local Education Authorities (LEAs). It also regulates childcare. It is one of the best examples of providing the public with easily accessible and free information through its inspection reports online. You can get other free publications from the Ofsted Publications Centre – Tel: 07002 637 833; Fax: 07002 693 274 – or by email to freepublications@ofsted.gov.uk

What you'll really want to get your hands on are the actual reports, and these are all publicly available online at www.ofsted.gov.uk/ reports. You can search alphabetically or by location.

General Teaching Council of England

www.gtce.org.uk
Victoria Square House, Birmingham B2 4AJ
Tel: 0870 001 0308 (Help Desk and registration information)
Publication scheme: follow links from FOI section of website

The General Teaching Councils are regulatory bodies and therefore subject to the FOIA. You can find the minutes from the full council online at www.gtce.org.uk/AboutTheGTC/CouncilBusiness/, though they very often go into private session and this part of the meeting is not publicly available. A list of disciplinary orders and decisions naming individual teachers can be accessed at: www.gtce.org.uk/standards/hearings/96364/bailey

General Teaching Council of Wales
www.gtcw.org.uk
4th Floor, Southgate House, Wood Street, Cardiff CF10 1EW
Tel: 029 2055 0350
Fax: 029 2055 0360
Email: registration@gtcw.org.uk

General Teaching Council of Scotland
www.gtcs.org.uk
Clerwood House, 96 Clermiston Road, Edinburgh EH12 6UT
Tel: 0131 314 6000
Fax: 0131 314 6001
Email: gtcs@gtcs.org.uk

Higher Education Funding Council for England
www.hefce.ac.uk
Help Desk (FOI Unit), Northavon House, Coldharbour Lane,
Bristol BS16 1QD
Tel: 0117 931 7438 (help desk)
Fax: 0117 931 7463
Email: foi@hefce.ac.uk
Publication scheme: www.hefce.ac.uk/AboutUs/foi/

The Council is the place to direct queries about public funding for teaching and research in England's 130 universities and higher education colleges. All the funding councils are public bodies under the Freedom of Information Act.

The Scottish Further and Higher Education Funding Council
www.sfc.ac.uk
Donaldson House, 97 Haymarket Terrace, Edinburgh EH12 5HD
Tel: 0131 313 6500 (switchboard)
FOI Officer: Simon Macauley, Legal Compliance and Customer Services Officer
Tel: 0131 313 6691
Email: informationaccess@sfc.ac.uk
Publication scheme: www.sfc.ac.uk/about/about_conduct_access.htm

The Council pays for teaching and research for Scotland's 43 colleges of further and higher education and 20 higher education institutions. In 2005–06, the Council distributed about £1.3 billion.

Higher Education Funding Council for Wales

www.hefcw.ac.uk
Linden Court, The Orchards, Ilex Close, Llanishen, Cardiff CF14 5DZ
Tel: 029 2076 1861
Fax: 029 2076 3163
Direct FOI requests to the Clerk to the Council
Email: info@elwa.ac.uk
Online FOI form: http://194.81.48.132/Publications/FOIForm.asp
Publication scheme: http://194.81.48.132/Publications/about_scheme.htm

The Welsh council distributes money for education and research to twelve higher education institutions. It also funds Open University teaching in Wales.

Joint Information Systems Committee (JISC)

www.jisc.ac.uk
Offices in London, Bristol and Nottingham
Tel: 0117 954 5083 (enquiries)
FOI Officer: Steve Bailey, Records & Information Manager
JISC Executive, 2nd Floor Beacon House, Queens Road, Bristol BS8 1QU
Tel: 07092 302 850
Email: s.bailey@jisc.ac.uk, but send FOI requests to: info@jisc.ac.uk
Publication scheme: www.jisc.ac.uk/about_foi_intro.html

JISC was established in 1993 to coordinate a strategic approach to IT networking and specialist information services. It adopted the role of centralised coordinator for the implementation of freedom of information across further and higher education institutions and has actively set about monitoring FOI use by conducting surveys, running an online FOI forum and building a central storehouse of information released under the Act. JISC is funded by the Higher Education Funding Councils for England, Scotland and Wales and is therefore itself a public body under the Act.

British Educational and Communications Technology Agency (Becta)

www.becta.org.uk
Milburn Hill Road, Science Park, Coventry CV4 7JJ
Tel: 024 7641 6994
Fax: 024 7641 1418

FOI Officer: Lesley Cox
Tel: 024 7679 7432
Email: lesley.cox@becta.org.uk, but send FOI requests to: foi@becta.org.uk
Publication scheme: follow the website links 'About Becta' > 'Freedom of information'

Becta is the public body covered by the FOIA, charged with delivering the government's e-strategy for primary and secondary schools and as such has received FOI requests for contracts it awards for IT and software in schools. Although Becta's remit is similar to the Joint Information Systems Committee, it has not provided a similar central FOI advisory role for schools nor conducted a survey to monitor how the Act is being used in schools. FOI Officer Lesley Cox says there are no future plans that this will change.

13
Private Companies

Private companies are not generally subject to the Freedom of Information Act, but you can still access a great deal of information about them from the many public authorities that do have to meet FOI obligations. Information is also available about private companies in two other areas – procurement (companies selling goods or services to public bodies) and public-private partnerships/ private finance initiatives. Huge sums of money are often involved in these projects so the possibility for corruption and mismanagement is great. Transparency and direct accountability are essential.

The FOIA gives the Lord Chancellor the power to designate as a public authority any person or private company that provides a public service either directly or under contract with a public authority. This means that numerous private companies could fall under the Act, though only for the parts of the business involved in operating a public service. So we could see, for example, Network Rail and the private companies running parts of London's Tube become public authorities in terms of the FOI law. Other companies such as Capita, Jarvis and Balfour Beatty could be classed as public authorities for their work operating public projects such as the London Congestion Charge, university residence halls and railway track maintenance. Unfortunately, the government is in no hurry to make these designations. Originally scheduled for January 2005, they had still not been made by summer 2006.

There is little case law about disclosing commercial information under the FOIA and Environmental Information Regulations. One noteworthy case is the UK Commissioner's decision in February 2006 ordering Derry City Council to disclose the terms of its six-year-old agreement with Ryanair. The Council used all the usual exemptions – prejudicial to economic, financial and commercial interests – but without even getting into the public interest balancing exercise, the Commissioner ruled that these exemptions did not apply. There have been other successes, too, particularly in obtaining contracts and tender details from public authorities.

Some contracts received under the FOIA:

- Kensington and Chelsea's parking enforcement contract with APCOA.
- British Library's contract with Building Zones to supply wireless access.
- Police Information Technology Organisation's contract and tender documentation for £122 million contract with Northrop Grumman to develop IDENT1 system of identification.
- Transport for London's PPP contracts with Metronet and Tube Lines.
- Various contracts and tender information regarding the House of Commons' information systems (www.flourish.org/foi for details).

These contracts were not always forthcoming and some of the pricing details were redacted, but just getting the bulk of the documents is a major step forward. Often of greater interest than the contract itself is the process by which it was awarded. By asking for correspondence, minutes and details of tender, it's possible to identify anti-competitive practices, such as awarding a contract without any advertisement, in a closed meeting, or with no public consultation.

The worry that FOI will discourage businesses from putting forward tenders to public authorities is purely speculative and not borne out by the experience in America where far greater transparency has not hindered the world's most competitive market. A greater hindrance to competitive tendering is the decision taken by some public authorities to charge businesses for the privilege.

The universities of Hertfordshire and Salford sparked criticism from small businesses when they introduced charges of between £75 and £120 just to release pre-qualification questionnaires for their contracts.[1] The British Printing Industries Federation used the Freedom of Information Act to investigate why the charges had been introduced, and soon after, the University of Hertfordshire backed down and rescinded the charging policy. Salford was scheduled to follow suit.

BUSINESS USERS OF FOI

In the United States, businesses are the biggest users of freedom of information, using the law to obtain contracts, tenders, the results from their own and competitors' regulatory investigations, and to

1. *Supply Management*, 13 April 2006, 'University U-turn on tender charges'.

obtain databases of official information, which they modify and sell for profit. In Ontario Canada, 27 per cent of the appeals received by the Commissioner in 2004 were from businesses.[2] Freedom of information plays an important role in keeping markets competitive. It exposes the sort of incestuous deals with the same few companies that are the hallmark of the private finance initiative scene in the UK.

Yet many public authorities are opposed to the use of FOI by businesses. They feel they should not have to provide information for free to profitable companies. 'There is concern about whether that was what was intended within the spirit of the Act,' Lydia Pollard from the local government organisation IDeA told MPs (28 March 2006). There is a legitimate point to the argument, but why should businesses be penalised for accessing publicly funded information? They are citizens just like anyone else (some might argue extremely productive citizens), but importantly, the law is purpose-blind meaning one's identity or reason for wanting information is immaterial. Even if you are a supplier seeking information about another supplier, that fact alone is not grounds for withholding information. A way around this dilemma would be to charge profit-making companies for information while introducing a fee waiver for those seeking information in the public interest (e.g. campaign groups, news media, activists, etc). This is the system currently operating in the United States.

Enterprise Act 2002

A major barrier preventing the release of private company information is Part 9 of the Enterprise Act 2002, which restricts disclosure of information about individuals and businesses. Some councils even cited this act as their reason for withholding restaurant inspections.

The Scottish Commissioner has stated that many local authorities want to release information because it is clearly in the public interest, but are concerned that this part of the Enterprise Act makes such disclosure a criminal offence. 'I have obtained legal opinion from senior counsel, which states that Part 9 of the Enterprise Act does not constitute a prohibition on disclosure. This is contrary to the view taken by the Department of Trade and Industry and the Department of Constitutional Affairs.' The Scottish Commissioner had not yet issued any decisions in relation to Part 9, but they were imminent so check his website for more details. Proposed changes to the Enterprise Act under the Company Law Reform Bill may also amend the restrictions of the Enterprise Act.

Until the situation is clarified on the Enterprise Act, I suggest you challenge any refusals by referencing the section of this law that states it does not prohibit ▶

---

2. Annual Report 2004, Information and Privacy Commissioner, Ontario, p. 34.

the disclosure of information 'held by a public authority to another person if the disclosure is required for the purpose of a Community obligation' (section 240). You could specifically reference an EC obligation requiring disclosure such as the Data Protection Act, Environmental Information Regulations or even the Human Rights directive. The law also says that a public authority can disclose information to the public 'for the purpose of facilitating the exercise by the authority of any function it has under or by virtue of this Act or any other enactment' (s. 241(1)). In this case the public authority has an obligation to uphold the FOIA.

PRIVATE FINANCE INITIATIVES

Public services are increasingly provided by private companies through private finance initiatives (PFIs) or public-private partnerships (PPPs). In March 2006, HM Treasury published a report showing that the public sector had already signed 700 PFI projects. Over the next four to five years the government had plans to begin another 200 projects worth £26 billion – making it the largest programme in the world. There are PFI projects to build, renovate or operate schools, hospitals, libraries, leisure centres, street lighting, waste collection, police facilities and magistrates' courts.

Information about PFIs is often shrouded in secrecy and until passage of the FOIA, the public were refused even the most basic contract information, even though it's public money being spent. These newly published contracts are remarkable in their complexity. Such complexity is very often used by private contractors to disguise the offloading of risk onto the taxpayer. Any rewards, obviously, go into the pocket of the private company.

There is heated debate about whether PFIs provide good value for money to the taxpayer. Often the short-term price seems lower but in the long-term the cost to the public is far higher. The Skye Bridge in Scotland provides a good example. In Scotland's first PFI deal, the bridge was designed, built and part-financed by the Skye Bridge Company. The bridge cost £39 million to build, of which £12 million came from a government grant. Tolls were £5.70 for a car and up to £27.90 for a lorry, one way! Up to June 2003, the company had collected about £27 million in tolls. The campaigner George Monbiot calculates that by 2005 the private company's actual outlay of capital came to just £15 million, yet the accumulated cost to taxpayers from tolls, government grants and services was £93million.[3] Soon after the

3. *Guardian*, 29 December 2004, 'A Scandal of Secrecy and Collusion'.

FOIA came into force, the tolls were abolished, and the government bought back the bridge.

There is also the danger of private companies refinancing PFI projects so they get a windfall of cash while saddling the public authority with more debt. Parliament's public accounts committee highlighted one such case involving the Norfolk and Norwich Hospital in May 2006. In that case, a consortium of businesses increased the debt from £200 million to £300 million taking the repayment time from 2017 to 2137. The investors pocketed £115 million from this deal, handing over just £34 million of it to the hospital trust.

Public access to PFI contracts is essential for ensuring projects run on time and on budget. Prior to the new access laws, there was no way for the public to scrutinise the IT system for the Child Support Agency contracted out to the American company EDS. It was delivered almost a year late and £50 million over budget, and it still doesn't work properly. In 2002, the government had to abandon a system being developed by EDS, IBM and KPMG that was meant to simplify buying and storing supplies for the army, but which did neither while still costing the taxpayer £140 million. And the Inland Revenue provoked outrage when it sold off some of its properties to Mapeley Steps, an offshore company that pays no British taxes.

Each fiasco has a similar theme – lack of public information and a resulting lack of public scrutiny. The secrecy is due primarily to restrictive confidentiality agreements and a narrow interpretation of what is 'commercially sensitive'.

At a bare minimum, public authorities should make public:

- the identity of the contractor
- the amount and terms of the contract.

In addition, any performance stipulations should be released along with reviews of the contractor's performance and any penalties incurred. Private companies should be under an obligation to provide any information they hold that the public authority needs to satisfy an FOI request. The terms for meeting the FOIA are set forth by the Office of Government Commerce in its Model Contracts for Local Authorities. These state that a private company and any subcontractors must keep and supply information to the public authority in a timely manner. The guidelines also specify that the decision to disclose rests solely with the public authority and while it may consult with the private company it is not under an obligation to do so. The contract terms and conditions are available on the Office of Government

Commerce website under 'Procurement': www.ogc.gov.uk/index. asp?id=1004889. These are the sections of interest:

34.2 The Contractor shall and shall procure that its sub-contractors shall:

(a) transfer the Request for Information to the Authority as soon as practicable after receipt and in any event within [2] Working Days of receiving a Request for Information;

(b) provide the Authority with a copy of all Information in its possession or power in the form that the Authority requires within [5] Working Days (or such other period as the Authority may specify) of the Authority requesting that Information; and

(c) provide all necessary assistance as reasonably requested by the Authority to enable the Authority to respond to a Request for Information within the time for compliance set out in section 10 of the FOIA [or regulation 5 of the Environmental Information Regulations].

34.3 The Authority shall be responsible for determining at its absolute discretion whether the Commercially Sensitive Information and/or any other Information:

(a) is exempt from disclosure in accordance with the provisions of the FOIA or the Environmental Information Regulations;

(b) is to be disclosed in response to a Request for Information, and in no event shall the Contractor respond directly to a Request for Information unless expressly authorised to do so by the Authority.

34.4 The Contractor acknowledges that the Authority may, acting in accordance with the Department for Constitutional Affairs' Code of Practice on the Discharge of Functions of Public Authorities under Part I of the Freedom of Information Act 2000, be obliged under the FOIA or the Environmental Information Regulations to disclose Information:

(a) without consulting with the Contractor, or

(b) following consultation with the Contractor and having taken its views into account.

34.5   The Contractor shall ensure that all Information produced in the course of the Agreement or relating to the Agreement is retained for disclosure and shall permit the Authority to inspect such records as requested from time to time.

There are two main exemptions in the FOIA that affect commercial information – section 41 (breach of confidence) and section 43 (information that would prejudice commercial interests). Guidance is available on the UK and Scottish Information Commissioner's website about both these exemptions. There are a few important points to note about these exemptions: section 41 can only be used for an actionable breach of confidence. This means the public authority must believe the other party would sue and also win. Although section 41 is an absolute exemption, within the law of confidence there is an in-built public-interest test. Section 43 is qualified by the public interest test. These restrictions should put an end to authorities' overuse of the 'commercially sensitive' excuse.

PROCUREMENT

All publication schemes ought to have a 'procurement' section that tells you where to access information about all their contracts and purchases. The reality is that very few do, and those that do, include only those contracts that the government has a legal duty to publish in the *Official Journal of the European Union*. The requirement is usually for tenders above £100,000. Transport for London publishes notices relating to procurement contracts with a value over £125,000, while central government publishes contracts above £100,410. The search facility on the EU website is not particularly user-friendly so public authorities would better serve the public by publishing their tender advertisements and final contracts on their own websites. If you can't find what you are looking for, then it is worth filing an FOIA request.

Official Journal of the European Union
Tenders Electronic Daily (TED)
www.ted.eur-op.eu.int/static/home/en

Office of Government Commerce
www.ogc.gov.uk
Service Desk, OGC, Rosebery Court, St Andrew's Business Park,
Norwich NR7 0HS

Fax: 01603 704 618
Email: ServiceDesk@ogc.gsi.gov.uk
Publication scheme: www.ogc.gov.uk/index.asp?id=2817

The OGC is an office of the Treasury charged with getting better deals for the public sector. The 'Better Projects' division manages the Gateway reviews that are designed to end the disasters of large-scale IT projects. The best way to keep track of such complex and costly projects is to operate in the open, so it is cause for concern that the OGC has itself refused all FOI requests for the detailed gateway reviews of government IT projects.

WHERE TO GET INFORMATION ABOUT COMPANIES

Health and Safety Executive

www.hse.gov.uk
Tel: 0151 951 4382 (information line)
FOI Officer: Sue Cornmell
Information Management Unit, Health and Safety Executive,
Magdalen House, Trinity Road, Bootle, Merseyside L20 3QZ
Tel: 0151 951 3407
Email: sue.cornmell@hse.gsi.gov.uk
Publication scheme: www.hse.gov.uk/publish/publicationscheme.htm

The HSE is an excellent source of business information as it covers a huge gamut of industry: nuclear installations, mines, factories, farms, hospitals, schools, offshore gas and oil installations, the safety of the gas grid, the movement of dangerous goods and substances, railway safety, and many others. It does not cover offices, shops or the service sector – but local authorities enforce health and safety in these places and report to the Health and Safety Commission. The HSE makes public the minutes from meetings of its many advisory committees on such topics as construction, railways, nuclear installations, toxic substances and genetic modification.

The HSE is covered by the FOIA and is a shining example of the kind of openness and accessibility that all public authorities should aspire to.

Industry health and safety violations – this is the most useful part of the HSE website as it shows which companies have been cited for health and safety violations. You can search the databases by name, type of industry, location or UK region. There are two databases, which you can find under the section 'Enforcement action' (www. hse.gov.uk/enforce/index.htm).

- Prosecutions database – includes details of all prosecution cases (which resulted in a conviction) and Crown censures since 1 April 1999: www.hse-databases.co.uk/prosecutions
- Notices database – includes details of all enforcement notices issued since 1 April 2001 – excluding those under appeal or withdrawn: www.hse-databases.co.uk/notices

Other useful databases on the HSE site include:

- register of licensed nuclear sites in Great Britain
- an A–Z subject index of industry research reports: www.hse. gov.uk/research/subject/index.htm
- statistics and information on work-related ill-health and injuries, dangerous occurrences and gas safety.

Department of Trade and Industry
www.dti.gov.uk
1 Victoria Street, London SW1H 0ET
Tel: 020 7215 5000 (general enquiries)
FOI Officer: Graham Rowlinson, Open Government Collection,
Room LG 139
Tel: 020 7215 6452
Fax: 020 7215 5713
Email: Graham.Rowlinson@dti.gsi.gov.uk
Publication scheme: www.dti.gov.uk/SMD3/publicationscheme.htm

The Department of Trade and Industry is the main government department that oversees commercial companies in the UK. Its stated goals are 'to champion UK business at home and abroad'. This broad remit involves enforcing a fair market system, protecting the rights of workers and consumers, and investing in science and technology. Several executive agencies (quangos) look after specific tasks as described below. General policy on trade and industry is held by the DTI, but more specific information particularly about the regulation of trade is the responsibility of various executive agencies, such as Companies House, the Financial Services Authority, the Patent Office, the Advisory, Conciliation and Arbitration Service (ACAS), Employment Tribunals Service and the Insolvency Service. The Shareholder Executive joined the DTI from the Cabinet Office in 2004. This section is worth probing with a few FOI requests as it covers the shares held by the government (i.e. taxpayers!). Government is the major shareholder in: British Energy, the Royal Mail, British Nuclear Fuels and the UK Atomic Energy Authority among others.

FOI Officer Graham Rowlinson advises requesters to make their FOI requests directly to the division or executive agency concerned rather than to his office. 'The default position is that if members of staff want to release information then that's fine,' he says. 'If the request is problematic and staff aren't sure what they can release or they want to refuse a request using one of the exemptions, then they should come to us for advice first.' However, in practice, the DTI is one of the less open sectors of government with a number of refusals under investigation by the Information Commissioner.

Executive agencies

Companies House
www.companieshouse.gov.uk
Crown Way, Maindy, Cardiff CF14 3UZ
Tel: 0870 333 3636 (enquiries line)
Email: enquiries@companies-house.gov.uk

Companies House is covered by the FOIA. It incorporates companies and maintains the public register of company documents and company names. According to Companies House, there are more than 1.8 million limited companies registered in Great Britain and over 300,000 new companies incorporate each year. The website has an online 'Webcheck' service that allows you to search for companies by name or registration number. You can order the latest filed accounts, annual report and appointments for a fee of between £1 and £2 per record.

Employment Tribunals Service
www.ets.gov.uk
5th Floor, Victory House, 30–34 Kingsway, WC2V 6EX
Tel: 0845 795 9775 (enquiry line)
FOI Officer: Tyrieana Long
Tel: 020 7273 8614
Email: tyrieana.long@tribunals.gsi.gov.uk
Publication scheme: www.ets.gov.uk/foi.htm

Tribunals, like courts, are not covered by the FOIA, but they have their own access rights. The Employment Tribunal and Employment Appeals Tribunal are extremely open, putting the minutes of their meetings online. You can also get decisions from the Employment Appeals Tribunal online from the British and Irish Legal Information Institute: www.bailii.org/uk/cases/UKEAT. Employment tribunals resolve disputes between employers and employees over employment rights. The Employment Tribunals Service *is* covered by the FOIA because it is an executive agency of the Department of Trade and Industry. The ETS deals with all the paperwork and administration related to the two tribunals (in much the same way that the Court Service handles administration for the courts), and is therefore a useful source of information, particularly for financial figures and the cost-effectiveness of the tribunals.

Insolvency Service

www.insolvency.gov.uk
Open Government Officer, HQ Secretariat, The Insolvency Service,
21 Bloomsbury Street, London WC1B 3QW
Tel: 020 7291 6895 (Insolvency); 0845 145 0004 (Redundancy)
Email: central.enquiryline@insolvency.gsi.gov.uk
Publication scheme: www.insolvency.gov.uk/pubsscheme

The Insolvency Service investigates and administers bankruptcy of individuals and companies. It is covered by the FOIA. The Service keeps a public register of bankruptcy orders and individual voluntary arrangements in England and Wales. Unhelpfully, these are not available online and you must either search the register in person, or fill out the appropriate form online and fax or mail it in. The information held on the register includes the bankrupt's name, last known address, details of the bankruptcy order or voluntary arrangement and, where known, the bankrupt's date of birth, occupation and trading details.

The Patent Office

www.patent.gov.uk
Louise Smyth, Open Government Liaison Officer, Room 3R11, Concept House, Cardiff Road, Newport, South Wales NP10 8QQ
Tel: 01633 813 784
Email: louise.smyth@patent.gov.uk
Publication scheme: www.patent.gov.uk/about/relationship/freedom

The Patent Office is responsible for registering claims on intellectual property in the UK, which includes copyright, designs, patents and trademarks. Covered by the FOIA.

UK Trade and Investment Agency

www.trade.uktradeinvest.gov.uk
Peter Westley, Open Government and Data Protection Liaison Officer
Strategy and Communications Group, UK Trade and Investment, Bay 134b,
Kingsgate House, 66–74 Victoria Street, London SW1E 6SW
Tel: 020 7215 4326
Email: peter.westley@dti.gsi.gov.uk
Publication scheme: www.trade.uktradeinvest.gov.uk/publication_scheme

This is the lead body responsible for fostering business competitiveness by helping UK firms secure overseas sales and investments, and for attracting high-quality foreign direct investment to the UK. It collects data on UK exports, which you can search online by country or sector (aerospace, drinks, engineering, and so on). It does not deal with arms exports, however. For that you will need to contact the Ministry of Defence, specifically the Defence Exports Services Organisation.

Office of Fair Trading

www.oft.gov.uk
Communications Division, Room GC/7A, Fleetbank House,
2–6 Salisbury Square, London EC4Y 8JX
Tel: 0845 722 4499 (general enquiries)
FOI Officer: Ian Bennett
Fax: 020 7211 8400
Email: Ian.Bennett@oft.gsi.gov.uk, or send requests to: foiaenquiries@oft.
gov.uk
Tel: 020 7211 8801
Publication scheme: follow links to FOI from homepage
Disclosure log: follow links to FOI from homepage

The OFT is covered by the FOIA. It is responsible for making sure commercial trading markets work correctly, and to do this it enforces competition and consumer protection laws. It holds useful information about market investigations (such as estate agents and private dentists) and keeps a number of public registers. Some of these are easily accessible online, such as the Competition Act 1998 Register and the Register of Orders and Undertakings. However, the ones most useful to the public – the register of prohibition orders against rogue estate agents, and the Consumer Credit Act 1974 Register (which lists information about all businesses that have consumer credit agreements for loans, financing and higher purchases of up to £25,000) – are not online and there is no publicity telling people where these registers are available, or that they even exist! Ian Bennett says the registers will be online by late 2006. In the meantime, the registers can be inspected from the Fleetbank HQ.

Financial Services Authority
www.fsa.gov.uk
FOI Publication Requests, Financial Services Authority,
25 The North Colonnade, Canary Wharf, London E14 5HS
Tel: 020 7066 4406
Fax: 020 7066 4407
Publication scheme: www.fsa.gov.uk/foi

The FSA is a public authority even though it is funded by the financial services industry rather than the taxpayer. The FSA regulates the financial industry and is an excellent source for information about financial companies, making its records easily available online. The FSA register will tell you if a money-management business is operating correctly. The register is a public record that lists all financial services firms, individuals and other bodies which fall under the FSA's regulatory jurisdiction as defined in the Financial Services and Markets Act 2000. You can search the register online – www.fsa.gov.uk/register – or in person at the Canary Wharf headquarters. The register includes the full names of major shareholders and details of any supervisory, disciplinary or civil regulatory action (but not criminal action), taken by the FSA. It's an excellent way to find out how many company boards an individual sits on and which businesses have been charged with violations.

Other sources
Export Credit Guarantee Department
www.ecgd.gov.uk
Communications Branch, ECGD, PO Box 2200, 2 Exchange Tower,
Harbour Exchange Square, London E14 9GS
Tel: 020 7512 7000 (switchboard)
Fax: 020 7512 7021
FOI Officer: Paul Redman
Email: information.access@ecgd.gsi.gov.uk

The ECGD helps UK manufacturers and investors trade overseas by providing them with insurance and/or backing for finance to protect against non-payment. Insurance is particularly comforting for companies who are looking to win contracts in the developing world or with buyers that they might be unfamiliar with. Arms deals seem to make up the bulk of the activity of the Export Credits Guarantee Department (www.ecgd.gov.uk), even though, according to the Campaign Against Arms Trade, arms exports comprise just 2–3 per cent of the UK's total visible export. This shady department is best cracked open with some well-framed freedom of information requests.

UK Trade Info

www.uktradeinfo.com
HM Revenue and Customs Statistics and Analysis of Trade Unit (SATU),
Alexander House, 21 Victoria Avenue, Southend on Sea, Essex SS99 1AA
Tel: 01702 367 485
Email: uktradeinfo@hmrc.gsi.gov.uk

Along with the UK Trade and Investment Agency, this is another major source for import/export data. It is run by HM Revenue and Customs and the data collected is 'the most complete, authoritative and up to date information on UK imports and exports available anywhere'. The figures are taken directly from the returns and reports required with every export and import consignment by HM Revenue and Customs. Although a public authority compiles these figures, there is an annual subscription fee of £1,500 to access the data, which puts it out of the range of most people. The primary use of UK trade data is currently market intelligence (identifying new trade opportunities and growth areas, measuring market share and analysing trade patterns). However, the public would find this data useful, too, as they could use it to compile information about UK trade in various industries such as armaments or toxic substances.

14
Information about Individuals

Getting information on living individuals, whether yourself or others, involves the Data Protection Act 1998, which came into force on 1 March 2000. The complexity of this law rivals even the Freedom of Information Act, so this chapter deals only with how the two laws interact and specifically how to make FOI requests about other people. These are known as third-party requests.

If you want information about yourself (known as a subject-access request), you will find some examples of how to do this throughout the book, such as accessing your medical records (Chapter 9) finding out if MI5 has a file on you (Chapter 5) or getting your school records (Chapter 12). The procedure for other requests for your own personal information will be similar. Your right to information about yourself is not absolute – the Data Protection Act has a number of exemptions. You can find out more about these by reading the Information Commissioner's guidance on the Act available on the Information Commissioner's website (www.informationcommissioner.gov.uk) or by contacting the Office. An important legal case – *Durant* v. *Financial Services Authority* – also radically narrowed the definition of what constitutes personal data. Again, the latest guidance on this is available from the Information Commissioner either online or on request.

Section 40 of the FOI Act appears to exempt all 'personal information', but this is not the case. The exemption has two parts. If the information you seek is about yourself, the request comes right out of the FOIA and is instead covered by the Data Protection Act. However, because neither Act requires you to name the law that gives you the right to request information, it doesn't matter whether you cite the DPA, the FOIA or no law at all. If you make a written request for personal information, the authority is required to deal with it under the DPA.

If the information is about someone else, it is covered by the Freedom of Information Act, but its release will be governed by the data protection principles laid out in the DPA.

The FOIA amends the definition of personal information defined in the Data Protection Act 1998 to include unstructured personal

---

How to make a subject-access request

1. Identify who holds the information about you. If you're not sure who this is, you can search the Information Commissioner's public register of data controllers online: http://forms.informationcommissioner.gov.uk/search.html
2. Write or email the data protection contact. Many organisations require some proof of identity to ensure you are who you say you are. Ask the organisation what they require.
3. If the organisation requires a fee, include it in your application.
4. The agency has 40 calendar days to respond. If you are unhappy with the agency's response you can complain to the agency, but unlike the FOIA there is no formal procedure for internal review of decisions under the DPA. If you remain unsatisfied, appeal to the Information Commissioner.

---

information held in manual form by a public authority. This means information in any kind of filing system, not just 'structured' files that are indexed or arranged. Existing types of personal information are electronic documents, CCTV footage, information in certain types of records (medical, social work, local authority, housing or credit reference, school), and information in structured manual records. Just because a file has your name on it doesn't mean that what's inside constitutes personal information. This used to be the way the DPA was interpreted, but the Court of Appeal narrowed the definition of what was considered 'personal information' in the case of *Durant* v. *Financial Services Authority*.[1] The court concluded that personal data 'is information that affects [a person's] privacy, whether in his personal or family life, business or professional capacity'. So identification alone no longer guarantees that data is 'personal'. It must also affect the named person's privacy. This more restrictive interpretation is bad news for those people expecting to receive a comprehensive listing of all the information a private company holds about them. On the other hand, it means that fewer requests about other people can be denied on the grounds that information is 'personal'. And any information about you held by a *public body* that no longer meets the definition of personal data should be accessible under the FOI Act.

You might not be interested specifically in information about other people, but while trying to get information about a topic it's quite likely that it will contain references to identifiable individuals such as public employees. The public have an interest, for example,

---

1. [2003] EWCA Civ 1746, Court of Appeal (Civil Division) decision of Lord Justices Auld, Mummery and Buxton dated 8 December 2003. A full text of the judgment is available from the County Service website at www. courtservice.gov.uk

in knowing the names and sponsoring companies of people on secondment to government departments, so they can ensure the process is above board and not a means of covert lobbying for lucrative government contracts. The public also have an interest in knowing the names and job descriptions of public officials who are carrying out work on behalf of the people. Public officials are spending public money, so the public have a right to know who these people are in order to hold them accountable.

If you do make requests that involve identifiable people, chances are that you will encounter a government official who is under the mistaken impression that the DPA prevents the release of *any* information about named individuals without their consent.

The Campaign for Freedom of Information and Friends of the Earth both report absurd interpretations of the DPA by government officials. On many occasions they have received letters where all names of individuals were redacted from documents. In one case the name of a minister, in a document with a ministerial letterhead, was redacted. In another case journalists' bylines were redacted from press clippings!

All the cases sent to the Commissioner for review involving the House of Commons related to refusals made under section 40 of the FOIA (personal information). It is to be hoped that recent decisions coming out of the Commissioner's Office and the Tribunal will clarify the situation.

But this is not a new problem. Back in 2003 police in Humberside mistakenly believed that the DPA prevented them from passing on sexual assault allegations made against Ian Huntley to the Soham school where he worked as a janitor before killing two schoolgirls. British Gas believed that the DPA meant they could not notify social services when they cut off the gas service to an elderly couple, both of whom subsequently died (one of hypothermia).

As early as 2002, the European Ombudsman warned that EU data protection rules (on which our Data Protection Act is based) were 'being used to undermine the principle of openness in public activities'.[2]

Privacy and public accountability may seem mutually exclusive, but as long as the principles of the Data Protection Act are followed, information about individuals can and should be released. It is worth

2. European Ombudsman Letters and Notes dated 25 September 2002: www. euro-ombudsman.eu/int/letters/en/20020925-1.htm

quoting the Information Commissioner's own guidance on personal information as the law is so often used incorrectly:

> It is often believed that the Data Protection Act prevents the disclosure of any personal data without the consent of the person concerned. This is not true. The purpose of the Data Protection Act is to protect the private lives of individuals. Where information requested is about the people acting in a work or official capacity then it will normally be right to disclose.[3]

The DPA is a needlessly complicated law full of vague concepts, which leads to the confusion. Even the Court of Appeal has called it 'a cumbersome and inelegant piece of legislation'. The Information Commissioner Richard Thomas agrees that 'the law is and does look very complicated', but that does not give people the right to shelter behind the law and blame it for operational failures. 'The Data Protection Act is very much about common sense and fairness,' Thomas said (BBC Radio 4, *Law in Action*, 6 February 2004).

Part of the confusion also results from the nature of privacy itself. Privacy is not a fixed right but operates along a continuum, with private individuals going about their private lives having the greatest expectation of privacy, and public officials conducting the public's business having the least. Ironically, the reality in the UK is almost the opposite, with the privacy of private citizens under constant assault by CCTV and increasingly repressive anti-terrorism laws that give the state broad powers to conduct surveillance and share information.

In January 2004, there were at least 4,285,000 CCTV cameras operating in Britain, according to Professor Clive Norris, deputy director of the Centre for Criminological Research in Sheffield. The average Londoner is caught on camera 300 times a day! Liberty estimates that up to 70 per cent of the surveillance systems in Britain are illegal in some way. Meanwhile, public officials and those carrying out public work routinely refuse to release even the most basic information, such as names and job descriptions to the public who are paying their wages. The names of MPs' staff, for example, are still secret even though their wages are being paid for with public money. The need for transparency is especially important in this case as many of the staff are MPs' relatives and the public have a right to

---

3. 'Freedom of Information Awareness Guidance No. 1: Personal information', issued by the Information Commissioner and available on the IC website: www.informationcommissioner.gov.uk

know if these people are doing any actual work. How can we know, if we can't even find out who is on the public payroll?

It is important to remember that this kind of secrecy can now be challenged. The Information Commissioner's guidance document states that 'when an applicant asks for third-party data, that request can only be refused if disclosure would breach any of the data protection principles'.

These are the eight data protection principles:

1. Data should be obtained and processed fairly and lawfully.
2. Data should only be held for specified (that is, registered) and lawful purposes.
3. Data shall be used and disclosed only for purposes and to persons described in the particulars entered in the register.
4. Personal data shall be accurate and, where necessary, kept up to date.
5. Personal data processed for any purpose or purposes shall not be kept for longer than is necessary.
6. Data should be processed in accordance with the rights of data subjects under the Act.
7. Appropriate technical and organisational measures should be taken against unauthorised or unlawful processing of personal data and against accidental loss, damage or destruction.
8. Data should not be transferred to a country or territory outside the European Economic Area unless that country or territory ensures an adequate level of protection for the rights and freedoms of data subjects in relation to the processing of personal data.

These principles should be viewed with common sense. It is good practice for public authorities to ask for consent before releasing personal information, but it is not essential and failure to get consent is not grounds for refusing an information request. One of the key concepts governing the release of personal information is 'fairness'. Such hard-to-define terms make the Data Protection Act open to subjective interpretation, but the Information Commissioner has issued clear guidance. The key question is whether the information sought relates to a person's private or public life, specifically:

Information which is about the home or family life of an individual, his or her personal finances, or consists of personal references, is likely to deserve protection. By contrast, information which is about someone acting in an official or work capacity should normally be provided on request unless there is some risk to the individual concerned.

The guidance document specifically warns against using the exemption 'as a means of sparing officials embarrassment over poor administrative decisions'. Following this logic, the Commissioner has listed the types of information that can and cannot be released.

Released:

- the names of officials
- job description and function
- decisions made in their official capacities
- expenses incurred in the course of official business
- pay bands, and for senior staff, salary details.

Withheld:

- home addresses
- family details
- internal disciplinary matters (although in some instances the public interest may warrant disclosure)
- bank account details
- activities unrelated to an official's public duties (if there is a concern about conflicts of interest, again the public interest may warrant disclosure).

For the latest guidance and decision related to the release of personal information see:

Information Commissioner
www.informationcommissioner.gov.uk
Wycliffe House, Water Lane, Wilmslow, Cheshire SK9 5AF
Data Protection Help Line: Tel: 01625 545 745
Email: mail@ico.gsi.gov.uk

Or consult:

Campaign for Freedom of Information
www.cfoi.org.uk
Suite 102, 16 Baldwins Gardens, London EC1N 7RJ
Tel: 020 7831 7477
Fax: 020 7831 7461
Email: admin@cfoi.demon.co.uk

Conclusion

The public's right to know is not just a noble ideal for an enlightened society; it is thoroughly practical. Freedom of information is the most effective and inexpensive way to stop corruption and waste, and enhance efficiency and good governance. It is as much for these practical reasons as for the more high-minded sentiments that nearly 70 countries from Antigua to Uzbekistan have adopted freedom of information laws over the past ten years.[1] Many were adopted in response to requirements by international money lenders such as the World Bank and International Monetary Fund. Other laws were passed as a reaction against government scandals or crises. In the UK a continuing string of government scandals led first to the voluntary Code of Access and then to the FOI Act. In the US, the major amendments strengthening FOI laws were made after the Watergate scandal was exposed.

The rise of global communications has made it easier to disseminate information to a wide audience and governments now find it harder to successfully suppress information from their citizens. There is a growing awareness and acceptance of human rights that is fuelling the public's demand for greater access to government information.

Three factors are necessary to ensure the Freedom of Information Act works for the people as intended.

1. CLEAR LINES OF ACCOUNTABILITY

One of the hardest things to find out in Britain is 'who is in charge?' Complex bureaucracies have grown up and thrived in the secrecy culture so that even those who work in the myriad government organisations aren't sure if they are working for an executive agency, a non-departmental public body, a ministerial department or any of the other created names of public services. What's lost in the confusion is the simple fact that all these organisations are funded by taxpayers' money and should therefore be accountable primarily to the public. By creating vast, complex and anonymous bureaucracies, the public is effectively locked out of the system. An early benefit of

1. See David Banisar's *Global Survery of FOI Laws Around the World*, updated annually at www.freedominfo.org

the FOIA is that these organisations are now having to justify – often for the first time in their existence – their purpose and describe their organisational structure.

Britain needs to embrace the idea that 'the buck stops here'. There must be total clarity about who is responsible for what. And by this I don't mean which department, in which office of which local authority. I mean the actual name of a person – a person that a member of the public can call (on their direct number) or write to (at their numbered office address) with their question, complaint or query. If you see litter in the street, you should not have to spend a week on the phone trying to find out whose job it is to clear it up. The best way to hold people accountable is to name names.

This applies not just to public officials but also to those they regulate. We need to do away with the ridiculous idea that there is something noble in protecting wrongdoers. Even the Information Commissioner's Office is reluctant to name those authorities who are utterly failing to implement a competent system to deal with the FOIA law or records management. Why are these laggards being protected? Shame and embarrassment are often more effective than legal enforcement, and certainly cheaper. These motivating factors need to be better utilised. The cost of protecting negligent organisations or individuals from shame or embarrassment is at the direct expense of the public – the negligent dentist continues to practise, the unhygienic restaurant continues to feed people, and the rogue trader defrauds more unwary customers.

2. INFORMATION MUST BE EASILY ACCESSIBLE

Ideally there should be little need to make formal information access requests. An authority that values public opinion will provide all its public registers and important information in its publication scheme or online for free. This is also the best way for a public authority to avoid having to divert resources to fulfilling information requests. One of the things that strikes me most about the British attitude to public information is that even where documents are defined as public and the public are given a right of access, there are always fees that are very often high or the public's information is copyrighted so you can't use it without buying a licence. It is a rare occasion when the public can access public information for free. The internet has introduced the idea that much more information should be available freely if accessed online, but many agencies are still charging even to access online public registers, such as the Land Registry. Fees serve one purpose – to discourage people from accessing information. They rarely bear any relation to the actual cost of complying with the request, and when you consider that the taxpayer is already paying the salaries of the public officials who have created this public information, it is remarkably short-sighted and greedy to ask the public to pay for the information a second time. If the government's much-stated goal of encouraging civic participation is to be believed, then fees should be minimal or waived except in rare cases. Public scrutiny may incur some meagre short-term costs, but the long-term savings are enormous. Think of how many millions would have been saved from the £800 million Millennium Dome bill if the public could have seen the figures!

3. USE IT OR LOSE IT

I have shown in this book the many ways in which the UK government shields itself from the scrutiny of those people it is meant to be representing. The need for accountability is becoming even greater as the government gathers ever more information about us. The introduction of ID cards, electronic health records, information sharing between agencies and anti-terrorism laws all give the government greater rights to collect information about private citizens. A strong FOI law is essential to ensure that the government gathers and uses this information correctly with proper regard for our civil liberties and privacy.

The enactment of the freedom of information law is the first step in shifting power back into the people's hands. But now the law is in place, it is time for the real work to begin. A law is only as good as how it is used and enforced, and it is worth remembering that even repressive countries like Zimbabwe have freedom of information laws on their books. In Zimbabwe, the law requires all media to register with the Media and Information Commission. So far, the Commission's contribution to greater freedom of information has been to shut down the country's main opposition newspaper and arrest and deport journalists who critically question the government.

You should not expect politicians to promote freedom of information. Why should they? They have a vested interest in controlling the public's access to information and thereby maintaining their grip on power. The UK's FOI Act is riddled with the kind of numerous and vague exemptions that are particularly vulnerable to abuse by politicians who favour secrecy. High fees, information refusals, obstruction, obfuscation and delays will all serve to increase the public's distrust and disengagement from Westminster and public officials.

Politicians may initially find it difficult to accept new standards of public accountability, but we must make the costs of not doing so even greater. The best way to do this is by publicly embarrassing and shaming those officials and departments who refuse to answer to the public.

The next few years will set the boundaries for openness in our society. If you make a request now it is likely that you will be determining these boundaries. That is why it is important to apply for information, don't accept 'no' for an answer and appeal for your rights to access information. It is only by putting cases forward to the Information Commissioner and courts that the case law for openness will be established.

Maybe you would prefer not to be bothered with how the government is run. If that's the case then you have no right to complain when your taxes are raised, or if your children's education is substandard, or you have to wait a year for a vital operation. Good government does not happen by itself but is the result of individual effort. One of the easiest and most effective things you can do is simply to ask for information. I hope I've given you the tools and confidence to do exactly that.

Appendix
Letters for Requesting Information

These letter templates can be adapted for most requests. Remember, requests under the FOIA, Data Protection Act or Environmental Information Regulations do not have to mention the law for it to be invoked. And sometimes it might be easier to just call up and ask for the information instead. These letters are for those instances when a more formal approach is needed.

To improve the chances of your request being successfully answered, be as specific as possible. If you have a broad request, ask for a specific time frame. Have a clear idea of what you want and don't be afraid to telephone first a department's records manager or Freedom of Information officer to help you formulate your query. The public authority is under a statutory duty to provide you with advice and assistance under section 16 of the FOIA. The FOI Officer is the main person who will do this, and that's why I have endeavoured to include their direct telephone number. A good example comes from a request I made to the Crown Prosecution Service for their conviction rates of various crimes across the UK. Before I made the request I talked to their FOI Officer about when the CPS switched from a manual to an electronic records system then asked about fields in their database, which gave me a better understanding of how they organised their information. I was then able to construct a successful request that gave me most of what I wanted while not putting an undue burden on the CPS. FOI is all about negotiation, so those public authorities refusing to provide direct contact with their FOI officers are simply making more work for themselves.

If you fear your letter might be ignored (for example if you're dealing with an agency that has a poor customer service reputation such as the Home Office), then send your request by registered mail. Alternatively, if you email the request, you can set your email-sending options to ask for a 'read receipt', and this will often show you the time and identity of the person who read the email. Follow up the email with a written letter and specify that the agency acknowledge receipt of your request. Then telephone if you don't hear anything after a week.

Keep a diary of the dates and details of any correspondence or conversations with the agency. And above all be tenacious. If it becomes apparent that you are not going to give up easily and go away, then someone might actually answer your request. If they do not, you have valid grounds to appeal to the Information Commissioner.

FREEDOM OF INFORMATION ACT REQUEST LETTER

[Your address]
[Your daytime telephone number]
[Your email address]

Freedom of Information Officer
[Name of organisation]
[Organisation's address]

[Insert date]

Dear [enter name]

I am writing to request information under the Freedom of Information Act 2000. In order to assist you with this request, I am outlining my query as specifically as possible.

[Give a description of your request here]

I would be interested in any information held by your organisation regarding my request. I understand that I do not have to specify particular files or documents and that it is the department's responsibility to provide the information I require. If you need further clarification, please contact me by [state your preferred contact method, i.e. phone, email, post].

I would like to receive the information in [specify your chosen format here: electronic, hard copy, and/or to inspect the documents onsite].

If my request is denied in whole or in part, I ask that you justify all deletions by reference to specific exemptions of the act. I will also expect you to release all non-exempt material. I reserve the right to appeal your decision to withhold any information or to charge excessive fees.

I would be grateful if you could confirm in writing that you have received this request. I look forward to your response within 20 working days, as outlined by the statute.

Regards,
[Your name]

FREEDOM OF INFORMATION ACT LETTER FOR A CONTRACT, TENDER OR OTHER COMMERCIAL INFORMATION

[Your address]
[Your daytime telephone number]
[Your email address]

Freedom of Information Officer
[Name of organisation]
[Organisation's address]

[Insert date]

Dear [enter name]

I would like to request the following information:

1) The contract (including all indexes, appendices and supplements) between [name of public authority] and [the private company]; (and/or)
2) Bids to tender for [specify service or project]; (and/or)
3) The annual revenue [public authority] receives from [private company] as a result of this contract.

I would like to receive the information in [specify your chosen format here: electronic, hard copy, and/or to inspect the documents on-site]. If one part of this request can be answered sooner than others, please send that information first followed by any subsequent data. If you need further clarification, please contact me by [state your preferred contact method, i.e. phone, email, post].

Many public authorities release their contracts with private vendors in line with the Freedom of Information Act. The exemption for commercial interest under the Act (section 43) is a qualified exemption, which means information can only be withheld if it is in the public's interest. The public have an interest in knowing the terms of contracts awarded by public authorities, whether or not public money changes hands immediately.

If you are relying on section 41 (the exemption for legal breach of confidence) then I would like to know the following:

- When these confidentiality agreements were agreed
- All correspondence and email in which these confidentiality agreements were discussed
- The precise wording of the confidentiality agreements.

I ask these questions because guidance issued by both the Lord Chancellor (draft guidance on FOI implementation) and the Office of Government Commerce (Model terms and conditions for goods and services) specifically state that public authorities should not enter into these types of agreements; they go directly against the spirit of the laws of disclosure. I would also point to the Information Commissioner's guidance on accepting blanket commercial confidentiality agreements: 'Unless confidentiality clauses are necessary or reasonable, there is a real risk that, in the event of a complaint, the Commissioner would order disclosure in any case.'[1]

Finally, within the law of confidence there is also a public interest test. Therefore, the contracts should be disclosed in full. If any parts are redacted they must be for information that can be proven to be a legal breach of confidence in court, and only then where secrecy can be shown to be in the public interest. These are difficult positions to argue when public money is at stake or where a public authority is offering a private company a monopoly to charge its stakeholders.

I reserve the right to appeal your decision to withhold any information or to charge excessive fees, and understand that under the act, I am

1. 'Freedom of Information Awareness Guidance 5: Commercial Interests' Office of the Information Commissioner, Page 10, www.informationcommissioner. gov.uk/eventual.aspx?id=102

entitled to a response within 20 working days. I would be grateful if you could confirm in writing that you have received this request.

Regards,
[Your name]

FREEDOM OF INFORMATION ACT APPEAL LETTER

[Your address]
[Your daytime telephone number]
[Your email address]

Agency Director or Appeal Officer
[Name of organisation]
[Organisation's address]

[Insert date]

Re: Freedom of Information Act Appeal

Dear **[enter name]**

I would like to appeal your organisation's refusal to positively answer my request for information made **[insert date of request]** under the Freedom of Information Act 2000.

My request was assigned the following reference number: **[insert reference number here]**. On **[insert date of denial]**, I received a response to my request from **[insert name of official]** who denied my request. Under the terms of the FOIA, I am exercising my right to seek an internal review of this decision.

[Optional] The documents that were withheld should be disclosed under the FOIA because **[they do not meet the exemption criteria and/or disclosure is in the public interest –** *make your argument about why the public interest favours disclosure citing the factors listed in Chapter 3*].

[Optional] I appeal the decision to require me to pay **[insert fee amount here]** in fees for this request as the information I requested

is in the public interest and the information should therefore be easily accessible to the public. The FOIA states that an authority can only charge 'reasonable' fees and this amount is unreasonable. If the fee decision is upheld, I require a full breakdown of how the total amount was calculated and a justification of how this amount can be considered 'reasonable'.

Thank you for your consideration of this appeal.

Regards,
[Your name]

LETTER REQUESTING ENVIRONMENTAL INFORMATION

[Your address]
[Your daytime telephone number]
[Your email address]

Agency Director or FOI Officer
[Name of organisation]
[Organisation's address]

[Insert date]

Dear [enter name]

I am writing to request information under the Environmental Information Regulations 2004/Freedom of Information Act 2000. In order to assist you with this request, I am outlining my query as specifically as possible.

[Give a description of your request here]

I would be interested in any information held by your organisation regarding my request. I understand that I do not have to specify particular files or documents and that it is the department's responsibility to provide the information I require. If you need further clarification, please contact me by [state your preferred contact method, e.g. phone, email, post].

I would like to receive the information in [**specify your chosen format here: electronic, hard copy, and/or to inspect the documents on-site**].

If my request is denied in whole or in part, I ask that you justify all deletions by reference to specific exemptions of the act. I will also expect you to release all non-exempt material. I reserve the right to appeal your decision to withhold any information or to charge excessive fees. If you plan to charge a fee for this information, I would ask that you pay particular attention to the ruling on fees made by the Information Tribunal 28 March 2006: *Mr David Markinson* v. *Information Commissioner*.

This decision makes clear that public authorities cannot charge an unreasonable amount for environmental information. It directed King's Lynn and West Norfolk Borough Council to overturn their charging structure and adopt instead a price of 10p per photocopied A4 page. Section 44 of the Tribunal decision states that a public authority can only exceed the guide price if it can demonstrate a good reason to do so, and in considering whether any such reason exists the public authority should:

(i)   take due regard of the guidance set out in the Code of Practice on the discharge of the obligations of public authorities under the Environmental Information Regulations 2004 and the Guidance to the Environmental Information Regulations 2004, both published by DEFRA, to the effect that any charge should be at a level that does not exceed the cost of producing the copies;
(ii) disregard any costs, including staff costs, associated with the maintenance of the information in question or its identification or extraction from storage; and
(iii) disregard any factors beyond the number and size of sheets to be copied, in particular, the real or perceived significance of the content, or the effect that any charging structure may have on the Council's revenue or its staff workload.

I look forward to your response within the 20-working-day time limit, and would be grateful if you could confirm in writing that you have received this request.

Regards,
[**Your name**]

REQUEST FOR PERSONAL RECORDS

[Your address]
[Your daytime telephone number]
[Your email address]

Data Protection/FOI Officer
[Name of organisation]
[Organisation's address]

[Insert date]

Re: Request for [insert type of records sought: health/school/ personal] records

Dear [enter name]:

This is a request made under the Data Protection Act 1998 to request a copy of any information or records about me held by your organisation.

To help you to locate my records, I have had the following contacts with your organisation: [insert identifying references such as school attendance dates (school records), periods of employment, customer or reference number, National Insurance number (health records), etc.].

Please consider that this request is also made under the Freedom of Information Act and any other applicable laws of access, so please provide any additional information about me that may be available under these laws.

[*Optional*] Enclosed is [check the identification requirements of the agency and include either a bank statement, copy of passport or other required identifying documents] that will verify my identity.

I would be grateful if you could confirm in writing that you have received this request, and I look forward to your response within the statutory time limits. Thank you for your consideration of this request.

Regards,
[Your name]

LETTER TO AMEND PERSONAL RECORDS

[Your address]
[Your daytime telephone number]
[Your email address]

Data Protection/FOI Officer
[Name of organisation]
[Organisation's address]

[Insert date]

Dear [enter name]

This is a request under the Data Protection Act 1998 to amend records about myself maintained by your organisation.

The following information is not correct [describe the incorrect information as specifically as possible].

The information is incorrect because it is [out of date, inaccurate, incomplete, etc.]. [Explain the reasons why the information is incorrect]

[*Optional*] Enclosed are copies of documents that show the information is incorrect.

I request that the information be [deleted] [changed to read: ...].

Thank you for your consideration of this request.

Regards,
[Your name]

Index

Compiled by Sue Carlton

Made in the USA
San Bernardino, CA
22 June 2014